Just for the Middle Level ISEE

- **Test Prep Works materials are developed for a specific test and level, making it easier for students to focus on relevant content**

- **The Middle Level ISEE is for students applying for admission to grades 7-8 – see table at the end of this book for materials for other grades**

- **Two books are available from Test Prep Works to help students prepare for the Middle Level ISEE**

Success on the Middle Level ISEE: A Complete Course

- Strategies for each section of the test

- Reading and vocabulary drills

- In-depth math content instruction with practice sets

- 1 full-length practice test

The Best Unofficial Practice Tests for the Middle Level ISEE

- 2 additional full-length practice tests

TEST PREP WORKS, LLC.

Are you an educator?

Incorporate materials from Test Prep Works into your test prep program

- Use the materials developed specifically for the test and level your students are taking

- Customize our books to fit your program

    - Choose content modules from any of our books – even from multiple books

    - Add your branding to the cover and title page

    - Greet your students with an introductory message

    - Create custom books with a one-time setup fee[1], then order copies at list price[2] with no minimum quantities

- Volume discounts available for bulk orders of 50+ copies

You provide the expertise – let us provide the materials

Contact *sales@testprepworks.com* for more info

1 - Setup fees start at $199 per title, which includes branding of the cover and title page and a customer-provided introductory message. Additional customization will incur additional setup fees.

2 - The list price for custom books is the same as the list price of the corresponding title available for retail sale. If the content of a book is modified so that it no longer corresponds to a book available for retail sale, then Test Prep Works will set the list price prior to assessing any setup fees.

TEST PREP WORKS, LLC.

SUCCESS

ON THE Middle Level ISEE

A Complete Course

Christa Abbott, M.Ed.

Published by:
Test Prep Works, LLC
PO Box 100572
Arlington, VA 22210
www.TestPrepWorks.com

For information about buying this title in bulk, or for editions with customized covers or content, please contact us at sales@testprepworks.com or (703) 944-6727.

The ISEE is a registered trademark of the ERB. They have not endorsed nor are they associated in any way with this book.

Neither the author nor the publisher of this book claims responsibility for the accuracy of this book or the outcome of students who use these materials.

ISBN: 978-1-939090-06-5

Contents

About the Author

Christa Abbott has been a private test prep tutor for over a decade. She has worked with students who have been admitted to and attended some of the top independent schools in the country. Over the years, she has developed materials for each test that truly make the difference.

Christa is a graduate of Middlebury College and received her Masters in Education from the University of Virginia, a program nationally known for its excellence. Her background in education allows her to develop materials based on the latest research about how we learn so that preparation can be an effective and efficient use of time. Her materials are also designed to be developmentally appropriate for the ages of the students taking the tests. In her free time, she enjoys hiking, tennis, Scrabble, and reading. Her greatest joy is spending time with her husband and three children.

Christa continues to work with students one-on-one in the Washington, D.C., area. She also works with students internationally via Skype. If you are interested in these services, please visit www.ChristaAbbott.com.

About Test Prep Works, LLC

Test Prep Works, LLC, was founded to provide effective materials for test preparation. Its founder, Christa Abbott, spent years looking for effective materials for the private school entrance exams but came up empty-handed. The books available combined several different tests and while there are overlaps, they are not the same test. Christa found this to be very, very overwhelming for students who were in elementary and middle school and that just didn't seem necessary. Christa developed her own materials to use with students that are specific for each level of the test and are not just adapted from other books. For the first time, these materials are available to the general public as well as other tutors. Please visit www.TestPrepWorks.com to view a complete array of offerings as well as sign up for a newsletter with recent news and developments in the world of admissions and test preparation.

Notes for Parents

What is the ISEE?

ISEE stands for Independent School Entrance Exam. It is published by the Education Records Bureau (ERB). If you have students already in independent school, you may have seen ERB scores before. You may also have heard of another independent school entrance exam – the SSAT. The schools that your student is applying to may accept either the SSAT or the ISEE, or they may exclusively use one test or the other. It can also depend upon what grade your child is applying for. Contact each school to which your child will apply to be sure that he or she is taking the correct test.

- Contact schools so that your child takes the right test

What level should I register my child for?

This book is designed to help students who are taking the Middle Level ISEE. If students are applying for grade 7 or grade 8, then they should be taking the Middle Level ISEE. If this does not describe your student, please visit www.TestPrepWorks.com to order the correct materials for the level that your student will be taking.

- Middle Level is for students applying to grade 7 or grade 8

What do I need to know about registering my child?

The most important fact that families need to know is that a child can only take the test once in a six-month period. Do not have your child take the test "just to see how he does" because he or she will not be able to take the test again in the same admissions season!

- Students can only take the test once in each admissions season, or six month period

Registration is done through the ERB. Their website is www.erblearn.org. On this site, you can also download a copy of *What to Expect on the ISEE*. The beginning of *What to Expect on the ISEE* includes sample problems and the end of the book has a complete practice test. I would recommend that you wait to give your student this practice test until after he or she has completed other preparations. Practice tests from the actual writers of the test are a valuable commodity, so save the practice test from *What to Expect on the ISEE.*

↖ Use other practice tests first

- Download *What to Expect on the ISEE*
- Feel free to have your student work through sample problems in the beginning of the book, just save the practice test for after your student has done other preparations

The test can be taken in a paper form or online at a testing center. The paper format is given at a number of schools in a large group setting. It can also be given in a small group setting at the ERB's New York offices or at a very limited number of sites in other locations. In the most recent ISEE student guide, small group testing sites are listed for Connecticut, Florida, Massachusetts, New York, Pennsylvania, Texas, China, South Korea, and Turkey. Outside of these areas, small group testing with the paper form is not available.

- Most students take the paper format at a school in a large group setting
- A very limited number of sites give the paper test in a small group setting – the list of these sites is in the ISEE Student Guide

Students can also take a computer-based form of the test at Prometric centers nationwide. The test is the exact same as the paper format test. Students can still go back and change answers. The only difference is that the students who take the computer-based test get to type their essays but students who take the paper form have to handwrite their essays. If you do go the testing center route, just make sure that your student knows that there will be people of all ages there taking a variety of tests. You can choose the time and date that works best for your student if you go the computer-based route.

- The ISEE can be taken at a testing center on the computer
- The computer-based test offers flexibility with date/time

You must request accommodations if your child needs them. If your child has an IEP or receives accommodations in school, then start the paperwork with the ERB promptly. Don't wait until the last minute as this is very stress inducing for both you and your student. If your child is going to get extended time, he or she should know that as he or she works through practice sections. Also, since your child can only take the ISEE once per admissions season, you won't have a "do over" if your child takes the test without accommodations.

Just how important is the ISEE to the admissions process?

Every school uses the test differently. In general, the more competitive the school, the more test scores are going to matter, but there are certainly exceptions to that rule. Reading through a school's literature is a great way to figure out whether or not a school emphasizes or deemphasizes testing. Also, call the admissions office where your child will be applying. Admissions officers are often quite candid about what the testing profile of their admitted students tends to be.

- Talk to the schools that your child is applying to in order to get a sense of the scores they look for

How can I help my student?

Keep your own cool. Never once has a student gotten a higher score because mom or dad freaked out. Approach this as a project. Good test taking skills can be learned and by working through the process with your child in a constructive manner, you are providing them with a roadmap for how to approach challenges in the future. We want them to be confident, but to earn that confidence through analysis, self-monitoring, and practice.

- Keep a positive attitude

What are the key elements of successful test preparation?

Analysis

It is important that students don't just do practice problem after practice problem without figuring out what they missed, and most importantly, WHY they missed those problems. Is there a particular type of problem that they keep missing? One issue that many students have is categorizing problems. When you go through a problem that they are stuck on, be sure to point out the words in the problem that pointed you in the correct direction.

- Teach your child to analyze why he or she missed a question

Self-monitoring

Students should develop a sense of their strengths and weaknesses so that they can best focus preparation time. This book provides many practice opportunities for each section, but your child may not need that. For example, if he or she is acing the math problems, then he or she shouldn't keep spending valuable time doing more of those problems. Maybe his or her time would be better spent on vocabulary. This is a great opportunity, and your student is at the perfect age, to be learning how to prioritize.

- Help your student prioritize material to work on

Practice

While it is important for a student to understand WHY he is doing what he is doing, at a certain point it just needs to become automatic. This is a timed test and you want the strategies to spring to mind without having to reinvent the wheel every time. Practice will make this process fast and easy. On test day all that practice will kick in to make this a positive and affirming experience for your student.

- Teach your child that he or she needs to practice what he or she has learned so that it is automatic on test day

How To Use This Book

This book is designed to teach you what you need to know in order to maximize your Middle Level ISEE performance.

There are strategies for each of the four multiple-choice sections as well as advice on the essay.

This book also includes a lot of content practice. There is a complete vocabulary section and detailed instruction for the math concepts that are tested on the ISEE.

You may find that you don't need to complete all of the content instruction. It is important to prioritize your time! If vocabulary is a weakness for you, then spend your time working through the vocabulary lessons. If some of the math concepts are challenging, then you should spend your study time working through the math sections.

At the end of this book is a practice test. This will give you a good idea of how you are doing with timing and what it feels like to take a longer test. There are included score charts, but please keep in mind that these are very rough estimates. It is very, very tough to accurately determine percentiles without a huge amount of data, so we have included percentiles just as a rough guideline of how the scoring works.

After you complete the practice test in this book, complete the practice test in *What to Expect on the ISEE*. That will give you your best estimate of performance on the actual ISEE.

I have spent years studying the test and analyzing the different question types, content, and the types of answers that the test writers prefer. Now you can benefit from my hard work! I will show how to approach questions so that you can raise your score significantly.

Let's get started!

The Format of the Middle Level ISEE

You can expect to see four scored sections plus an essay. The sections are listed below in the order that they will appear on the ISEE. One great thing about the ISEE is that it has a very predictable format.

The Four Scored Sections

✓ Verbal Reasoning
- 40 total questions
- 17-23 vocabulary (or synonyms) questions
- 17-23 sentence completion questions
- 20 minutes to complete

✓ Quantitative Reasoning
- 37 total questions
- 18-21 word problems
- 14-17 quantitative comparisons
- 35 minutes to complete

✓ Reading Comprehension
- 36 total questions
- 6 passages, each with 6 questions about it
- 35 minutes to complete

✓ Mathematics Achievement
- 47 math questions
- Questions probably look more like questions that you see in school than Quantitative Reasoning questions do
- 40 minutes to complete

The Essay

- Prompt for students to respond to
- 30 minutes to complete
- Two lined pieces of paper to write response on
- NOT scored, but a copy of the essay is sent to schools that student applies to

Now, on to the strategies and content! The strategies covered in this book will focus on the multiple-choice sections since those are what is used to determine your score. Please also see the tips for the essay found on page 401.

What Students Need To Know For the ISEE– Just the Basics

Here is what you really need to know to do well on the Middle Level ISEE:

How the Scoring Works

On the ISEE, your score is determined just by how many questions you answer correctly. They do not take off any points if you answer a question incorrectly.

When To Guess

On the ISEE, you want to answer absolutely everything, even if you haven't even looked at the question. You may answer the question correctly and they don't take off any points for questions that you answer incorrectly. If you are running out of time or don't understand a question, just blindly guess – you may choose the right answer!

The Percentile Score

You will get a raw score for the ISEE based upon how many questions you answer correctly. This raw score will then be converted into a scaled score. Neither of these scores are what schools are really looking at. They are looking for your percentile scores.

Percentile score is what schools are really looking at

The percentile score compares you to other students that are in your grade. For example, let's say that you are an eighth grader and you scored in the 70th percentile. What this means is that out of a hundred students in your grade, you would have done better than 70 of them.

- Your percentile score compares you only to other students in your grade

Many students applying to independent schools are used to getting almost all the questions correct on a test. You will probably miss more questions on this test than you are used to missing, but because the percentile score is what schools are looking at, don't let it get to you.

- You may miss more questions than you are used to, but that is OK as long as other students your age also miss those questions

You should also look at the scoring charts in *What to Expect on the ISEE*. These charts will give you a rough idea of how many questions you need to answer correctly to achieve different percentile scores.

Students always want to know, "What is a good percentile score?" Well, that depends on the schools you are applying to. The best resources are the admissions officers at the schools that you want to attend.

The Mother of All Strategies

Use the Process of Elimination, or "Ruling Out"

If you remember nothing else on test day, remember to use process of elimination. This is a multiple-choice test, and there are often answers that don't even make sense.

When you read a question, you want to read all of the answer choices before selecting one. You need to keep in mind that the test will ask you to choose the answer choice that "best" answers the question. Best is a relative word, so how can you know which answer choice best answers the question if you don't read them all?

- After you read the question, read ALL of the answer choices
- Look for the "best" answer, which may just be the least wrong answer choice

After you have read all of the answer choices, rule them out in order from most wrong to least wrong. Sometimes the "best" answer choice is not a great fit, but it is better than the others. This process will also clarify your thinking so that by the time you get down to only two answer choices, you have a better idea of what makes choices right or wrong.

- Rule out in order from most wrong to least wrong

On the ISEE, they don't take off for wrong answer choices, so it can be tempting to just blindly guess if you are confused. However, put a little of work into the question before you do that. Even if you are having trouble understanding a question, there may be one or two answer choices that don't even make sense.

- Use ruling out before you guess, even if the question leaves you totally confused

Verbal Section- Basic Strategies

In the verbal section you will see two question types:

- Synonyms
- Sentence completions

On the synonym questions, you will be given one question word and then you have to choose the answer choice that has the word that comes closest in meaning to that question word.

Synonym questions look something like this:

1. JOYOUS:

    (A) crying
    (B) happy
    (C) loud
    (D) mad

Out of all the answer choice words, happy comes closest in meaning to joyous. Choice B is correct.

The synonym questions won't all be that easy, but you get the idea.

The sentence completion questions give you a sentence in which a dashed line has replaced one word. Your job is to figure out which answer choice should be inserted instead of that dashed line so that the sentence makes the most sense.

The sentence completion questions look something like this:

2. The student was afraid that she had not done well on the test, but when she got her scores back she was pleasantly -------.

   (A) boisterous
   (B) panicked
   (C) surprised
   (D) worried

In this case, the beginning of the sentence tells us that the student thinks she hasn't done well. We then have the conjunction "but" which tells us that the second part of the sentence will contradict the first, so something good must have happened. Choice C fits the bill and it is the correct answer choice.

These are the basic question types that you will see in the Verbal Reasoning section. They are very different, so we have different strategies for each question type.

Synonym strategies

There are several strategies that we can use on the synonyms section. Which strategy you use for an individual question is up to you. It depends on what roots you know, whether or not you have heard the word before, and your gut sense about a word.

Think of these strategies as being your toolbox. Several tools can get the job done.

Here are the strategies:

- Come up with your own word
- Use positive or negative
- Use context
- Look for roots or word parts that you know

Strategy #1: Come up with your own word

Use this strategy when you read a question and a word just pops into your head. Don't force yourself to try to come up with your own definition when you aren't sure what the word means.

- Use this strategy when the definition pops into your head

If you read a question word and a synonym pops into your head, go ahead and jot it down. It is important that you write down the word because otherwise you may try to talk yourself into an answer choice that "seems to come close". One of the biggest enemies on any standardized test is doubt. Doubt leads to talking yourself into the wrong answer choice, and physically writing down the word gives you the confidence you need when you go through the answer choices.

- Physically write down the definition – don't hold it in your head

After you write down the word, start by crossing out answer choices that are not synonyms for your word. By the time you get down to two choices, you will have a much better idea of what you are looking for.

- Cross out words that don't work

The following drill contains words that you may be able think of a definition for. You should focus on creating good habits with these questions. Even if you see the correct answer, go ahead and write down the word that you were thinking of.

What are good habits?

- Jot down the definition – this will actually save time in the long run
- Use ruling out – physically cross out answer choices that you know are incorrect

Drill #1

1. RAPID:

   (A) exhausted
   (B) marvelous
   (C) professional
   (D) swift

2. DAINTY:

   (A) delicate
   (B) long
   (C) surprising
   (D) warm

3. TIMID:

   (A) alive
   (B) damp
   (C) shy
   (D) upset

4. SUBDUE:

   (A) abandon
   (B) overpower
   (C) stun
   (D) wander

5. ILLUSTRATE:

   (A) demonstrate
   (B) kneel
   (C) nudge
   (D) sacrifice

(Answers to this drill are found on page 39)

Strategy #2: Use positive or negative

Sometimes you see a word, and you couldn't define that word, but you have a "gut feeling" that it is either something good or something bad. Maybe you don't know what that word means, but you know you would be mad if someone called you that!

- You have to have a "gut feeling" about a word to use this strategy

To use this strategy, when you get that feeling that a word is either positive or negative, then write in a "+" or a "−" sign next to the word. Then go to your answer choices and rule out anything that is opposite, i.e., positive when your question word is negative or negative when your question word is positive.

- Physically write a "+" or "−" sign after the question word

To really make this strategy work for you, you also need to rule out any words that are neutral, or neither positive nor negative. For example, let's say the question word is DISTRESS. Distress is clearly a negative word. So we could rule out a positive answer choice, such as friendly, but we can also rule out a neutral word, such as sleepy. At night, it is good to be sleepy, during the day it is not. Sleepy is not clearly a negative word, so it goes.

- Rule out neutral words

To summarize, here are the basic steps to using this strategy:

1. If you have a gut negative or positive feeling about a word, write a "+" or "−" sign next to the question word.
2. Rule out any words that are opposite.
3. Also rule out any NEUTRAL words.
4. Pick from what is left.

Here is an example of a question where you may be able to use the positive/negative strategy:

1. CONDEMN:

    (A) arrive
    (B) blame
    (C) favor
    (D) tint

Let's say that you know that condemn is bad, but you can't think of a definition. We write a "−" sign next to it and then rule out anything that is positive. That means that choice C can go because it is positive. Now we can also rule out neutral words because we know condemn has to be negative. Arrive and tint are neither positive nor negative, so choices A and D are out. We are left with choice B, which is correct.

On the following drill, write a "+" or "−" sign next to each question word. Then rule out answer choices that are opposite or neutral. Pick from what is left. Even if you aren't sure if the question word is positive or negative, take a guess at it! You may get more right than you would have imagined.

1. HUMANE:

   (A) compassionate
   (B) invalid
   (C) portable
   (D) restricted

2. PROSPEROUS:

   (A) depressed
   (B) humid
   (C) resourceful
   (D) successful

3. TARNISH:

   (A) express
   (B) qualify
   (C) stain
   (D) thrill

4. LOATHE:

   (A) gobble
   (B) hate
   (C) land
   (D) pierce

5. GAUDY:

   (A) ahead
   (B) gloomy
   (C) practical
   (D) showy

(Answers to drills are found on page 39)

Strategy #3: Use context – Think of where you have heard the word before

Use this strategy when you can't define a word, but you can think of a sentence or phrase where you have heard the word before.

- This strategy only works when you have heard the word before

To apply this strategy, think of a sentence or phrase where you have heard the question word before. Then try plugging the answer choices into your phrase to see which one has the same meaning within that sentence or phrase.

- Think of where you have heard the word before
- Plug answer choice words into that sentence or phrase

Here is an example:

1.   ENDORSE:

   (A) drain
   (B) import
   (C) prowl
   (D) support

Let's say that you can't think of a definition for the word "endorse", but you have heard people say that they "endorse a candidate" for political office. Now we plug our answer choices into that phrase and see what would have the same meaning. Would it make sense to "drain a candidate"? Nope. Answer choice A is out. Would it make sense to "import a candidate" or "prowl a candidate"? No and no. Answer choices B and C are out. Finally, would it make sense to say that you "support a candidate"? Absolutely. Answer choice D is correct.

In the following drill, if you have heard the word before, then come up with a sentence or phrase and practice our strategy. If you have not heard the word before, you can't use the strategy of thinking where you have heard the word before! Use another strategy and ruling out to answer the question anyway. You may not answer every question correctly, but remember, nothing ventured, nothing gained.

Keep in mind that all of these words would be among the toughest on the test – the whole test will not be this hard! We just want to make sure you have practice for when the going gets tough.

Drill #3

1. WILY:

   (A) cunning
   (B) flattering
   (C) serious
   (D) tough

2. PROPHESY:

   (A) copy
   (B) mystify
   (C) predict
   (D) quiver

3. ABOLISH:

   (A) end
   (B) liberate
   (C) manage
   (D) salute

4. FATHOM:

   (A) ditch
   (B) nag
   (C) raid
   (D) understand

5. BRAWNY:

   (A) awake
   (B) coarse
   (C) strong
   (D) tiny

(Answers to drills are found on page 39)

Strategy #4: Look for roots or word parts that you know

This strategy works when you recognize that a word looks like another word that you know or when you recognize one of the roots that you have studied in school or in this book.

If you see something familiar in the question word, underline the roots or word parts that you recognize. If you can think of the meaning of the root, then look for answer choices that would go with that meaning. If you can't think of a specific meaning, think of other words that have that root and look for answer choices that are similar in meaning to those other words.

- Underline word parts that you recognize
- Think of the meaning of that word part
- If you can't think of a meaning for that word part, think of other words with that same word part

Here is an example of a question that uses a word with recognizable word parts:

1. EXCLUDE:

   (A) drift
   (B) find
   (C) prohibit
   (D) send

There are two word parts in the word "exclude" that can help us out. First, we have the prefix "ex-", which means out (think of the word exit). Secondly, "clu" is a word root that means to shut (think of the word include). Using these word parts, we can see that exclude has something to do with shutting out. Choice C comes closest to this meaning, so it is correct.

For the following drill, try to use word parts to come up with the correct answer choice. If you can't think of what the word root, prefix, or suffix means, then think of other words that have the same root, prefix, or suffix.

Drill #4

1. POSTPONE:

    (A) allow
    (B) delay
    (C) recruit
    (D) tease

2. SUBTERRANEAN:

    (A) faded
    (B) partial
    (C) tragic
    (D) underground

3. CERTIFY:

    (A) confirm
    (B) debate
    (C) ponder
    (D) toss

4. IMPERFECT:

    (A) abandoned
    (B) defective
    (C) separate
    (D) upward

5. BENEFICIAL:

    (A) brisk
    (B) expensive
    (C) helpful
    (D) trim

(Answers to drills are found on page 39)

Sentence Completion strategies

We have several strategies in our toolbox for sentence completion questions.

They include:

- Underlining the key idea
- Look for sentences showing contrast
- Look for sentences showing cause or sequence
- Use our strategies for synonyms when you don't know the meaning of one or more of the answer choices

Strategy #1: Underlining the key idea

Perhaps our most powerful strategy is underlining what the sentence is about.

If you are unsure of what to underline, look for the part of the sentence that if you changed that word or phrase, you would change what you were looking for.

- Look for the part of the sentence that if you changed it, you would change what word or phrase would fit in the blank
- Underline this key word or phrase

After you underline the key word or phrase, try coming up with your own word or phrase that would fit in the blank. This will help you easily rule out answer choices that are not like your word.

- After you underline the key word/phrase, fill in your own word or phrase in the blank

Here is an example:

1. The artist spent his days ------ the walls in the cave.
2. The scientist spent his days ------ the walls in the cave.

Do you see how changing just one word changed what we would put in that blank? If the person was an artist, we might expect him to be painting the walls in the cave. If the person was a scientist, however, we would expect him to maybe be studying the walls in the cave or analyzing the walls in the cave.

Following is a drill for you to try. For this drill, you should underline the key word or phrase and then fill in a word that would work for the blank. There are no answer choices for these questions because we just want you to focus on the process of underlining the key word or phrase and filling in your own word at this point.

Drill #5

Underline the key word or phrase. Then jot down a word that would work for the blank

1. Author Charles Dickens ------ class structure in Victorian London.

   Word to fill in the blank?

2. The company received ------ calls after they placed an ad in a widely read publication.

   Word to fill in the blank?

3. The path seemed to wander in a ----- manner, twisting and turning through the woods.

   Word to fill in the blank?

4. The impulsive shopper swooped into the store and filled her cart -------.

   Word to fill in the blank?

(Answers to drills are found on page 39)

Strategy #2: Look for sentences showing contrast

Some sentences show contrast. With these sentences, the end of the sentence changes direction from the beginning of the sentence.

These sentences often use the words "but", "although", "however", "rather", and "even though". If you see any of these words, circle them.

The first step in answering these questions is to underline the key word or phrase. We need to know what we are contrasting with. The next step is to circle the words that show contrast, such as "but", "although", "however", "rather", and "even though".

- Underline key word or phrase
- Circle words that show contrast such as "but", "although", "however", "rather", and "even though"

Here is an example:

1. Although the student tried to stay interested, her expression clearly showed that she was
   -------.

   (A) bored
   (B) jealous
   (C) mysterious
   (D) positive

In this question, we circle the word "although" since it shows contrast. Then we underline the word "interested" since the sentence is about the student staying interested (if we changed that word, we would change what the blank would be). Since we have the word "although" we know that we are looking for a word that contrasts with interested. Since bored is the opposite of interested, choice A is correct.

For the following drill, be sure that you:

- Underline the key word or phrase
- Circle any words that show contrast
- Fill in your own word for the blank
- Use ruling out to get to the right answer

Drill #6

1. His teachers always predicted that Sam would not be successful as an adult but he founded a company that -------.

   (A) failed
   (B) limped
   (C) managed
   (D) thrived

2. Although Kara was often tardy, on the day of her birthday she was always -------.

   (A) active
   (B) happy
   (C) prompt
   (D) tense

3. Critics said that the musician's new album would be a flop, but album sales were instead------.

   (A) definite
   (B) limited
   (C) slender
   (D) strong

4. Even though there was a big crowd at the event, it was surprisingly --------.

   (A) impolite
   (B) mellow
   (C) rowdy
   (D) tedious

Continued on the next page

Drill #6 (continued)

5. People often think of China as having a large population, however, there are several regions of China that have ----- inhabitants.

   (A) beloved
   (B) few
   (C) regular
   (D) typical

6. Although Ansel Adams was unsuccessful as a student, he later -------- as a photographer.

   (A) built
   (B) discussed
   (C) prospered
   (D) travelled

7. In contrast to the Senate where it is very rare for a candidate to run unopposed, -------- elections are much more common in the House of Representatives.

   (A) dismal
   (B) honorable
   (C) late
   (D) uncontested

(Answers to drills are found on page 39)

Strategy #3: Look for sentences showing cause or sequence

Many sentences in the sentence completions section use the cause or sequence relationship. In these sentences, one thing leads to another. Sometimes one directly causes the other, but sometimes one just happens to come after the other.

- Look for sentences where one thing leads to another
- Think about what the effect of the given action would be

Sometimes you will see the words "because", "when", or "after" in these sentences, but there is often no one particular word that indicates cause.

- If you see the words "because", "when", "after", or other words showing sequence, you usually have a sentence showing cause or sequence
- There may be no one word that indicates this relationship in a sentence

Here is an example:

1. Years of floods and fires left the former resort ------.

   (A) busy
   (B) effective
   (C) patriotic
   (D) wrecked

To answer this question, we have to ask ourselves what years of floods and fires would lead to. While you could say that the resort would be left busy because they had lot of clean up work to do, the more direct answer would be that it was left wrecked. Choice D is the correct answer.

Here is a drill for you to try. Remember to look for the answer choice that shows the clearest cause or sequence relationship.

Drill #7

1. In the early 1800s there was a high demand in New England for cleared pastureland and lumber which led to rapid -------- in the region.

   (A) deforestation
   (B) decline
   (C) growth
   (D) looting

2. John F. Kennedy's vision of a national center for performing arts was fulfilled in 1971 when the Kennedy Center ----- holding performances.

   (A) annexed
   (B) commenced
   (C) halted
   (D) limited

3. When George entered a room where he didn't know anyone, he felt rather-------.

   (A) apprehensive
   (B) backward
   (C) defensive
   (D) quaint

4. The increase in the number of students forced the school district to consider ----- existing schools.

   (A) adding
   (B) limiting
   (C) painting
   (D) supplementing

5. The damage caused by the tornado was ------.

   (A) apathetic
   (B) catastrophic
   (C) efficient
   (D) musty

6. When part of their habitat was destroyed, the number of lynx cats in the area -------.

   (A) increased
   (B) returned
   (C) waned
   (D) yielded

7. As the excitement over the upcoming summer break increased, the students became more and more --------.

   (A) efficient
   (B) gallant
   (C) inattentive
   (D) restrained

(Answers to drills are found on page 39)

Strategy #4: Use our strategies for synonyms when you don't know the meaning of one or more of the answer choices

Sometimes you know what kind of word you are looking for, but the problem is that you don't know the meaning of some of the answer choices. If this is the case, ask yourself:

- Am I looking for a positive or negative word?
- Do any of the answer choices have roots or prefixes that I can use?
- Have I heard any of the answer choices used in a sentence or phrase before?

In the following drill, practice using our strategies of looking for a positive or a negative word, looking for roots or word parts that you know, or thinking of where you have heard an answer choice before. You may not be certain of the answer choice that you choose, but by using ruling out you are more likely to answer questions correctly.

Drill #8

1. The majestic mountain views often leave visitors feeling ------.

    (A) awe
    (B) candid
    (C) excluded
    (D) sorrowful

2. Since the mall was nicely redone and more parking was added, the restaurant business there has --------.

    (A) crumbled
    (B) flapped
    (C) thrived
    (D) vanished

3. Mother Teresa showed her ------ by helping people who lived in poverty.

    (A) bashfulness
    (B) compassion
    (C) finesse
    (D) technique

4. Henry Thoreau took off to the woods of Concord, Massachusetts by himself in a search for --------.

    (A) accuracy
    (B) conversation
    (C) revulsion
    (D) solitude

5. The sides of the shape are not all the same size, rather they are ------.

    (A) adjoining
    (B) buckled
    (C) familiar
    (D) irregular

6. When Paul Revere saw the British troops approaching, he took off with ------- to warn the other rebels as quickly as he could.

    (A) dispatch
    (B) haughtiness
    (C) laxity
    (D) silence

7. When the runner won the marathon, the local press praised her ------- performance.

    (A) lucid
    (B) neutral
    (C) superlative
    (D) troubled

Now you have the skills that you need to do well on the Verbal Reasoning section of the ISEE! An important part of improving your verbal reasoning score is also studying vocabulary. Be sure to spend time with the following vocabulary section.

Answers to Drills

Drill #1

1. D
2. A
3. C
4. B
5. A

Drill #2

1. A
2. D
3. C
4. B
5. D

Drill #3

1. A
2. C
3. A
4. D
5. C

Drill #4

1. B
2. D
3. A
4. B
5. C

Drill #5

1. Underline author, fill in a word like *describes*
2. Underline widely read, fill in a word like *many*
3. Underline twisting and turning, fill in a word like *indirect*
4. Underline impulsive, fill in a word like *quickly*

Drill #6

1. D   5. B
2. C   6. C
3. D   7. D
4. B

Drill #7

1. A   5. B
2. B   6. C
3. A   7. C
4. D

Drill #8

1. A   5. D
2. C   6. A
3. B   7. C
4. D

Vocabulary Review

A key component of improving your verbal score is increasing your vocabulary. Following are ten lessons that will help you do just that.

Each lesson has twenty new words for you to learn. There are good words, there are bad words, and there are even words with roots. Exciting, eh?

After you learn the words, complete the activities for each lesson. The best way to learn new words is to think of them in categories and to evaluate how the words relate to one another. The activities will help you do this.

The activities also give you practice with synonyms and sentence completions. You will be working on strategy while you are learning new words – think of it as a two for one! Be aware that the synonym and sentence completion questions may have a different form of the word than is given in the word list. This is by design so that you get used to looking for words that are similar to the words that you have learned.

- The synonym and sentence completion practice may use a different form of the word from the list

If there are words that you have trouble remembering as you work through the lessons, go ahead and make flashcards for them. Continue to review these flashcards until the words stick. There may also be words that you run across in the analogies or synonyms practice that you do not know the meaning of. Make flashcards for these words as well.

- Make flashcards for the words that you have trouble remembering

After each lesson are the answers. Be sure to check your work.

Now, on to the lessons!

Lesson 1

Words to Learn

Below are the twenty words used in Lesson 1; refer back to this list as needed as you move through the lesson.

Expel: to force out
Disband: to break up
Chasm: gorge (a seemingly endless one)
Conscientious: responsible
Dispense: distribute (hand out)

Dismantle: take apart
Abyss: never-ending gulf
Propel: drive (to push forward)
Discontent: unhappiness
Reliable: trustworthy

Compel: to force
Disbelief: doubt
Crevice: a crack (or gap)
Judicious: wise
Precipice: a cliff

Dislodge: to loosen
Repel: to force away
Brink: edge
Prim: proper (maybe even a little uptight)
Disembark: to get off (generally from a plane, train, car, etc.)

Expel
Disband
Chasm
Conscientious
Dispense

Word List Practice

Use the words from the Lesson 1 list to answer the following questions.

1. If you were working on a group project, what three words describe the kind of people that you would like to have in your group?

   a.

   b.

   c.

2. Your mom might want you to hang out with this kind of person in hopes that you would pick up his or her good manners:

   a.

3. What two words describe a deep crack in the earth that doesn't seem to end?

   a.

   b.

4. What word could describe a crack in the earth that maybe isn't as deep?

5. You must be very careful if you are standing on the _____ of a_____ and looking into a chasm or abyss.

Roots Practice

The root "dis" can mean either not or away/apart.

1. In what two words from our list does the "dis" root mean not?

   a.
   b.

2. There are five words from our list in which the "dis" root means away from or apart. What are they?

   a.
   b.
   c.
   d.
   e.

3. There are four words from our list that have the "pel" root. What are they?

   a.
   b.
   c.
   d.

4. From these words, what do you think the root "pel" means?

Make sure to study the words before you do these practice questions. Try not to look back at the list.

Synonyms Practice

1. DISCONTENT:

   (A) boredom
   (B) crevice
   (C) surface
   (D) unhappiness

2. BRINK:

   (A) edge
   (B) lever
   (C) reliability
   (D) scuffle

3. CHASM:

   (A) abyss
   (B) formula
   (C) mountain
   (D) precipice

4. DISLODGE:

   (A) confine
   (B) fetch
   (C) loosen
   (D) propel

5. COMPEL:

   (A) disband
   (B) force
   (C) illustrate
   (D) suspect

Sentence Completions Practice

1. Some people apply Eucalyptus oil to their skin in order to -------- mosquitoes on summer nights.

   (A) dispense
   (B) hide
   (C) repel
   (D) writhe

2. Many inventors, such as Benjamin Franklin, were known to ------ everyday objects to see how they worked.

    (A) dismantle
    (B) expel
    (C) provide
    (D) receive

3. During the Great Depression, many families had to spend their money in a ------- manner since unemployment rates were very high.

    (A) disbelieving
    (B) judicious
    (C) possible
    (D) reckless

4. After more than two months at sea, the settlers aboard the Mayflower were overjoyed to ------- from the ship.

    (A) disembark
    (B) manufacture
    (C) navigate
    (D) plead

5. Although Craig had a reputation for turning in his homework late, his homework grade showed that he was actually quite ------- when it came to handing in assignments on time.

    (A) absent
    (B) conscientious
    (C) daring
    (D) prim

Lesson 1 Answers

Word List Practice

1. a. conscientious
   b. judicious
   c. reliable
2. prim
3. a. chasm
   b. abyss
4. crevice
5. first blank: brink
   second blank: precipice

Roots Practice

1. a. disbelief
   b. discontent
2. a. disband
   b. dislodge
   c. dispense
   d. dismantle
   e. disembark
3. a. expel
   b. compel
   c. propel
   d. repel
4. to force

Synonyms Practice

1. D
2. A
3. A
4. C
5. B

Sentence Completion Practice

1. C
2. A
3. B
4. A
5. B

Lesson 2

Words to Learn

Below are the twenty words used in Lesson 2; refer back to this list as needed as you move through the lesson.

Abode: home
Misconduct: bad behavior
Frank: honest (really, really honest)
Novel: new
Clarify: explain (to make clear)

Deflect: to bend away
Misguided: mistaken
Confirm: validate (to say something is true)
Deprive: withhold (to keep something needed away from another person)
Flounder: to struggle

Dwelling: place to live
Mistrust: doubt
Deplore: to disapprove
Certify: guarantee
Destitute: without food, clothing, and shelter

Divulge: to reveal (something that is secret)
Depress: to push down
Mishap: accident
Verify: to prove true
Novice: beginner

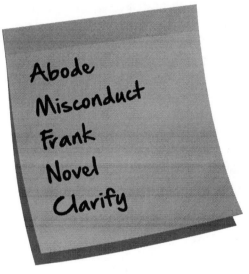

Word List Practice

Use the words from the Lesson 2 list to answer the following questions.

1. If you need to know if something is true, you might ask someone to do what three things?

    a.

    b.

    c.

2. If you just need more details, then what would you ask someone to do?

3. If you just need the truth, what might you ask someone to be?

4. If you tell a friend a deep, dark secret, what are you hoping that he or she will not do?

5. When you try something new, what might you do at first?

6. What two words describe a place where you could live?

    a.

    b.

Roots Practice

1. The "de-" prefix can mean down or away. What three words from our list have the "de-" prefix that means down or away?

   a.

   b.

   c.

2. The "de-" prefix can also mean without. What two words have the "de-" prefix that means without?

   a.

   b.

3. We have two words in our list that have the "nov" root. What are they?

   a.

   b.

4. From these words, what do you think the "nov" root means?

5. We have four words in our list that have the "mis-" prefix. What are they?

   a.

   b.

   c.

   d.

6. From these words what do you think the "mis-" prefix means? (Hint: mistake also has the mis- prefix)

Make sure to study the words before you do these practice questions. Try not to look back at the list.

Synonyms Practice

1. CONFIRM:

    (A) depress
    (B) fragment
    (C) linger
    (D) verify

2. DWELLING:

    (A) abode
    (B) kitchen
    (C) mishap
    (D) portfolio

3. DIVULGE:

    (A) clarify
    (B) plan
    (C) reveal
    (D) trust

4. FRANK:

    (A) certified
    (B) honest
    (C) qualified
    (D) sustained

5. NOVICE:

    (A) beginner
    (B) expert
    (C) soldier
    (D) trainer

Sentence Completion Practice

1. The fall of the czar in 1917 left many members of the Russian ruling class ------- and struggling to provide the basic necessities for their families.

    (A) busy
    (B) destitute
    (C) misguided
    (D) responsible

2. If a mirror is placed in the beam of light created by a laser then the beam of light is -----
and changes direction.

   (A) clarified
   (B) deflected
   (C) divulged
   (D) redeemed

3. When Richard Nixon ordered his workers to spy on his opponent, he committed an act
of -------- that led to his resignation as president of the United States.

   (A) misconduct
   (B) misfortune
   (C) mishap
   (D) mistrust

4. Benjamin Franklin was known for coming up with ------ solutions to common problems, such as when he invented bifocals because he kept losing his own eyeglasses.

   (A) deplorable
   (B) frequent
   (C) lively
   (D) novel

5. When a person tries to ------- himself of food and calories, the strategy often backfires
and that person winds up consuming more calories than he would have otherwise eaten.

   (A) certify
   (B) condense
   (C) deprive
   (D) flounder

Lesson 2 Answers

Word List Practice

1. a. verify
   b. certify
   c. confirm
2. clarify
3. frank
4. divulge it to someone else
5. flounder
6. a. abode
   b. dwelling

Roots Practice

1. a. deflect
   b. depress
   c. deplore (to deplore someone is to put him or her down, or see him or her as less)
2. a. deprive
   b. destitute
3. a. novel
   b. novice
4. new
5. a. misconduct
   b. mishap
   c. misguided
   d. mistrust
6. wrong or bad

Synonyms Practice

1. D
2. A
3. C
4. B
5. A

Sentence Completions

1. B
2. B
3. A
4. D
5. C

Lesson 3

Words to Learn

Below are the twenty words used in Lesson 3; refer back to this list as needed as you move through the lesson.

Benediction: blessing
Advocate: support
Era: period of time
Overdue: late
Frigid: freezing (really, really cold)

Beneficial: helpful
Adaptable: flexible (can be changed)
Eternity: forever
Encore: repeat performance
Torrid: scorching (very hot)

Elapse: time passing by
Rash: careless (doing something without thinking it through)
Episode: an incident
Arid: dry (extremely dry)
Adjacent: touching (next to)

Perpetual: constant
Momentary: brief
Sultry: hot and humid
Punctual: on time
Abrupt: sudden

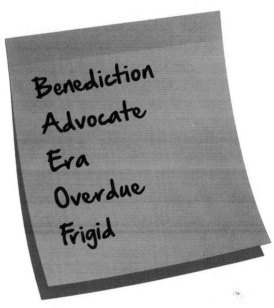

Word List Practice

Use the words from the Lesson 3 list to answer the following questions.

1. What is longer, an era or an episode?

2. What word from our list means a time period much greater than an era?

3. If you are going to meet friends at the movies, would you rather they be punctual or overdue?

4. What two words from our list could describe actions that are sudden and not thought through?

    a.
    b.

5. What would it mean if someone said that "15 minutes has elapsed"?

6. Would it be better if your chores were perpetual or momentary?

7. After a concert, the band often walks off the stage and then comes back to do what?

8. What two words from our list mean hot?

9. What is the difference between these two words?

10. What word would we use to describe a desert climate?

11. What word would describe the arctic or North Pole?

Roots Practice

1. We have three words in our list with the "ad-" prefix. What are they?

    a.
    b.
    c.

2. The "ad-" prefix means to or toward. How does the word adaptable relate to this meaning?

3. We have two words with the "bene" root in them. What are they?

    a.
    b.

4. From these two words, do you think that the "bene" root has a positive or negative meaning?

Make sure to study the words before you do these practice questions. Try not to look back at the list.

Synonyms Practice

1. ADVOCATE:

    (A) elapse
    (B) lecture
    (C) paralyze
    (D) support

2. MOMENTARY:

    (A) brief
    (B) pleasant
    (C) rash
    (D) sultry

3. OVERDUE:

    (A) eternal
    (B) final
    (C) late
    (D) torrid

4. BENEDICTION:

    (A) aptitude
    (B) blessing
    (C) era
    (D) moment

5. PERPETUAL:

    (A) adaptable
    (B) constant
    (C) punctual
    (D) uneasy

Sentence Completion Practice

1. There are often border disputes between countries that are -------.

    (A) adjacent
    (B) frigid
    (C) punctual
    (D) wealthy

2. Due to its ------ climate, the Sahara desert is one of the most dangerous places in the world for a traveller to get lost.

   (A) abrupt
   (B) arid
   (C) beneficial
   (D) visible

3. Al Gore, an environmentalist, has long ------- for stricter guidelines for reducing pollution.

   (A) advocated
   (B) elapsed
   (C) refused
   (D) trended

4. Many performers claim to retire and then return to the stage for one more -------.

   (A) benediction
   (B) conduct
   (C) difference
   (D) encore

5. Television dramas often have a cliffhanger at the end of each ------- so that viewers will return to find out what happens next.

   (A) core
   (B) disbelief
   (C) episode
   (D) label

Lesson 3 Answers

Word List Practice

1. An era is longer. An era is usually measured in years but an episode happens just once.
2. Eternity
3. It would be better if they were punctual (on time) than overdue (late).
4. a. rash
   b. abrupt
5. 15 minutes has gone by.
6. It would be better if chores were momentary because then doing them would end quickly. If chores were perpetual, it would mean that you would have to keep doing chores again and again.
7. perform an encore
8. torrid and sultry
9. Torrid implies a scorching dry heat and sultry is hot and very humid.
10. arid
11. frigid

Roots Practice

1. a. adjacent
   b. advocate
   c. adaptable
2. If something is adaptable, then it can change to its environment.
3. a. benediction
   b. beneficial
4. positive

Synonyms Practice

1. D
2. A
3. C
4. B
5. B

Sentence Completions

1. A
2. B
3. A
4. D
5. C

Lesson 4

Words to Learn

Below are the twenty words used in Lesson 4; refer back to this list as needed as you move through the lesson.

Detract: diminish (to take away from)
Contract: to draw in
Adversary: opponent
Contradict: challenge
Discord: disagreement

Extract: pull out
Desolate: bleak (abandoned)
Agitate: irritate (stir up trouble)
Diverge: separate
Abate: decrease

Abstract: not literal OR to take out
Isolate: separate
Antagonize: to anger
Fray: battle
Retract: take back

Absolute: pure
Belligerent: hostile
Defensive: guarded (on the look out)
Besiege: to attack
Abolition: end

Detract
Contract
Adversary
Contradict
Discord

Word List Practice

Use the words from the Lesson 4 list to answer the following questions.

1. We have a lot of fighting words in this section. What two words describe how you might feel if you were looking for a fight?

   a.
   b.

2. Before a fight begins, what two things might you do to an adversary?

   a.
   b.

3. If one group besieged another group, what might result?

4. There is an expression "to sow the seeds of discord". What does this mean?

5. If your opinion diverges from another person's, what does that mean?

6. Would you be happy or mad if your parents contradicted you about your bedtime?

Roots Practice

1. We have five words with the "tract" root in them. What are they?

   a.

   b.

   c.

   d.

   e.

2. From these words, what do you think the "tract" root means?

3. How does the word tractor relate to this root?

4. We have three words with the "sol" root in them. What are they?

   a.

   b.

   c.

5. The "sol" root means alone. How does the word absolute relate to this meaning?

6. We have four words with the "ab-" prefix in them. What are they?

   a.

   b.

   c.

   d.

7. The "ab-" prefix means away from. How does this meaning relate to the word abate?

Make sure to study the words before you do these practice questions. Try not to look back at the list.

Synonyms Practice

1. BELLIGERENT:

   (A) abstract
   (B) bleak
   (C) hostile
   (D) sudden

2. ABATE:

   (A) antagonize
   (B) decrease
   (C) detract
   (D) discord

3. ADVERSARY:

   (A) ally
   (B) counselor
   (C) opponent
   (D) uneasy

4. ISOLATE:

   (A) contradict
   (B) irritate
   (C) join
   (D) separate

5. DISCORD:

   (A) abolition
   (B) assent
   (C) consent
   (D) disagreement

Sentence Completion Practice

1. The army generals prepared a -------- strategy in case their troops were attacked.

   (A) defensive
   (B) desolate
   (C) punctual
   (D) rash

2. The rescuers have to wait for the floodwaters to -------- before they can safely access the damaged homes.

   (A) abate
   (B) agitate
   (C) isolate
   (D) support

3. Arguing with your mother when she is clearly exhausted will likely just -------- her instead of getting her to see your point of view.

   (A) accomplish
   (B) antagonize
   (C) contradict
   (D) discord

4. The decay in Tom's tooth was so widespread that the dentist had no choice but to ------- the entire tooth.

   (A) annoy
   (B) contract
   (C) detract
   (D) extract

5. Slaves became legally free when President Lincoln's Emancipation Proclamation in 1863 called for the -------- of slavery in the United States.

   (A) abolition
   (B) episode
   (C) legend
   (D) spectator

Lesson 4 Answers

Word List Practice

1. a. belligerent
   b. defensive
2. a. agitate
   b. antagonize
3. a fray
4. "To sow the seeds of discord" is to take actions that will lead to disagreement and conflict.
5. It means that your opinion is different from the other person's.
6. You would probably be mad since most kids want to stay up later than their parents let them.

Roots Practice

1. a. detract
   b. extract
   c. abstract
   d. contract
   e. retract
2. to pull
3. A tractor is a machine that pulls things.
4. a. desolate
   b. absolute
   c. isolate
5. If something is absolute, it stands alone. For example, the absolute winner means that there was one clear winner.

6. a. abate
   b. abolition
   c. abstract
   d. absolute
7. Abate usually means to reduce, or move away from, a problem. For example, the problem of flooding can be abated with higher sea walls.

Synonyms Practice

1. C
2. B
3. C
4. D
5. D

Sentence Completions

1. A
2. A
3. B
4. D
5. A

Lesson 5

Words to Learn

Below are the twenty words used in Lesson 5; refer back to this list as needed as you move through the lesson.

Dejected: depressed
Fortify: strengthen (make stronger)
Decoy: a fake
Feint: imitation
Harmonious: peaceful

Eject: push out
Counterfeit: a copy (made to look real)
Assent: agree
Sham: a trick
Deceit: dishonesty

Mimic: to copy
Trajectory: path
Impostor: a fraud (someone who pretends to be someone else)
Accord: agreement
Farce: mockery (a funny imitation)

Fortitude: strength
Hoodwink: to trick
Pedestrian (as an adjective): boring
Project (as a verb): to look forward
Forthright: honest (even when being honest isn't easy)

Word List Practice

Use the words from the Lesson 5 list to answer the following questions.

1. We have four words that describe something that is a fake. What are they?

   a.

   b.

   c.

   d.

2. What three words relate to purposely tricking someone?

   a.

   b.

   c.

3. In a farce, what does an actor do?

4. We have three words in out list that relate to being peaceful and in agreement. What are they?

   a.

   b.

   c.

5. What word would describe watching paint dry on a wall?

Roots Practice

1. We have four words with the "ject" root in them. What are they?

   a.

   b.

   c.

   d.

2. The "ject" root means to throw. How does this relate to the word trajectory?

3. In the word dejected, we have the "de-" prefix that means down or away and the "ject" root which means to throw. What is being thrown down with the word dejected?

4. We have three words with the "fort" root in them. What are they?

   a.

   b.

   c.

5. The "fort" root means strong. If you are being forthright, what are you showing strength of?

Make sure to study the words before you do these practice questions. Try not to look back at the list.

Synonyms Practice

1. COUNTERFEIT:

   (A) fortitude
   (B) impostor
   (C) remedy
   (D) victory

2. FORTHRIGHT:

   (A) dejected
   (B) generous
   (C) honest
   (D) impulsive

3. PEDESTRIAN:

   (A) boring
   (B) harmonious
   (C) honest
   (D) quaint

4. HOODWINK:

   (A) deceive
   (B) mimic
   (C) project
   (D) wither

5. SHAM:

   (A) core
   (B) donation
   (C) ejection
   (D) trick

Sentence Completion Practice

1. At the Yalta Conference, the United States, Britain, and Russia came together to sign a(n) -------- that would permit the occupation of postwar Germany.

   (A) accord
   (B) brink
   (C) guide
   (D) leader

2. Physicists must take into account the rotation of the Earth when they predict the -------- of rockets.

   (A) feint
   (B) label
   (C) residue
   (D) trajectory

3. Battlements are defensive structures that were added to castles in medieval times in order to -------- the castle and keep its inhabitants safe from attack.

   (A) eject
   (B) fortify
   (C) hoodwink
   (D) permit

4. In comic books, the villains often use ------ so that the hero will follow the wrong person while the real culprit escapes.

   (A) accord
   (B) captives
   (C) decoys
   (D) growth

5. The weather was very hot and Gil hoped his mother would ------- to taking him to the pool to cool off.

   (A) assent
   (B) hate
   (C) postpone
   (D) secure

Lesson 5 Answers

Word List Practice

1. a. impostor
   b. decoy
   c. counterfeit
   d. feint
2. a. hoodwink
   b. deceit
   c. sham
3. mimic another person in a funny way
4. a. accord
   b. assent
   c. harmonious
5. pedestrian

Roots Practice

1. a. dejected
   b. eject
   c. project
   d. trajectory
2. A trajectory can be the path that something takes when it is thrown.
3. someone's spirit
4. a. fortify
   b. fortitude
   c. forthright
5. character

Synonyms Practice

1. B
2. C
3. A
4. A
5. D

Sentence Completions

1. A
2. D
3. B
4. C
5. A

Lesson 6

Words to Learn

Below are the twenty words used in Lesson 6; refer back to this list as needed as you move through the lesson.

Continuity: persistence (remaining the same)
Creed: belief (set of beliefs)
Pious: religious
Disapprove: criticize
Pauper: beggar (poor person)

Converge: combine (come together)
Incredible: unbelievable
Disciple: follower
Disdain: disrespect
Zealot: overly enthusiastic person

Discredited: disgraced (proven wrong)
Fanatic: radical (overly enthusiastic person)
Chide: criticize
Coincide: happen at the same time
Jeer: ridicule (make fun of someone)

Righteous: moral
Spendthrift: a big spender (someone who spends money wastefully)
Jilt: to reject
Devout: religious (very religious)
Doctrine: teachings of a church or group

Word List Practice

Use the words from the Lesson 6 list to answer the following questions.

1. What three adjectives could describe someone who attends church regularly, but isn't an extremist?

   a.
   b.
   c.

2. If a group follows a very strict set of beliefs, what are the group members (or followers) called?

3. What two words could describe a religious extremist?

   a.
   b.

4. What two words could describe the set of beliefs that a religious person follows?

   a.
   b.

5. There are five words in our list that are related to people being just plain mean. What are they?

   a.
   b.
   c.
   d.
   e.

6. If you are a spendthrift, what might you become?

Roots Practice

1. We have three words with the "co-" prefix. What are those words?

   a.

   b.

   c.

2. From these words, what do you think the "co-" prefix means?

3. What two words in our list have the "cred" root in them?

   a.

   b.

4. The "cred" root means to believe. What other word in our list is related to the "cred" root? (Hint: it looks very similar to cred)

Make sure to study the words before you do these practice questions. Try not to look back at the list.

Synonyms Practice

1. INCREDIBLE:

   (A) disapproving
   (B) lonesome
   (C) superb
   (D) unbelievable

2. PIOUS:

   (A) devout
   (B) jilted
   (C) luxurious
   (D) ordinary

3. ZEALOT:

   (A) aviator
   (B) fanatic
   (C) horde
   (D) soldier

4. DISCIPLE:

   (A) bandit
   (B) comedian
   (C) follower
   (D) host

5. CREED:

   (A) doctrine
   (B) farce
   (C) precipice
   (D) retraction

Sentence Completion Practice

1. The bus stop is often very busy because the pick up times for the elementary school, middle school, and high school all -------.

   (A) coincide
   (B) jeer
   (C) rotate
   (D) wander

2. Although many people once believed that the sun orbited the Earth, that theory was ----- when it was discovered that the Earth really orbited the sun.

    (A) converged
    (B) discredited
    (C) elapsed
    (D) settled

3. During the roaring '20s, many people acted like -------, throwing lavish parties overflowing with expensive food and drinks.

    (A) advocates
    (B) decoys
    (C) paupers
    (D) spendthrifts

4. Henry the VIII was obsessed with producing a male heir to take over the throne so that family ------- would be maintained within the British monarchy.

    (A) continuity
    (B) contempt
    (C) isolation
    (D) righteousness

5   It is rude to -------- someone in front of other people.

    (A) assent
    (B) chide
    (C) praise
    (D) relinquish

Lesson 6 Answers

Word List Practice

1. a. devout
   b. pious
   c. righteous
2. disciples
3. a. fanatic
   b. zealot
4. a. doctrine
   b. creed
5. a. disdain
   b. chide
   c. disapprove
   d. jeer
   e. jilt
6. a pauper

Roots Practice

1. a. continuity
   b. converge
   c. coincide
2. together or with
3. a. incredible
   b. discredited
4. creed

Synonyms Practice

1. D
2. A
3. B
4. C
5. A

Sentence Completion Practice

1. A
2. B
3. D
4. A
5. B

Words to Learn

Below are the twenty words used in Lesson 7; refer back to this list as needed as you move through the lesson.

Adhere: stick to
Pact: agreement
Insolent: disrespectful
Deluge: downpour (or flood)
Petty: unimportant or small-minded

Amiable: friendly
Cohesive: unified (bound together)
Wayward: disobedient (not following the rules)
Douse: drench (cover with water)
Sullen: gloomy

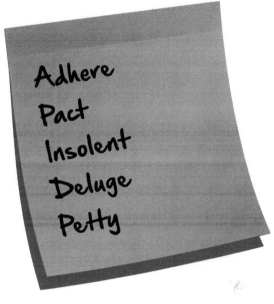

Clique: exclusive group
Adhesive: sticky
Pacify: to calm
Haughty: snobbish (believing you are better than other people)
Ruthless: heartless (willing to do anything to win)

Congregation: group (often a group of church members)
Unruly: uncontrollable
Cordial: welcoming
Impudent: insulting (or rude)
Menagerie: an unusual collection (often of people or animals)

Word List Practice

Use the words from the Lesson 7 list to answer the following questions.

1. We have three words in our list that mean group.

   a. Which word describes a group that excludes other people?

   b. Which word describes a group that attends a church together?

   c. Which word describes a group with unusual members?

2. What two words relate to being soaked?
   a.
   b.

3. What eight words from our list would you NOT want to be called?

   a.
   b.
   c.
   d.
   e.
   f.
   g.
   h.

4. What two words from our list would describe a friendly person?

   a.
   b.

Roots Practice

1. We have three words in our list that have the "her/hes" root in them. What are they?

   a.
   b.
   c.

2. From these words, what do you think that the "her/hes" root means?

3. We have two words in our list with the "pac" root. What are they?-

   a.
   b.

4. The "pac" root means peace. How does the word pact relate to this meaning?

Make sure to study the words before you do these practice questions. Try not to look back at the list.

Synonyms Practice

1. UNRULY:

   (A) cohesive
   (B) dejected
   (C) righteous
   (D) wayward

2. CORDIAL:

   (A) amiable
   (B) impudent
   (C) sullen
   (D) valiant

3. PACIFY:

   (A) calm
   (B) douse
   (C) hoodwink
   (D) isolate

4. HAUGHTY:

   (A) adhesive
   (B) petty
   (C) ruthless
   (D) snobbish

5. INSOLENT:

   (A) amiable
   (B) disrespectful
   (C) fortified
   (D) momentary

Sentence Completion Practice

1. During the American Revolution, the colonists made a ------ with France so that France would provide naval support to the colonists.

   (A) congregation
   (B) fray
   (C) pact
   (D) transfer

2. The travelling circus brought with them an enormous ------- of exotic animals.

   (A) adherence
   (B) disregard
   (C) menagerie
   (D) shortage

3. Teachers often try to prevent ------- from forming so that no student feels left out.

   (A) attitudes
   (B) cliques
   (C) distractions
   (D) games

4. During storms, environmental damage is often caused when a rapid ------- overwhelms the drainage system and dirty water spills into places with fragile ecosystems.

   (A) deluge
   (B) fanatic
   (C) impostor
   (D) thunder

5. Napoleon was known as a quite ------- military leader willing to sacrifice anything to win a battle.

   (A) forthright
   (B) cohesive
   (C) pious
   (D) ruthless

Lesson 7 Answers

Word List Practice

1. a. clique
   b. congregation
   c. menagerie
2. a. douse
   b. deluge
3. a. sullen
   b. unruly
   c. insolent
   d. haughty
   e. ruthless
   f. wayward
   g. impudent
   h. petty
4. a. amiable
   b. cordial

Roots Practice

1. a. adhere
   b. adhesive
   c. cohesive
2. to stick
3. a. pacify
   b. pact
4. A pact is often an agreement between two parties that leads to peace.

Synonyms Practice

1. D
2. A
3. A
4. D
5. B

Sentence Completion Practice

1. C
2. C
3. B
4. A
5. D

Lesson 8

Words to Learn

Below are the twenty words used in Lesson 8; refer back to this list as needed as you move through the lesson.

Foresight: anticipation (looking into the future)
Obstruct: stop (prevent something from happening)
Dwindle: decrease
Meager: small
Fiend: demon

Swindle: to cheat
Foreboding: dread
Obscure: unclear or unknown
Corrode: to rust (or eat away)
Sparse: inadequate (not enough of something)

Culprit: guilty person
Stealthy: sneaky
Ebb: decline
Foretell: predict
Obstinate: stubborn

Brittle: fragile
Caper: practical joke
Foremost: most important
Obsolete: outdated (no longer in use)
Pilfer: steal

Word List Practice

Use the words from the Lesson 8 list to answer the following questions.

1. We have two words that mean to get smaller. What are they?

   a.

   b.

2. We have two words that describe quantities that are already small. What are they?

   a.

   b.

3. What word describes a process that would make something more brittle?

4. In order to pull off a caper, what must you be?

5. An honest person does not do what two things from our list?

   a.

   b.

6. What two words from our list describe people who have not been behaving themselves?

   a.

   b.

Roots Practice

1. We have four words in our list with the "fore" root. What are they?

   a.

   b.

   c.

   d.

2. From these words, what do you think the "fore" root means?

3. How does the meaning of the word foremost relate to the meaning of the "fore" root?

4. We have four words in our list that have the "ob" root. What are they?

   a.

   b.

   c.

   d.

5. From these words, do you think the meaning of the "ob" root is positive or negative?

Make sure to study the words before you do these practice questions. Try not to look back at the list.

Synonyms Practice

1. OBSTINATE:

   (A) foremost
   (B) misunderstood
   (C) radiant
   (D) stubborn

2. DWINDLE:

   (A) crush
   (B) ebb
   (C) nestle
   (D) skid

3. PILFER:

   (A) corrode
   (B) foretell
   (C) steal
   (D) trespass

4. FOREBODING:

   (A) caper
   (B) dread
   (C) fiend
   (D) sacrifice

5. STEALTHY:

   (A) brittle
   (B) obsolete
   (C) relaxed
   (D) sneaky

Sentence Completion Practice

1. A special coating must be applied to metal parts on a ship since salt water can cause metal to -------.

   (A) corrode
   (B) gleam
   (C) lather
   (D) swindle

2. The human population in Alaska is so -------- that the United States government actually pays residents in order to encourage population growth.

    (A) cohesive
    (B) divergent
    (C) obscure
    (D) sparse

3. People were surprised when a seemingly innocent elderly woman turned out to be the ------- in a robbery scandal.

    (A) culprit
    (B) foresight
    (C) obstruction
    (D) spendthrift

4. In developing countries, it is often difficult for families to buy the basic necessities with their ------ salaries.

    (A) brittle
    (B) meager
    (C) perpetual
    (D) understood

5. The telegraph was made ------- when the telephone was invented and people found it much easier to use the telephone than the telegraph.

    (A) foremost
    (B) isolated
    (C) obsolete
    (D) stealthy

Lesson 8 Answers

Word List Practice

1. a. dwindle
   b. ebb
2. a. meager
   b. sparse
3. corrode
4. stealthy
5. a. pilfer
   b. swindle
6. a. culprit
   b. fiend

Roots Practice

1. a. foresight
   b. foreboding
   c. foretell
   d. foremost
2. previous (or before)
3. If something is foremost, it comes before everything else in order of importance.
4. a. obstruct
   b. obscure
   c. obsolete
   d. obstinate
5. It is negative – the "ob" root means against.

Synonyms Practice

1. D
2. B
3. C
4. B
5. D

Sentence Completion Practice

1. A
2. D
3. A
4. B
5. C

Lesson 9

Words to Learn

Below are the twenty words used in Lesson 9; refer back to this list as needed as you move through the lesson.

Encircle: surround
Abhor: to hate
Gruesome: horrible
Navigable: passable (capable of being navigated or travelled through)
Enrich: improve

Malicious: hateful
Encompass: include
Rove: wander
Ample: plenty
Endear: to become beloved to someone else

Abominable: revolting (shockingly bad)
Envelop: surround (or cover) completely
Aghast: horrified
Bloated: swollen
Wretched: terrible

Entrust: to give responsibility to someone else
Dire: dreadful
Jaunt: expedition (usually a short one)
Amass: accumulate (to gather)
Entice: tempt

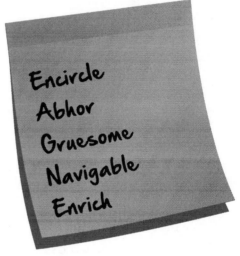

Encircle
Abhor
Gruesome
Navigable
Enrich

Word List Practice

Use the words from the Lesson 9 list to answer the following questions.

1. Our list has four adjectives that describe when things are really bad. What are they?

   a.

   b.

   c.

   d.

2. If something really bad happened, what word describes how you would feel?

3. What word would describe a person who is just plain mean?

4. If you abhor the color pink, what does that mean?

5. We have three words that relate to being an adventurer. What are they?

   a.

   b.

   c.

6. In order to have ample supplies before a camping trip, what should you do?

7. If you have too many supplies, what might your backpack become?

Roots Practice

1. We have seven words with the "en-" prefix. What are they?

   a.

   b.

   c.

   d.

   e.

   f.

   g.

2. From these words, what do you think the "en-" prefix means?

3. When you endear yourself to someone else, what are you putting yourself into?

4. How does the word entice relate to the meaning of the "en-" prefix?

Make sure to study the words before you do these practice questions. Try not to look back at the list.

Synonyms Practice

1. AMPLE:

   (A) dire
   (B) fine
   (C) plenty
   (D) sparse

2. BLOATED:

   (A) abominable
   (B) brittle
   (C) different
   (D) swollen

3. WRETCHED:

   (A) cordial
   (B) gruesome
   (C) haughty
   (D) unruly

4. ENVELOP:

   (A) encircle
   (B) enrich
   (C) isolate
   (D) rove

5. JAUNT:

   (A) adversary
   (B) endearment
   (C) expedition
   (D) foresight

Sentence Completion Practice

1. The city of Washington, D.C. is located where it currently is because the Potomac River was not -------- any further upstream and earlier settlers relied upon ships being able to come up the Potomac.

   (A) abhorred
   (B) divergent
   (C) navigable
   (D) pedestrian

2. The so-called "robber barons" were able to ------- considerable wealth by making a good profit while developing railroads in the United States.

   (A) amass
   (B) entrust
   (C) obstruct
   (D) verify

3. It is more humane to use bait to --------- unwanted animals so that they can be trapped and released elsewhere.

   (A) amass
   (B) entice
   (C) obscure
   (D) repel

4. The spectators were left -------- when the tiger attacked the performer at the circus.

   (A) aghast
   (B) dynamic
   (C) malicious
   (D) respectable

5. The boundaries of Canada -------- millions of acres of undeveloped land.

   (A) abhor
   (B) encompass
   (C) jaunt
   (D) swindle

Lesson 9 Answers

Word List Practice

1. a. dire
   b. abominable
   c. gruesome
   d. wretched
2. aghast
3. malicious
4. That you really, really don't like the color pink.
5. a. jaunt
   b. rove
   c. navigable
6. amass supplies
7. bloated

Roots Practice

1. a. encircle
   b. encompass
   c. envelop
   d. endear
   e. entrust
   f. enrich
   g. entice
2. The "en-" prefix means in.
3. His or her affection.
4. To entice another person is to draw them in.

Synonyms Practice

1. C
2. D
3. B
4. A
5. C

Sentence Completion Practice

1. C
2. A
3. B
4. A
5. B

Lesson 10

Words to Learn

Below are the twenty words used in Lesson 10; refer back to this list as needed as you move through the lesson.

Expend: use up
Unanimous: uncontested (everyone agrees)
Dauntless: courageous
Homage: respect
Valiant: brave

Exterminate: abolish (get rid of completely)
Unison: agreement
Decisive: making decisions easily
Sublime: extraordinary
Articulate: well-spoken

Elude: escape
Unique: singular (one of a kind)
Evade: avoid
Glorify: to honor
Ingenious: clever or original

Exclude: prohibit (keep something or someone out)
Formidable: threatening (and strong)
Idolize: adore
Exempt: to excuse (from a responsibility)
Commend: praise

Expend
Unanimous
Dauntless
Homage
Valiant

Word List Practice

Use the words from the Lesson 10 list to answer the following questions.

1. What two words from our list describe someone who is creative and well-spoken?

    a.
    b.

2. What five words could describe a superhero?

    a.
    b.
    c.
    d.
    e.

3. What four words relate to putting someone up on a pedestal?

    a.
    b.
    c.
    d.

Roots Practice

1. We have six words in our list with the "e/ex" root. What are they?

    a.
    b.
    c.
    d.
    e.
    f.

2. Based on these words, what do you think the "e/ex" root means?

3. We have three words from our list that have the "uni" root. What are they?

    a.
    b.
    c.

4. The "uni" root means one and the "anim" root means spirit. Based on these meanings, what do I mean if I say that a vote was unanimous?

5. How are the words unique and special different?

Make sure to study the words before you do the following practice questions. Try not to look back at the list.

Synonyms Practice

1. DAUNTLESS:

    (A) decisive
    (B) enriched
    (C) obstinate
    (D) valiant

2. ELUDE:

    (A) amass
    (B) evade
    (C) glorify
    (D) pilfer

3. UNIQUE:

    (A) different
    (B) formidable
    (C) sublime
    (D) singular

4. HOMAGE:

    (A) continuity
    (B) exclusion
    (C) respect
    (D) souvenir

5. COMMEND:

    (A) praise
    (B) soothe
    (C) train
    (D) welcome

Sentence Completion Practice

1. Although the bill had a lot of support, the final vote was not -------- with several members voting against it.

   (A) articulate
   (B) exempt
   (C) meager
   (D) unanimous

2. Sometimes a complex problem can be solved with a simple yet --------- solution that uses everyday objects in a new way.

   (A) expendable
   (B) ingenious
   (C) momentary
   (D) obscure

3. Snakes are extremely resilient and it can be very tough to truly -------- them from a home.

   (A) commend
   (B) divulge
   (C) exterminate
   (D) hoodwink

4. When the teacher asked if the class would like extra recess, the class answered in --------- that they would like more time outside.

   (A) continuity
   (B) dejection
   (C) foresight
   (D) unison

5. The Beatles were -------- by the fans who would fawn over them and scream in excitement every time the musical group entered a room.

   (A) idolized
   (B) mistrusted
   (C) swindled
   (D) watched

Answers to Lesson 10

Word List Practice

1. a. articulate
   b. ingenious
2. a. dauntless
   b. decisive
   c. formidable
   d. sublime
   e. valiant
3. a. glorify
   b. idolize
   c. commend
   d. homage

Roots Practice

1. a. expend
   b. exterminate
   c. elude
   d. evade
   e. exclude
   f. exempt
2. out or out of
3. a. unanimous
   b. unison
   c. unique
4. That everyone who voted was of the same spirit, or voted for the same person or thing.
5. Something that is special is unusual. Something that is unique, however, is one of a kind.

Synonyms Practice

1. D
2. B
3. D
4. C
5. A

Sentence Completion Practice

1. D
2. B
3. C
4. D
5. A

ISEE Reading Comprehension Section

In the ISEE reading section, you are given passages and then asked questions about those passages. There are six passages in the reading comprehension section and each passage has six questions. For the entire section, there will be a total of thirty-six questions. You will have thirty-five minutes to complete the section. There will be only one reading section on your test.

- 6 passages
- 6 questions for each passage
- 36 total questions
- 35 minutes to complete section
- Only one reading section

You may be thinking, "I know how to read, I am good on this section." However, most people applying to independent schools know how to read. In order to get around the 50th percentile score for seventh graders on the reading section, you need to answer a little more than half of the questions correctly. This means that half the seventh graders taking this test are getting less than that.

- To get the median score for 7th grade, you need to answer a little more than half of the questions correctly

The issue is that not every student can get a perfect score on the reading section, so the test writers have to create a test where some students who know how to read are going to miss several questions.

So how do the test writers get you to answer so many questions incorrectly? First of all, the questions can be very detail-oriented. Think of this not as a reading test, but as looking for a needle in a haystack – with very little time to find it. Secondly, they include answer choices that take the words from the passage, but those words are describing something else. Students often see these answer choices and think that if the words show up in the passage, it must be the correct answer. However, the words are describing something else. Lastly, they use your own brain against you! How do they do this?? They include answer choices that would be a logical conclusion, but aren't mentioned in the passage, so they are wrong.

- Very detail-oriented questions
- Test writers take words from another part of the passage and put them in the incorrect answer choices
- Some answer choices are logical conclusions, but aren't mentioned in the passage so they are not correct

By making a plan and sticking to it, however, you can overcome these obstacles and beat the average score – by a lot!

In this section, first we will cover the general plan of attack and then we will get into the details that make the difference.

Reading section plan of attack

Students can significantly improve their reading scores by following an easy plan:

Step 1: Plan your time.
You have almost six minutes per passage, so be sure to lay out your time before you begin.

Step 2: Prioritize passages.
Play to your strengths. Don't just answer the passages in the order that they appear.

Step 3: Go to the questions first.
Mark questions as either specific or general. You want to know what to look for as you read.

Step 4: Read the passage.
If you run across the answer to a specific question, go ahead and answer that. But do not worry if you miss an answer.

Step 5: Answer specific questions.
If there are any specific questions that you did not answer yet, go back and find the answers.

Step 6: Answer general questions.

Answer any questions that ask about the passage as a whole.

Step 7: Repeat steps 3-6 with next passage.

You've got it under control. Just keep cranking through the section until you are done.

Keep in mind that this section is not a test of how well you read. It is a test of how well you test. You need to manage your time and think about the process.

Step #1- Plan your time

Before you do anything, take thirty seconds to plan out your time. You have a little less than six minutes per passage, and there are six passages. Give yourself five minutes for the first passage since this should be the easiest one.

- Just under six minutes per passage
- Five minutes for the first passage, six minutes each for the rest

Look at the starting time and make a quick chart of when you should finish each passage at the top of your first page. For example, let's say you start at 9:23, then your chart should look like this:

Start – 9:23
1 – 9:28
2 – 9:34
3 – 9:40
4 – 9:46
5 – 9:52
6 – 9:58

We make a chart like this because we won't be answering the passages in the order that they appear. You don't have to follow the pacing chart exactly, but you should be close. If you finish the first passage in 3 minutes, then you are moving way too quickly. If it takes you 8 minutes to finish the first passage, then you will know that you need to speed up.

- Timing chart is a rough guideline

Drill #1

Let's say that you start the reading section and the start time is 9:32. Fill in the chart below:

Start –

1 –

2 –

3 –

4 –

5 –

6 –

(Answers to this drill are found on page 135)

Step #2- Prioritize passages

Take a quick look at your passages. You can even quickly read the first sentence to get an idea of what the passage is about. If you see a passage with a topic that you have studied in school, do that first. While you do not need any background information to answer the passage questions, it is easier to understand what is going on quickly if you are familiar with the topic. If there are any passages that stand out as being really long, save those for last.

- Look for passages with a familiar topic
- Save really long passages for last

The following are the types of passages that you may see:

Narrative

These passages read like a story. The story may be true or it may be fiction. Some of the types of narrative that you may see include biographical narrative (tells a story about a historical figure), personal narrative (an author shares an experience he or she has had), or fictional narrative (a made-up story). These passages tend to have more questions that require drawing a conclusion or figuring out what is implied.

- In the form of a story
- Can be fiction or non-fiction
- Questions tend to be more about drawing conclusions and figuring out what is implied

Expository

Expository passages explain something. The goal of an expository passage is to explain, not to tell a story. You may see passages that compare and contrast, describe a historical event, or explain a scientific occurrence. The questions for these passages tend to be more detail-oriented.

- Explain something
- Questions more detail oriented

Persuasive

These passages are designed to convince the reader of something. Persuasive passages may offer an opinion, give pros and cons, or present a problem and a solution. Questions for these types of passages tend to require following an argument or deciding which evidence supports the argument.

- Convince the reader
- Questions may ask reader to follow an argument or decide which evidence supports an argument

Descriptive

The purpose of descriptive passages is to describe something so clearly that it creates a picture in the reader's mind. Questions for descriptive passages tend to test details since the passage is mainly composed of details.

- Creates a picture in your mind
- Questions are very detail-oriented

So what passage types should you answer first? That depends on what you are good at! If you are good at finding picky details, then the expository or descriptive passages might be better for you. If inferring ideas and understanding arguments is your strength, then persuasive or narrative passages may be easier for you. In general, you want to do passages that are easier for you first and save the toughest one for the end.

- Different people will find different passages easy or hard
- Do the passages that are easier for you first

Drill #2

You start the reading section. After a quick scan of each passage, you have to prioritize the order of answering the passages. Quickly number the passages below in the order that you would answer them.

Passage topics:

Passage about the invention of the unicycle: #_____

Essay about the importance of school nutrition: #_____

Description of the creation of the first American Flag: #_____

Passage about why we have Leap Day: #_____

Passage from a novel #_____

Newspaper article about the Battle of the Bulge #_____

(Answers to this drill are found on page 135)

Step #3- When you start a passage, go to the questions first

It is important that you identify specific (S) and general (G) questions before you begin to read. You may come across the answer to a specific question as you read, so you also want to underline what the question is asking about for specific questions.

- Mark general questions with a "G"
- Mark specific questions with an "S"
- For specific questions, make sure you underline what the question is about if it references a particular topic

So how do you know if a question will be specific or general? Become familiar with the question types that follow.

General Questions

On the ISEE, you will see the following types of questions that are general:

- Mark these question types with a "G"

Main Idea Questions

These questions ask you for the overall theme of the passage.

Here are some examples:

- The primary purpose of this passage is to
- Which of the following best states the passage's main idea?
- This passage is mainly concerned with

Main idea questions are definitely general questions. You should mark them with a "G" for general and remember to answer them after any specific questions

- Mark main idea questions with a "G" for general
- Answer them at the end

Organization Questions

Organization questions ask you to look for the structure of the passage and see how the parts all fit together.

Here is what they look like:

- The function of the second paragraph is to
- Which of the following would be most logical for the author to discuss next?
- Which of the following best describes the organization of the passage as a whole?

These are general questions, so mark them with a "G". These questions want you to look at the passage as a whole. To tackle these questions, write a word or two next to each paragraph that summarizes what that paragraph is about. Look at these labels to see the flow of the passage. From this, you should be able to figure out how one paragraph functions in the passage or what would make sense to discuss next. Don't worry too much about these questions, you may see only a couple of them on the entire reading section.

- Mark organization questions with a "G"
- Answer them at the end
- Jot down a word or two next to each paragraph so that you can see the structure of the passage as a whole
- There won't be very many of these questions, don't worry too much about them

Tone or Attitude Questions

These questions ask you to identify the tone of a piece or writer or how the writer feels about something.

They might look like these:

- Which best expresses the author's attitude about _____?
- The tone of the passage can best be described as

These are general questions, so we mark them with a "G". In general, we look for moderate answers for these questions. An author is not likely to be "enraged" on the ISEE, but they might be "annoyed". This is the least common question type on the reading section – you might only see one of them!

- Mark tone or attitude questions with a "G"
- Look for moderate answers
- Least common question type in the whole reading section

Specific Questions

There are also question types for specific questions:

- Remember to mark specific questions with an "S"
- If there is a key word in a specific question (i.e. what the question is asking about), be sure to underline it

Supporting Idea Questions

These questions are looking for details.

Here are some examples:

- The passage states that which of the following people helped Johnny Appleseed?
- Which question is answered by the passage?
- Which statement about the spring equinox is supported by the passage?

These questions are definitely specific questions. They are looking for details from the passage that are directly stated and not asking you to pull together information from different places. For these questions, you should be able to underline the correct answer restated in the passage.

- Mark supporting idea questions with an "S" for specific
- You should be able to underline the correct answer in the passage

Inference Questions

Inference questions ask you to draw a conclusion from the text. They might ask you how two ideas or people compare, to interpret what the author states, or to predict what might happen.

Here are some examples of inference questions:

- Charles Dickens clearly believed
- According to the passage, both Susan B. Anthony and Elizabeth Cady Stanton
- In the second paragraph, the author implies
- Which of the following best characterizes bacterial growth as the passage describes it?

These are specific questions because you will find the answer in just small portion of the passage. Mark these questions with an "S" and remember that you must be able to underline the answer.

Inference questions are one of the most common question types on the ISEE. The key to these questions is that you may not be able to underline just one sentence in the passage that contains your answer, but you should be able to underline the evidence for the correct answer.

- Mark inference questions with an "S"
- Underline the evidence in the passage for the correct answer – it may show up in more than one place but you should be able to underline all of it
- Practice these questions – they show up a lot!

Vocabulary Questions

These questions ask you to use the context of the passage to figure out what a word means.

Here are some examples:

- In line 14, the word "capable" most nearly means
- In line 25, "captivate" most nearly means to

These are specific questions because they require you to use just a small part of the passage. You cannot underline the correct answer for these questions, however. For vocabulary questions, we have a different approach. We actually find the word in the passage, cross it out, and then plug in the answer choices to see what makes sense in that sentence. It is important that you practice this strategy – vocabulary questions are one of the most common question types in the reading section. In fact, there is usually a vocabulary question for every single passage.

- Mark vocabulary questions with an "S"
- Cross out the word in the passage and then fill in answer choices to see which has the same meaning as the question word
- Get good at vocabulary questions – there is one for almost every passage!

As you can see, there are definitely more specific questions than general questions on the ISEE reading section.

To practice identifying whether questions are specific or general, complete the drills that follow by identifying each question as general or specific. Time yourself on each drill to see how you improve! If you aren't completely sure of whether a question is specific or general, don't get too worried or spend a lot of time on that. The goal of this strategy is to save time in the long run and it is easy to change your mind as you work through a passage.

Drill #3

1. This passage is primarily about

2. As used in line 7, "graciously" most nearly means

3. It can be inferred from the passage that which statement about types of grasses is true?

4. According to the passage, how long did it take to travel across the country on the first transcontinental railway?

5. The function of the third paragraph is to

Time:

(Answers to this drill are found on page 135)

Drill #4

1. Which of the following statements does the passage provide evidence for?

2. The sounds referred to in the passage were

3. According to the author, the musicians stopped playing because

4. An "emu" is probably a type of

5. The tone of this passage can best be described as

Time:

(Answers to this drill are found on page 135)

Drill #5

1. The sound that came from the floorboards can best be described as

2. It can be inferred that from the passage that earlier setters did not have windows in their homes because

3. What made the citizens call a town meeting?

4. As it is used in line 15, the word "substantial" most nearly means

5. Which of the following questions is answered by information in the passage?

Time:

(Answers to this drill are found on page 135)

Drill #6

1. Which of the following best states the main idea of the passage?

2. In line 4, John Adams' use of the word "furious" is ironic for which of the following reasons?

3. How does Adams' speech reflect the idea that government is "for the people, by the people"?

4. The purpose of Adams' speech was to

5. Why does Adams use the word "mocking" in line 13?

Time:

(Answers to this drill are found on page 135)

Step #4- Read the passage

Now, you can go ahead and read the passage. If you happen to run across the answer to one of your specific questions, go ahead and answer it. If not, don't worry about it.

You have to be a little zen about looking for the answers while you read. You can spend five minutes obsessing over finding the answer for one particular question, but if you just move on, you are likely to come across the answer later.

- It's a little like love, sometimes you just have to let it go and trust that it will come back to you

Step #5- Answer specific questions

After you finish reading, answer any specific questions that you have not yet answered. For these questions, think of it as a treasure hunt. The right answer is there, you just have to find it. Generally, you should be able to underline the exact answer paraphrased in the passage or evidence for the correct answer. If you can't do that, you just haven't found it yet. Keep looking. You should also think about what category the question fits into (we will work on those in just a minute).

When you are looking for the answer to a specific question, skim! Don't read every word, you have already done that. Look quickly for the words that you underlined in the question. Also, remember our old friend ruling out.

- Skim when looking for the answers for specific questions
- Use ruling out
- For specific questions, you should be able to underline the correct answer restated in the passage or evidence for the correct answer
- Think about what category questions fit into

Now, we are going to work on practicing strategies for each particular type of specific question.

The following passage can be used for all of the question type practice drills. Go ahead and tear this passage out from the book. We want you to develop good habits of underlining and marking the passages, which is hard to do if you are flipping back and forth.

Passage for Drills 7-12

1   During World War II, propaganda advertisements were commonly used in the
2   United States to both vilify the enemy and encourage patriotism. The incredible
3   expenses of the war – upwards of a few hundred billion dollars – made it necessary
4   for the government to request the assistance of everyday citizens. To help counter
5   the military's costly demands, the government created rations and initiated special
6   programs on the home front. These programs provided Americans with different
7   avenues they could take to demonstrate their support for their war.
8   One of the largest and most well-known programs was the sale of U.S. War Bonds.
9   Called "Defense Bonds" prior to the attack on Pearl Harbor, War Bonds were
10 marketed as a way for Americans to invest in their country. A person might contrib-
11 ute $18.75 in exchange for a ten-year bond. Then after the ten-year window had
12 passed, they could exchange the bond for $25 – a small increase per single bond, but
13 a much larger sum when multiple bonds were purchased together.
14   People who couldn't afford to secure the bonds outright could buy stamps to
15 save toward the purchase of a bond. Or they could save quarters in a special folio
16 with designated slots for the right amount of coins. For wealthier Americans and
17 corporations, the bonds could also be purchased in larger dominations.
18   However, above and beyond any financial benefits the bonds offered Americans,
19 the main appeal was the idea of participating in a higher cause – of doing one's
20 patriotic duty to support the military in its fight against evil forces. These emotional
21 motivations were exactly what the government and advertising agencies attempted
22 to appeal to in their war bond advertisements.
23   The ads were distributed as radio commercials and appeared as spreads in
24 newspapers and magazines and on posters. Many used images of small children or
25 mothers with babies to evoke fear of what could happen to them if bonds weren't
26 bought. Pictures of soldiers were also commonly used to suggest that Americans
27 buying bonds were as much a part of the fight as soldiers wielding weapons overseas.
28   Some of the campaigns even targeted children directly by using famous cartoon
29 characters. And many famous celebrities of the time were hired to participate in
30 national tours promoting the bonds. Movie theaters and sporting arenas also offered
31 special events, with the purchase of a bond as the price of admission.
32   Such widespread efforts to urge Americans to purchase war bonds were met
33 with great success throughout the war. Not only did a majority of Americans buy
34 war bonds, but the total amount purchased by individuals and companies reached
35 well over $100 billion dollars.

This page left intentionally blank so that passage can be removed from book to use for drills.

Supporting Idea Questions

Supporting idea questions are looking for a picky detail. When you read through this type of question, you want to underline specifically what the question is asking about. For example, if the question is "How many years did it take for the transcontinental railroad to be built?", you would underline "how many years". The whole passage is probably about the transcontinental railroad, so underlining that would not help you pinpoint where to find the answer.

- Underline the detail in the question that will tell you where to find your answer, if appropriate

Some supporting idea questions do not have a detail to underline. For example, questions such as "Which question is answered by the passage?" and "Which statement is supported by the passage?" do not have a detail in the question that we can skim for.

- Not every supporting idea question has something to underline in the question

The key to answering this type of question is to underline the correct answer restated in the passage. If you can't do that, you simply have not yet found the answer – keep looking!

- Correct answer can be underlined in the passage

The following is a drill for practicing this type of question. The questions refer to the passage about war bonds.

We want to be sure that you develop good habits. So what are good habits for supporting idea questions?

- Underline in the question what it is asking about (if appropriate)
- Underline the evidence for the correct answer in the passage

Drill #7

1. According to the passage, people who did not have money to buy bonds could do which of the following?

    (A) join the army instead
    (B) market bonds to their neighbors
    (C) buy severely discounted bonds
    (D) save quarters in specially designed folders

2. According to the passage, why did the American government start the war bonds program?

    (A) in response to the attack on Pearl Harbor
    (B) to require more Americans to participate in the war
    (C) to finance the military during World War II
    (D) to limit the involvement of corporations

3. The passage provides evidence for which statement?

    (A) All Americans supported World War II.
    (B) Advertising agencies were used to help sell war bonds.
    (C) Children were the largest buyers of war bonds.
    (D) War bonds are still being sold today.

(Answers to this drill are found on page 135)

Inference Questions

On the ISEE, inference questions ask you to draw conclusions from what the author has written. These questions often use the words "implies", "it can be inferred", and "the author suggests".

*   If you see the words infer, imply, or suggest, it is probably an inference question

The trick to these questions is that they aren't looking for some deep conclusion. They are not asking you to read into a character's motivation or determine what another person thinks or feels. That would be too hard for a multiple-choice test! The correct answer for this type of question is the answer choice that has the most evidence in the passage. Also, look for answers that are less extreme. For example, an author is more likely to suggest that an animal is a pest than to suggest that an animal should be completely eliminated.

- Look for the answer choice with the most evidence
- Look for less extreme answers

For the following drill, use the passage about war bonds to answer the questions. Remember to underline evidence for the correct answer.

- Underline evidence in the passage

1. The passage implies that using pictures of small children and mothers with babies was meant to

   (A) scare citizens about the safety of children if America did not win the war.
   (B) support soldiers in the field.
   (C) help advertising agencies make more money.
   (D) demonstrate the strength of American families.

2. The passage suggests which of the following?

   (A) War bonds were not successful.
   (B) The primary purpose of war bonds was to make soldiers feel supported.
   (C) War bonds were supported in the entertainment industry.
   (D) War bonds will be used again.

(Answers to this drill are found on page 135)

Vocabulary Questions

On the ISEE reading section, they test whether or not you can use context to figure out the meaning of a word. The words tend to be higher-level words that you may not know the definition of.

The best way to answer these questions is to go back to the passage and actually cross out the word that the question asks about. Then plug the answer choices into that space in the sentence and see which answer choice gives you the same meaning.

- Cross out word in passage
- Plug in answer choices to see what makes sense

For the following drill, use the passage about war bonds. Remember to physically cross out the word – don't just do it in your head!

Drill #9

1. In line 4, the word "counter" most nearly means

   (A) argue with.
   (B) compensate for.
   (C) limit.
   (D) continue.

2. In line 25, the word "evoke" most nearly means

   (A) control.
   (B) accuse.
   (C) silence.
   (D) encourage.

(Answers to this drill are found on page 135)

Step #6- Answer general questions

After answering the specific questions, you have probably reread the passage multiple times. The trick for the general questions is not to get bogged down by the details, however. How do we do this? By rereading the last sentence of the entire passage before we answer general questions. This will clarify the main idea.

- Reread last sentence of passage before answering general questions

Main Idea Questions

Main idea questions are looking for you to identify what the passage is about. You can identify them because they often use the words "main" or "primarily".

- Often have the words "main" or "primarily" in them

The trick to main idea questions on the ISEE is that incorrect answers are often details from the passage. Students see these answer choices, remember reading about that detail, and then choose that answer because it shows up in the passage. The problem is that these answers are details from the passage and not the main idea.

- Wrong answer choices are often details from the passage

For the following drill, use the war bonds passage. Remember to practice good habits.

- Reread the last sentence before answering a general question
- Don't choose a detail from the passage

Drill #10

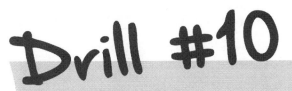

1. The primary purpose of this passage is to

   (A) explain how bonds were marketed.
   (B) explore the differences between stocks and bonds.
   (C) examine the success of a wartime program.
   (D) describe all the ways that citizens supported soldiers during World War II.

(Answer to this drill is found on page 136)

Organization Questions

Organization questions ask about why an author has chosen to include a particular part of the passage or ask about what the author would discuss next. These questions are testing your ability to see the organization of the passage or the function of a particular section.

To answer these questions, jot down a word or two next to each paragraph that summarizes what that paragraph is about. Look for the flow and what each paragraph contributes.

- Jot down a word or two next to each paragraph
- Look at these labels to see how the pieces fit together

For the following drill, use the passage about war bonds.

1. The primary purpose of the fourth paragraph (lines 18-22) is

   (A) to explain one motivation for buying bonds.
   (B) to summarize the war bonds program.
   (C) to introduce an argument.
   (D) to provide the evidence contrary to the main argument.

2. Which best describes the organization of this passage?

   (A) A thesis is presented and then evidence is provided to refute it.
   (B) A concept is introduced and then further explained.
   (C) Two competing theories are presented and then evaluated.
   (D) Several viewpoints on one topic are presented.

(Answers to this drill are found on page 136)

Tone or Attitude Questions

Tone or attitude questions on the ISEE ask you to draw your own conclusion about how the author approaches the topic. Are they annoyed? Trying to be informative?

Since these are general questions, we want to reread the last sentence before we answer them. It is also particularly important to use ruling out on these questions. Remember that we are looking for the "best" answer, which in some cases might just be the least wrong answer choice.

- Reread last sentence
- Use ruling out

There are a couple of tricks to these types of questions. First of all, look for moderate answers. For example, the test writers are not likely to choose a writer that is either ecstatic (extremely happy) or enraged (really, really mad). Also, don't be afraid of words that you do not know! Just because you don't know what the word "objective" means doesn't mean that it can't be the right answer.

- Look for moderate answers
- Don't avoid answer choices with words that you do not know

Finally, if it is a tone question, think about what type of writing the passage is. A fiction passage might have a tone that is lively, nervous, excited, etc. A non-fiction passage might have a tone that is objective, informative, interested, etc.

- If it is a tone question, think about what would be appropriate for fiction or non-fiction

The following drill refers to the war bonds passage.

Drill #12

1. Which best expresses the author's tone in discussing war bonds?

   (A) disrespectful
   (B) elated
   (C) conflicted
   (D) informative

(Answer to this drill is found on page 136)

Step #7- Move on to your next passage and repeat!

When you complete a passage, check your time against the chart you created before starting the section and then move on to the next passage.

- Keep track of time
- Just keep on truckin'

A note about what types of answers to look for

On the ISEE, the test writers have to make sure that not everyone gets a perfect score. As a matter of fact, they have to make sure that students who are good readers still miss several questions. The art of answering reading questions correctly often comes down to:

- On general questions, be sure not to pick a detail as an answer
- On specific questions, watch out for answer choices that take words from the passage but change them slightly so that the meaning is different

Secret #1: On general questions, be sure not to pick an answer that is a detail

The test writers need students to miss general questions. Generally, if a student sees an answer choice that was mentioned in the passage, this answer choice will be really tempting! These answer choices are wrong, however, because they are details and not the main idea. The best way to focus in on the real main idea is to reread the last sentence before answering a general question.

- Look out for answers that are details – these are the wrong answers for main idea questions
- Reread the last sentence before answering a general question

Following is a short passage followed by a general question. See if you can pick out the answers that are tricks!

Drill #13

1   In the late 1870's, King David Kalakaua sat in his palace in
2 Honolulu reading by the light of a gas lamp. At that time, there were
3 no electric lights in Honolulu, Hawaii. As a matter of fact, there were
4 very few electric lights in the world.
5   It wasn't until 1879 that Thomas Edison invented a filament
6 light bulb that could burn for 40 hours. There were other light bulbs
7 before this but they burned out too quickly to be practical. Thomas
8 Edison's new light bulb changed everything.
9   After reading about this new light bulb and its inventor, King
10 Kalakaua decided that he must meet this great inventor. In 1881 he
11 had the chance. King Kalakaua was on a world tour and met with
12 Edison in New York.
13   It took five long years before a light bulb shined in the palace.
14 On July 26, 1886, a demonstration of the new electric light was held
15 at the palace. It was a huge event with a tea party thrown by two
16 princesses. The military band played and troops marched to
17 celebrate.
18   After the exhibit, a power plant was built on the palace grounds
19 that could power more than just one light. On Friday, March 23,
20 1888, Princess Kaiulani, threw the switch and turned on the new
21 power system. In that moment, Iolani Palace officially became the
22 first royal residence in the world to be lit by electricity. Electricity
23 had come to the Hawaiian Islands.

1. The primary purpose of this passage is to

(A) describe the friendship between King Kalakaua and Thomas Edison.

(B) explain why Thomas Edison's lightbulb was better than the light-bulbs that came before it.

(C) relate how the Hawaiian islands came to have electricity.

(D) show how much King David Kalakaua cared for his people.

What is the correct answer? Which answer choices were tricks?

(Answer to this drill is found on page 136)

Secret #2: On specific questions, watch out for answer choices that have words from the passage

On the ISEE, answer choices often have words from the passage, but they might insert another word or two so that the meaning is different. Some answer choices also have words from the passage, but they are not the correct answer to that particular question.

- Be cautious when choosing an answer that repeats words from the passage

Here is an example. Let's say that the passage states:

John was upset when Sam got into the car with Trish.

The question may look something like:

1. Which of the following is implied by the author?

   (A) John was upset with Trish when he got into the car.
   (B) Sam and Trish were upset when John got into the car.
   (C) John and Sam were cousins.
   (D) John was not happy when Sam rode with Trish.

Answer choices A and B use words from the passage, but do not have the same meaning as what the passage says. Choice C is just unrelated – which happens on the ISEE. Choice D restates what the passage says.

In the following drill there is a sentence from a passage. There is then a list of answer choices. You have to decide whether the answer choice has the same meaning as the passage, or whether the words have been twisted around to mean something else.

Drill #14

Passage: When the morning sun rose high above the horizon, a small boy could be spotted as he carried a bucket along the ridge of a hill in the distance.

Answer choice:	Same meaning	Twisted meaning
1. A small boy was spotted along the horizon, looking almost like a bucket on the hill.		
2. Along the ridge, a child was carrying a pail in the morning.		
3. The small boy spotted the sun rising over a ridge as he carried a bucket.		
4. Far away, it was possible to see a boy carrying a bucket as he walked along the top of a hill in the morning sun.		

(Answers to this drill are found on page 136)

Full reading passages

We are going to finish up the reading section with three full passages.

Remember to apply what we have learned. What are the good habits that we are looking for?

1. Mark questions "S" (specific) or "G" (general) before looking at passage.
2. Answer specific questions first.
3. Underline the correct answer for specific questions in the passage.
4. Reread the last sentence before answering general questions.
5. Rule out any answer choices that are details for general questions.

Also, be sure to time yourself. It is important that you don't stop answering questions when the six minutes is up, however, since it will take you longer at first to use our strategies. Just be aware of the time so that you know if you need to work on speeding things up.

Drill #15

Time: 6 minutes

1   The field of archeology can often be incredibly unpredictable. An experi-
2 enced archeologist may research a particular location for several years, with
3 little to no significant findings. And a random person may accidentally stum-
4 ble upon an amazing archeological discovery. Such was the case with two of
5 the most significant archeological discoveries ever made.
6   In 1888, while tracking cattle in Colorado, two cowboys spotted some-
7 thing strange. From their view on the edge of a canyon, they saw what looked
8 like a living area inside the walls of a cliff. After exploring further, the two
9 men designated the ancient array of rooms as Cliff Palace. It was just one of
10 hundreds of cliff dwellings that would be discovered at the site known as
11 Mesa Verde. For hundreds of years beginning around 600 AD, the Ancient
12 Puebloans occupied the area. After initially living in villages on top of the
13 canyons, they then expanded out and built large settlements inside the canyon
14 walls. Then suddenly, in the late 1200s, the Puebloans abandoned the cliff
15 dwellings.
16   Although archeologists are still not entirely sure why the group left the
17 region, they have developed several theories that are accepted as plausible.
18 Some scientists support the idea that disagreements, either with an outside
19 enemy, or amongst the Puebloan people themselves, caused the group to
20 disperse to areas further south. Others point to physical evidence, such as
21 logs that indicate a severe drought, to suggest that harsh environmental condi-
22 tions coupled with food shortages are what inspired the move. Whether or
23 not the mystery is ever solved, the breathtaking beauty and intrigue of the
24 Mesa Verde National Park still offers a unique glimpse into the lives of the
25 ancient Pueblo people.
26   Similarly, across the globe near the city of Xi'an, China, another
27 spectacular archeological discovery offers people a first-hand encounter with
28 an ancient culture. It too was discovered entirely by accident.
29   In 1974, workers were digging a well when they found a single clay
30 soldier, positioned as if ready to engage in battle. They called in archeologists
31 to the site, and upon investigating further, the archeologists were astounded to
32 discover that the soldier was just one of thousands of clay soldiers arranged
33 in organized lines. For over two thousand years, the soldiers had stood unde-
34 tected, protecting the tomb of the first emperor of China, Qin Shi Huang Di.
35 According to one ancient account, more than 700,000 workers were used to
36 build the mausoleum and create the horses, chariots, and guards that protect it.
37 After its discovery, the site was quickly established as a museum, and has since
38 become one of the most visited historical sites in all of China.
39   Both of these discoveries serve to demonstrate that people may never
40 know what lies just below their feet. One can only venture a guess at what
41 ancient mystery will be uncovered next.

Drill #15

1. The primary purpose of this passage is to

    (A) explain how the Pueblo caves were discovered.
    (B) describe the soldiers at Xi'an.
    (C) argue that archaelogists rarely make the truly important finds.
    (D) point out that important discoveries are often made when no one is looking for them.

2. Which statement about Puebloans is most clearly supported by the passage?

    (A) They left the cliff dwellings because of fighting among themselves.
    (B) They originally lived on the plateau above the cliff dwellings.
    (C) The Puebloans frequently fought with local cowboys.
    (D) The Puebloans named the cliff dwellings the Cliff Palace.

3. According to the passage, the soldiers at Xi'an

    (A) were created to guard a grave.
    (B) were first discovered by archaelogists looking for the soldiers.
    (C) are not frequently visited.
    (D) represent the greatness of the second emperor of China.

Continued on the next page

Drill #15 (continued)

4.   In line 17, the word "plausible" is closest in meaning to

   (A) unlikely.
   (B) proven.
   (C) possible.
   (D) wonderful.

5.   Which word best describes the tone of this passage?

   (A) passionate
   (B) informative
   (C) critical
   (D) disinterested

6.   Which best describes how this passage is organized?

   (A) An argument is presented and then evidence is provided to refute the argument.
   (B) A problem is introduced and then several solutions are offered.
   (C) A common view is challenged.
   (D) An observation is made and then a couple of examples are given to support this observation.

(Answers to this drill are found on page 136)

Be sure to check your answers and figure out WHY you missed any questions that you answered incorrectly before moving on to the next drill.

Drill #16

Time: 6 minutes

1   As you travel deep into the ocean, the water becomes progres-
2 sively colder, darker, and less accommodating to life. In the zone
3 closest to the surface, the sun warms the water, and aquatic life
4 thrives; but further below, thousands of miles from the surface,
5 impenetrable darkness, high pressure, and freezing conditions
6 threaten all forms of life. Animals found at this level are able to
7 survive in such severe environmental conditions by relying on
8 special biological adaptations.
9   For many years, it was difficult, if not impossible, for scientists
10 to study the life forms at these deep levels. Only more recently, with
11 the development of advanced technological equipment and
12 machines, have scientists been able to travel farther into previously
13 unexplored territories to discover the menagerie of strange creatures
14 living in the deep ocean.
15   In fact, many of the animals found in these realms have such
16 bizarrely unique physical characteristics that some people may say
17 they more closely resemble science fiction monsters than actual
18 living species found elsewhere on Earth. For example, in order to
19 cope with the absolute darkness, some of the creatures have
20 extremely large or bulging eyes. Many others are bioluminescent.
21 Amongst the pitch blackness, bright blue light flashes from biolumi-
22 nescent animals as their bodies process chemical reactions and
23 create light energy.
24   This luminosity is often used for protection from predators, or
25 in some instances, as a strategy to lure and deceive prey. A squid fish
26 may emit a flash to surprise a predator and then escape from it while
27 it is distracted. Other animals are able to distract their predators by
28 actually detaching a piece of their bodies and leaving it behind.
29 While the predators hunt after the glowing piece of flesh, the trick-
30 ster animal escapes the scene with the rest of its body intact.
31   Rather than escape from its predators, a hatchetfish uses light to
32 hide in plain sight. While its predators hunt from below, the hatchet
33 fish's body creates a light that matches the light from above and
34 disguises its shadows so that it blends in with the surface of the water.
35 On the other hand, an angler fish uses its bioluminescence to lure
36 and attack its prey. Above an angler fish's mouth, an appendage
37 protrudes from its body and emits a light that attracts other fish.
38 Once the fish approach, the angler fish launches toward them and
39 chomps down with its huge, protruding teeth.
40   Whether an animal uses its light to escape from a predator or
41 catch its own prey, its techniques are demonstrative of the incredible
42 adaptations that are often necessary for survival in extreme
43 environments.

Drill #16

1. According to the passage, the hatchetfish is able to use bioluminescence to camouflage itself because

   (A) predators are hunting from below the hatchetfish and therefore the hatchetfish blends in with the light from above.
   (B) the deep sea is a surprisingly well lit environment.
   (C) the hatchetfish can detach part of its body.
   (D) other deep sea creatures can not see very well.

2. The passage implies that the squid fish

   (A) does not taste good to other sea creatures.
   (B) lacks speed.
   (C) uses a flash of light to stun predators.
   (D) has enormous teeth that it uses to attack.

3. Which of the following statements is best supported by the passage?

   (A) Animals that live in the deep sea environment are often slow to adapt.
   (B) It is easier for animals to survive in the shallow zones near the shoreline.
   (C) It is dangerous for a fish to produce a flash of light in a dark environment because predators can them see the fish.
   (D) Recent technology has not changed our understanding of sea creatures.

Continued on the next page

Drill #16 (continued)

4. The main purpose of the third paragraph (lines 15-23) is to

   (A) introduce evidence that is contrary to a previous claim.
   (B) further explain how technological improvements have improved research.
   (C) to shift focus from the shallow water area to the deep sea environment.
   (D) to reintroduce a concept and begin to provide examples.

5. In line 13, the word "menagerie" most nearly means

   (A) animal.
   (B) disturbance.
   (C) collection.
   (D) limits.

6. The primary purpose of this passage is to

   (A) explain how different animals have changed to survive in deep water conditions.
   (B) describe technological advances in marine biology.
   (C) offer information contrary to popular opinion.
   (D) question a theory.

(Answers to this drill are found on page 136)

Be sure to check your answers and figure out WHY you missed any questions that you answered incorrectly before moving on to the next drill.

Drill #17

Time: 6 minutes

1   Paulo finished the concerto and flipped back through the pages to
2 start again. Not only was it the most difficult piece he had ever played,
3 but soon it would also be the most important one. Tomorrow was his
4 audition for the orchestra and his only chance of being hired was
5 entirely dependent on his performance of the concerto. The formal
6 rules for the auditions mandated that all applicants should only be
7 allowed 24 hours to practice their audition pieces, and Paulo had just
8 received the sheet music early yesterday morning.
9   In the past 20 hours, Paulo had played each and every note in
10 succession at least 100 times. Over and over again, he cycled through
11 the pages until his fingers were numb. But this display of determina-
12 tion was nothing new. From the time Paulo was five years old and saw
13 a concert of the New York Symphony Orchestra on a television special,
14 his dream was to become an instrumentalist in a professional orchestra.
15 He often imagined himself wearing a crisp tuxedo with a neat bowtie,
16 enthusiastically playing a Beethoven Symphony alongside his fellow
17 musicians. Although Paulo's parents had limited financial resources,
18 they were able to rent a violin for him and sign him up for weekly
19 violin lessons at the local community center. Despite the difficult
20 nature of the violin, Paulo had an innate talent that was immediately
21 obvious, and any gaps in his talent were filled in by his dedication to
22 practice.
22   After packing up his violin, Paulo went through the motions of
23 walking the two blocks to the subway station, riding the train, and then
24 taking a seat inside the auditorium at the auditions, all the while
25 absorbed in his own thoughts. No outside stimuli could penetrate the
26 mental barrier surrounding him like a soundproof bubble.
27   In the dark of the auditorium, he sat in a row by himself awaiting
28 his turn to perform. He closed his eyes and focused on the music play-
29 ing through the headphones that sat tight against his ears. It was a
30 recording of him playing the audition concerto and in some way, it was
31 allowing him to practice the piece one last time before his critical
32 moment before the judges.
33   As soon as the music finished, he heard his name being called by
34 the judges. This was it—the moment he had been dreaming of since he
35 was a five-year-old little boy. He released a deep breath, picked up his
36 bow, and began playing from memory. His eyes flew over the notes
37 etched in his mind and his bow moved like a boat gliding over smooth
38 waters. Despite his intense nervousness, it was actually a relief for him to
39 know that his destiny was no longer in his hands alone.

Drill #17

1. Which statement would the author be most likely to agree with?

    (A) The chances of Paolo being chosen for the orchestra were slim.
    (B) Paolo should have started practicing his audition piece earlier.
    (C) Paolo's family could not support his ambition.
    (D) Paolo had been dedicated to becoming a performance musician for a long time.

2. In line 20, the word "innate" most nearly means

    (A) natural.
    (B) practiced.
    (C) stubborn.
    (D) lazy.

3. Paolo's attitude toward his audition can best be described as one of

    (A) defeat.
    (B) anxiety.
    (C) confidence.
    (D) disinterest.

4. In lines 25-26, "No outside stimuli could penetrate the mental barrier" can best be interpreted as meaning that

    (A) Paolo was physically separated from other people.
    (B) there were many distractions on the way to the audition.
    (C) Paolo did not let the outside world into his thoughts.
    (D) earphones prevented Paolo from hearing what was going on around him.

Continued on the next page

5. The purpose of the last paragraph (lines 33-39) is to

    (A) create a sense of suspense about whether or not Paolo will be accepted into the orchestra.
    (B) describe Paolo's audition.
    (C) explain the importance of hard work.
    (D) change subjects.

6. Which word best describes Paolo as he is described in the passage?

    (A) unfocused
    (B) determined
    (C) young
    (D) skeptical

(Answers to this drill are found on page 136)

Answers to Reading Comprehension Drills

Drill #1

Drill #1
Start – 9:32
1 – 9:37
2 – 9:43
3 – 9:49
4 – 9:55
5 – 10:01
6 – 10:07

Drill #2

There is no right order to answer the passages for everyone. It depends upon what you find interesting! If you find the passage interesting, you are likely to pick up on a lot more of the details.

Drill #3

1. G
2. S
3. S
4. S
5. G

Drill #4

1. S
2. S
3. S
4. S
5. G

Drill #5

1. S
2. S
3. S
4. S
5. S

Drill #6

1. G
2. S
3. S or G – it depends on what the whole passage is about. Remember, we have to stay flexible when we do this.
4. G
5. S

Drill #7

1. D
2. C
3. B

Drill #8

1. A
2. C

Drill #9

1. B
2. D

Continued on the next page

Drill #10

1. C

Drill #11

1. A
2. B

Drill #12

1. D

Drill #13

1. Choice C is the correct answer choice. Choices A and B are traps.

Drill #14

1. Twisted meaning
2. Same meaning
3. Twisted meaning
4. Same meaning

Drill #15

1. D
2. B
3. A
4. C
5. B
6. D

Drill #16

1. A
2. C
3. B
4. D
5. C
6. A

Drill #17

1. D
2. A
3. B
4. C
5. B
6. B

Quantitative Reasoning and Mathematics Achievement

On the ISEE, there are two math sections. One is Quantitative Reasoning and the other is Mathematics Achievement. There are no open response math questions on the ISEE – they are all multiple-choice.

- Two math sections
- All multiple-choice

The first math section is the Quantitative Reasoning section. On the Middle Level ISEE, this section has word problems and quantitative comparisons. Some of the word problems require you to do calculations, but some do not. The problems that do not require you to do calculations are testing your ability to understand operations and interpret equations. The quantitative comparison questions may or may not require calculations as well. The quantitative comparison questions ask you to determine which of two quantities is greater, if the quantities are equal, or if it cannot be determined.

- Quantitative Reasoning has word problems and quantitative comparisons on the Middle Level ISEE
- Not all problems require calculations
- 37 questions
- 35 minutes
- A little less than a minute per problem

The Mathematics Achievement section of the test will look a little more like questions that you might be asked in school. All of the problems on the Mathematics Achievement section require calculations. There are 47 questions and you will have 40 minutes to complete the section. This means that you have a little less than one minute per problem.

- More like questions you might see in school
- All of the problems require calculations
- 47 questions
- 40 minutes
- A little less than one minute per question

Since the two math sections are similar, we will study them together.

Now, on to the strategies!

Quantitative Sections– Basic Strategies

On the quantitative sections, there are problems from arithmetic, algebra, and geometry. The math is really not that hard. The ISEE is more about applying what you have learned than answering complicated questions.

You will NOT be allowed to use a calculator on the ISEE. By using strategies, however, we can get to the right answers, often without using complicated calculations.

- No calculator allowed

The goal here is for you to get a general understanding of the key strategies for the math section. Following the basic strategies are content lessons where you will get to apply these new strategies.

Drumroll, please! The strategies are:

- Estimate – this is a multiple-choice test!
- If there are variables in the answer choices, try plugging in your own numbers
- If they ask for the value of a variable, plug in answer choices

Strategy #1: Estimate

You can spend a lot of time finding the exact right answer on this test, or you can spend time figuring out what answers couldn't possibly work and then choose from what is left.

For example, let's say the question is:

1. Use the pictures below to answer the question.

The pictures above show two jars that each hold 1 liter of liquid when they are full. They are not currently full (as shown). If the liquid from the two jars was combined, about how many liters of liquid would there be in total?

(A) $\dfrac{9}{20}$

(B) $1\dfrac{1}{5}$

(C) $1\dfrac{1}{2}$

(D) $2\dfrac{1}{4}$

We could read each jar and see that one jar has $\dfrac{1}{4}$ of a liter in it and the other jar has $\dfrac{1}{5}$ of a liter in it and then add those fractions together. However, we don't need to do that! We can clearly see that each jar is less than half full. That means that the total volume of the two combined would have to be less than a liter. Only answer choice A is less than a liter, so we can answer the question correctly without doing involved calculations.

You can use estimates on many of the problems, but in particular estimate when the question tells you to! You may see questions that ask for a "reasonable estimation" or "the closest estimate".

-   Always estimate if the question tells you to

Sometimes you will need to do a little legwork before you estimate. In particular, it is often necessary to break a number down into its factors and then divide. It can also make our life easier if we use the commutative property ($A \times B = B \times A$) to rearrange the factors.

- Sometimes you need to break a number into factors before you estimate
- Remember to use the commutative property ($A \times B = B \times A$) as well

For example, let's say we need to estimate the following problem:

$$(79 \times 81) \div 700$$

Now we are going to rewrite this problem so that we can more easily see what is going on.

$$\frac{79 \times 81}{700}$$

Since we are looking for an estimate, we can round off 79 and 81 at this point.

$$\frac{80 \times 80}{700}$$

Now we can break apart each number into factors. They don't have to be prime factors, but we do need to think about factors that cancel.

$$\frac{8 \times 10 \times 8 \times 10}{7 \times 10 \times 10}$$

Now can you see how the two tens on the top cancel out the two tens on the bottom? We are left with:

$$\frac{8 \times 8}{7} = \frac{64}{7}$$

Since 7 goes into 64 nine times with 1 left over, the answer is approximately 9.

Here is one for you to try:

2. Ms. Kline gave her students the expression $(69 \times 71) \div 600$. She asked them to estimate an answer. Which of the following is the closest estimate?

   (A) 7
   (B) 8
   (C) 80
   (D) 90

We can't estimate the answer to the expression without first doing a little rearranging and cancelling.

First, let's rewrite the given expression:

$$\frac{69 \times 71}{600}$$

Now let's round off:

$$\frac{70 \times 70}{600}$$

Our next step is to break down each number into factors:

$$\frac{7 \times 10 \times 7 \times 10}{6 \times 10 \times 10}$$

Now we can cancel the tens from the top and the bottom. We are left with:

$$\frac{7 \times 7}{6} = \frac{49}{6} \approx 8$$

Answer choice B is correct.

Here is another one for you to try:

3. The expression $\frac{75(47 + 52)}{3}$ is equivalent to which of the following?
    (A) 1,975
    (B) 2,475
    (C) 4,975
    (D) 7,475

This question does not tell us to estimate, but the answer choices are all far enough apart that we can estimate to find the answer.

Before we estimate, let's break the 75 down into factors and cancel out:

$$\frac{3 \times 25(47 + 52)}{3}$$

This makes it easy to see that we can cancel out a 3 from both the top and the bottom. We are left with:

$$25(47 + 52)$$

Now we're ready to round off:

$$25(50 + 50) = 25(100) = 2,500$$

Answer choice B is closest and is the correct answer.

Another question type that requires estimating is questions that involve square roots of numbers that are not perfect squares. We can't find an exact answer since we do not have a calculator.

The trick to these questions is to find a range that the square root must fall between.

- For square root questions, find a range in order to estimate

For example, let's say we need to estimate the square root of 130.

Let's think of the numbers both higher and lower than 130 that are perfect squares and then come up with a range.

$$\sqrt{121} = 11$$
$$\sqrt{130} = ??$$
$$\sqrt{144} = 12$$

From this we can see that the square root of 130 must fall between 11 and 12.

Here is one for you to try:

4. Which is closest to the square root of 89?

    (A) 8
    (B) 9
    (C) 20
    (D) 45

First, let's establish a range that the answer should fall within using the perfect squares that are greater than and less than 89.

$$\sqrt{81} = 9$$
$$\sqrt{89} = ??$$
$$\sqrt{100} = 10$$

Here is an example for you to try:

6.   The graph below shows the number of sunny days in Smithville for the last 6 months.

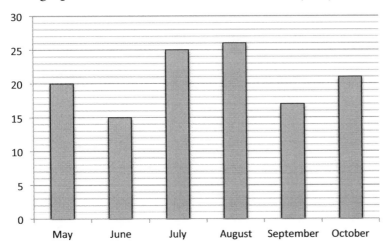

According to the graph above, what is the mean monthly number of sunny days?

(A)   15
(B)   20.67
(C)   25
(D)   26

Before we do any math, we can estimate. If we look at the graph, it looks like the average should be around 20. There are some values higher and some values lower, but we should rule out and see what remains. We can rule out choice A because it is the lowest value (a mean is never the lowest value unless all the values are the same). Now we can rule out choices C and D because choice C is way above our estimate of 20 and choice D is even higher. We are left with choice B, which is very close to our estimate. We were able to find the correct answer without doing a lot of math by estimating.

Here is another one for you to try:

7.   If a soda machine dispenses $\frac{4}{7}$ of a cup of soda in one minute, how many minutes would it take for the soda machine to dispense a full cup of soda?

(A)   0.5 minutes
(B)   1 minute
(C)   1.75 minutes
(D)   2 minutes

Before we do any math, let's think about an estimate. We know that it would take more than one minute to fill a cup since it takes a minute to fill $\frac{4}{7}$ a cup. This allows us to rule out choices A and B. Now let's think about how much of a cup could be filled in 2 minutes. We multiply $\frac{4}{7}$ by 2 to figure out how many cups could be filled in 2 minutes. Without doing the math, we can see that $\frac{4}{7}$ is greater than one-half, so $2 \times \frac{4}{7}$ is greater than one cup. That allows us to rule out choice D. Answer choice C is correct.

Some of the best questions to use estimating to answer are questions that you give you a figure and ask for lengths.

- Can use estimates for questions that give a figure and then ask for a side length

For these questions, you can compare the side lengths that you are given to the side lengths they are asking for and then use ruling out.

- Compare given side lengths to the side lengths they are asking for
- Use ruling out

Here is an example for you to try:

8. The triangles shown below are similar.

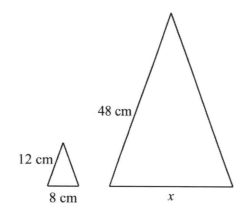

What is the value of *x?*

(A) 20 cm
(B) 32 cm
(C) 60 cm
(D) 72 cm

Let's use estimating to answer this question. If we look at the side labeled x, we can see that it is shorter than the side that is 48 cm long. This allows us to rule out choices C and D since they would make x longer than 48 cm. Now let's look at the two remaining choices. If x were 20 (choice A), that would make that side less than half the length of the side labeled 48 cm. Since we can see that is not true, we can rule out choice A. We are left with choice B.

Here is another one – remember to try to use estimating BEFORE you jump into trying to solve:

9.   Use the trapezoid below to answer the question.

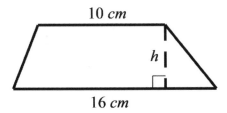

$$\text{Area of Trapezoid} = \frac{(b_1 + b_2)h}{2}$$

The area of the trapezoid shown is 65 cm². What is the height, h?

(A) 2.5 cm
(B) 5.0 cm
(C) 11.2 cm
(D) 14.8 cm

When we first read through this question, it is very tempting to jump right into plugging into the area equation given. Solving that equation for h would be a lot more work than just estimating, though. From the picture we can see that the height is shorter than the side that is 10 cm. This allows us to rule out choices C and D. Now we have to decide whether the height looks like half the length of the 10 cm side (choice B) or a quarter of the length of the 10 cm side (choice A). It looks more like half the length of the 10 cm side, so choice B is correct. If we were to actually do the math, we would see that choice B is in fact correct.

Some questions are more about figuring out how many digits the answer should have than actually being able to do the calculation. Always look at the answer choices before solving – sometimes they are far enough apart that we just have to figure out what the place value of the final answer should be.

- Look at answer choices to see if they are really far apart

Here are a couple of examples for you to try:

10. If Mona uses her calculator to multiply 802 by 196, then the answer should be approximately

    (A) 12,000
    (B) 16,000
    (C) 120,000
    (D) 160,000

To answer this question, we can round off 802 to 800 and 196 to 200. Now we multiply 800×200. We can do $8 \times 2 = 16$ and then add four zeroes since there are four zeroes in the original expression. Answer choice D is correct.

11. Which of the following problems would have three digits in the answer?

    (A) $889 \div 9$
    (B) $972 \div 9$
    (C) $12,692 \div 11$
    (D) $14,239 \div 11$

For this question, let's use ruling out. If we look at answer choice A, in order to get a 3-digit answer the number being divided by 9 would have to be at least 900. Since 889 is less than 900, we can rule out choice A. Choice B is a little more than 900, so we know that it would give us a 3-digit answer. If we want to be sure we have the right answer, we can keep going. If we multiply 11 by 1,000, we get 11,000. Since both choices C and D are greater than 11,000, we know that the answer in these cases would be at least 4 digits. We can eliminate choices C and D and choose choice B with confidence.

Now that you know how to estimate on the ISEE, be sure to complete the following practice drill to reinforce what you have learned.

Drill #1

1. Jack is making a juice cocktail. He combines $\frac{3}{4}$ cup of pineapple juice, $1\frac{1}{2}$ cup apple juice and $\frac{1}{3}$ cup of cranberry juice. How much total juice cocktail does he now have?

   (A) $1\frac{7}{8}$

   (B) $2\frac{7}{12}$

   (C) $3\frac{5}{12}$

   (D) $3\frac{7}{12}$

2. Carol did the following problem with her calculator.

   $$\frac{49 \times 592}{25}$$

   Which of the following would be a reasonable estimate for the answer that Carol's calculator showed?

   (A) between 900 and 1,300
   (B) between 1,300 and 1,500
   (C) between 1,500 and 1,800
   (D) between 1,800 and 2,100

3. A litter of four kittens was born. One kitten weighted 2 pounds, two kittens weighed 2.4 pounds each, and one kitten weighed 4 pounds. What was the mean weight of the four kittens?

   (A) 2 pounds
   (B) 2.4 pounds
   (C) 2.7 pounds
   (D) 4 pounds

Continued on the next page

4. The triangles below are similar.

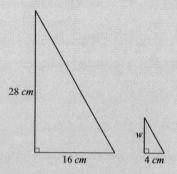

28 cm

16 cm

w

4 cm

What is the value of *w?*

(A) 7 cm
(B) 10 cm
(C) 12 cm
(D) 18 cm

5. Which is closest to the square root of 110?

(A) 9
(B) 10
(C) 20
(D) 55

6. The area of the Gates of the Arctic National Park is about 11,756 square miles. Which National Park has an area that is closest to $\frac{2}{3}$ that of the Gates of the Arctic National Park?

(A) Lake Clark National Park, which has an area of 4,093 square miles
(B) Glacier Bay National Park, which has an area of 5,038 square miles
(C) Katmai National Park, which has an area of 5,761 square miles
(D) Denali National Park, which has an area of 7,408 square miles

Continued on the next page

Drill #1 (continued)

7. Which is equal to the expression $\frac{15(14+36)}{3}$?

   (A) 200
   (B) 250
   (C) 554
   (D) 750

8. Use the trapezoid below to answer the question.

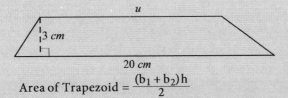

   Area of Trapezoid $= \frac{(b_1+b_2)h}{2}$

   If the area of the trapezoid above is 51 cm², what is the value of u?

   (A) 7 cm
   (B) 14 cm
   (C) 18 cm
   (D) 19 cm

9. The result of $9{,}020 \div 45$ is approximately

   (A) 2
   (B) 20
   (C) 200
   (D) 2,000

10. Which problem would have an answer with 4 digits?

   (A) 23×45
   (B) 99×110
   (C) 203×101
   (D) 504×20

(Answers to this drill are found on page 174)

Strategy #2: Plug in your own numbers if there are variables in the answer choices

What do I mean by variables in the answer choices? If you look at the answer choices and some or all of them have letters in addition to numbers, then you have variables in your answer choices.

- Look for letters in the answer choices

Here is how this strategy works:

1. Make up your own numbers for the variables.

   Just make sure they work within the problem. If they say that x is less than 1, do not make x equal to 2! If they say $x + y = 1$, then for heavens sake, don't make x equal to 2 and y equal to 3. Also, make sure that you write down what you are plugging in for your variables. EVERY TIME.

2. Solve the problem using your numbers.

   Write down the number that you get and circle it. This is the number you are trying to get with your answer choices when you plug in your value for the variable.

3. Plug the numbers that you assigned to the variables in step 1 into the answer choices.

   See which answer choice matches the number that you circled.

Here is an example:

1. Suzy has q more pencils than Jim. If Jim has 23 pencils, then how many pencils does Suzy have?

   (A) $q \div 23$
   (B) $q - 23$
   (C) $q + 23$
   (D) $23 - q$

Step 1: Plug in our own number.

Let's make q equal to 4. Suzy now has 4 more pencils than Jim.

Step 2: Solve using our own numbers.

If Jim has 23 pencils, and Suzy has 4 more than Jim, then Suzy must have 27 pencils. This is our target. Circle it. 27 is the number that we want to get when we plug in 4 for q in our answer choices.

Step 3: Plug into answer choices.

We are looking for the answer choice that would be equal to 27 when we plug in 4 for q.

(A) $q \div 23 = \dfrac{4}{23}$

(B) $q - 23 = 4 - 23 = -19$

(C) $q + 23 = 4 + 23 = 27$

(D) $23 - q = 23 - 4 = 19$

Choice C gives us 27, which is what we were looking for, so we choose C and answer the question correctly.

Sometimes the question will not be a word problem. We can still plug in our own numbers if there are variables in the answer choices, however.

Here is an example:

2. $7(M + 3) =$

    (A) $3M + 7$

    (B) $7M + 3$

    (C) $7M + 10$

    (D) $7M + 21$

We see variables in the answer choices, so we can plug in our own numbers. Our first step is to choose a number for the variable. To make our life easy, let's make $M = 2$. Now we will plug in 2 for M and solve $7(M + 3)$.

$7(M + 3) =$

$7(2 + 3) =$

$7(5) = 35$

We now know that our target is 35, so we will plug 2 in for M in our answer choices and see which answer choice gives us 35.

(A) $3M + 7 = 3(2) + 7 = 13$

(B) $7M + 3 = 7(2) + 3 = 17$

(C) $7M + 10 = 7(2) + 10 = 24$

(D) $7M + 21 = 7(2) + 21 = 35$

Since answer choice D gives us 35 (our target) when we plug in 2 for M, that is our correct answer.

You might be thinking that you didn't need to plug in for that one and you are right if you remembered to use the distributive property. However, if you did not see that you could just use the distributive property, this strategy gives you a way to still be able to answer the question. Sometimes the correct answer is not so easy to see, however, and you will need the strategy of plugging in to get to the right answer.

- Plugging in your own numbers for variables is particularly helpful on hard problems

Here is a hard one for you to try:

3. Which expression is equivalent to $\dfrac{h}{j}\left(\dfrac{j}{m} - \dfrac{h}{m}\right)$?

(A) $\dfrac{hj - 2h}{jm}$

(B) $\dfrac{hj - h^2}{j}$

(C) $\dfrac{h}{m}\left(1 - \dfrac{h}{j}\right)$

(D) $\dfrac{h}{m}\left(1 - \dfrac{1}{j}\right)$

This problem isn't as simple as just using the distributive property. If we simply distribute the $\dfrac{h}{j}$, we do not get one of the answer choices so the question must require further rearranging.

Let's plug in real numbers to see how it works.

Our first step is to choose numbers and write them down.

$h = 3$

$j = 4$

$m = 5$

Now we plug those values into the expression and solve for a target.

$$\frac{h}{j}\left(\frac{j}{m}-\frac{h}{m}\right)=\frac{3}{4}\left(\frac{4}{5}-\frac{3}{5}\right)=\frac{3}{4}\left(\frac{1}{5}\right)=\frac{3}{20}$$

Now we have our target, so we just need to plug our numbers into the answer choices and see what matches our target:

(A) $\quad\dfrac{hj-2h}{jm}=\dfrac{(3)(4)-2(3)}{(4)(5)}=\dfrac{6}{20}$

(B) $\quad\dfrac{hj-h^2}{j}=\dfrac{(3)(4)-3^2}{4}=\dfrac{3}{4}$

(C) $\quad\dfrac{h}{m}\left(1-\dfrac{h}{j}\right)=\dfrac{3}{5}\left(1-\dfrac{3}{4}\right)=\dfrac{3}{5}\left(\dfrac{1}{4}\right)=\dfrac{3}{20}$

(D) $\quad\dfrac{h}{m}\left(1-\dfrac{1}{j}\right)=\dfrac{3}{5}\left(1-\dfrac{1}{4}\right)=\dfrac{3}{5}\left(\dfrac{3}{4}\right)=\dfrac{9}{20}$

Since answer choice C matches our target of $\dfrac{3}{20}$ when we plug in our numbers, it is the correct answer choice.

Sometimes we will need to plug in for one variable and then solve for another variable. You will know that you need to do this if there is an equation (not an expression) in the question. For this type of question, we often don't find a target. Rather, we plug into the answer choices and see which one gives us an equation where the value is the same on both sides of the equal sign.

- If there is an equation (not an expression), you need to plug in for one variable and solve for the other one
- You won't find a target – rather you will find values for both variables and then plug those values into the answer choices to see which one gives us two sides that are equal

Here is an example:

4. Which is equivalent to $2q = 4m + 6$?

    (A) $2q + 4m = 6$
    (B) $2m + q = 6$
    (C) $2m + q = 3$
    (D) $q - 2m = 3$

We will start by plugging in for one variable and solving for the other. It doesn't really matter which variable we plug in for first, but in this problem it is a little easier to plug in for m and solve for q. For our example, we will plug in 3 for m.

$$m = 3$$
$$2q = 4(3) + 6$$
$$2q = 12 + 6$$
$$2q = 18$$
$$q = 9$$

For this type of question, we don't find a target. We just plug our values for the variables into the answer choices and see which answer choice gives us the same value on both sides of the equal sign.

(A) $2q + 4m = 6$
$$2(9) + 4(3) = 6$$
$$30 \neq 6$$

(B) $2m + q = 6$
$$2(3) + 9 = 6$$
$$15 \neq 6$$

(C) $2m + q = 3$
$$2(3) + 9 = 3$$
$$15 \neq 3$$

(D) $q - 2m = 3$
$$9 - 2(3) = 3$$
$$3 = 3$$

Since the equation in answer choice D works when we plug in our numbers, it is the correct answer choice.

Here is a harder one for you to try:

5. Which is equivalent to $b = \dfrac{c}{3} - 5$?

(A) $c + 5 = \dfrac{b}{3}$

(B) $3b + c = 5$

(C) $3(b + c) = 5$

(D) $\dfrac{1}{3}c = 5 + b$

Our first step is to plug into one variable and solve for the other one. We will start with plugging in for c because it makes our life a little easier than if we plug in for b. Also, we are going to plug in a number for c that is divisible by 3 since we do not have a calculator and the fractions could get ugly if c is not divisible by 3.

$$c = 9$$

$$b = \frac{c}{3} - 5 = \frac{9}{3} - 5 = 3 - 5 = -2$$

Now we plug our numbers into the answer choices.

(A) $c + 5 = \dfrac{b}{3}$

$$9 + 5 = \frac{-2}{3}$$

$$14 \neq -\frac{2}{3}$$

(B) $3b + c = 5$

$$3(-2) + 9 = 5$$

$$-6 + 9 = 5$$

$$3 \neq 5$$

(C) $3(b + c) = 5$

$$3(-2 + 9) = 5$$

$$3(7) = 9$$

$$21 \neq 9$$

(D) $\frac{1}{3}c = 5 + b$

$\frac{1}{3}(9) = 5 + (-2)$

$3 = 3$

There are not too many of this problem type on the ISEE. However, if you read through a problem and think, "this would be a lot easier if they gave us real numbers", then make up your own numbers! Sometimes the process of solving with real numbers will be enough to figure out what the correct answer is.

- If you think to yourself, "this problem would be a lot easier with real numbers", then plug in real numbers

Be sure to complete the following drill to practice this new skill:

Drill #2

1. $8(Q + 3) =$

    (A) $3Q + 8$
    (B) $8Q + 3$
    (C) $8Q + 11$
    (D) $8Q + 24$

2. If the width of a rectangle is 4 times the length, l, which of the following gives the perimeter of the rectangle?

    (A) $3l$
    (B) $5l$
    (C) $10l$
    (D) $2(4 + l)$

3. Use the figure below to answer the question.

    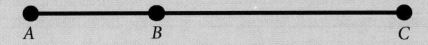

A	B	C

    The length of AB is g and the length of AC is h. What is the length of BC?

    (A) $h - g$
    (B) $h + g$
    (C) $g - h$
    (D) gh

4. If the perimeter of a rectangle is 18 in, which equation could be used to determine the length of that rectangle? ($P = 2l + 2w$, where P = Perimeter, l = length, and w = width.)

    (A) $l = \dfrac{18 - w}{2}$
    (B) $l = \dfrac{18 - 2w}{2}$
    (C) $l = 18 - w$
    (D) $l = 2(18) - w$

Continued on the next page

Drill #2 (continued)

5. Which is equivalent to $\frac{y}{3} = 2x + 5$?

(A) $y = 6x + 5$

(B) $2x - \frac{1}{3}y = 5$

(C) $2x - \frac{1}{3}y = -5$

(D) $3x - 2y = 5$

(Answers to this drill are found on page 174)

Strategy #3: If they ask for the value of a variable, plug in answer choices

On the ISEE, it is often easier to plug in answer choices and see what works. In particular, you may find this strategy most helpful on word problems. After all, this is a multiple-choice test so one of those answers has to work!

- Can often use this strategy on word problems
- This is a multiple-choice test

For this strategy, keep in mind that a variable is not always a letter. The problem might define x as the number of cars, or it might just ask you what the number of cars is. Either way, it is still asking for the value of a variable and you can use this strategy. The test writers might also throw in a symbol, such as a small square, instead of a letter.

- A variable may not always be a letter, it can be any unknown quantity
- Sometimes there is a symbol, such as a small square, instead of a letter

Whenever a question asks for the value of a variable, whether it is a letter or something like the number of bunnies, one of those answer choices has to work. Since this is a multiple-choice test, you just have to figure out which one. Ruling out is one of our most important strategies and this scenario is just another example of how valuable a tool ruling out can be.

- Remember the mantra: Ruling out is good

Here is an example:

1. If three times a number is 18, what is the number?

    (A) 3
    (B) 6
    (C) 12
    (D) 15

To answer this question, we can simply plug in answer choices. If we plug in answer choice A and multiply 3×3, the answer is 9 and not 18. That tells us to rule out answer choice A. Now let's try choice B. If we plug in 6 and multiply 6×3, we get 18 for an answer. That is what we were looking for, so choice B is correct.

The above problem was pretty simple and you may not have needed to plug in answer choices. However, with some harder questions, plugging in saves us steps, which makes errors less likely.

- Plugging in answers sometimes means fewer steps, which means less opportunity for making an error

Here is an example:

2. What is the value of y in $\dfrac{y+5}{y} = \dfrac{1}{6}$?

    (A) 6
    (B) 5
    (C) −1
    (D) −6

Instead of trying to solve a complicated equation, we will just plug in the answer choices for y and see which answer choice would give us a value equal to $\dfrac{1}{6}$ for $\dfrac{y+5}{y}$.

(A) $\dfrac{6+5}{6} = \dfrac{11}{6} \neq \dfrac{1}{6}$

(B) $\dfrac{5+5}{5} = \dfrac{10}{5} \neq \dfrac{1}{6}$

(C) $\dfrac{-1+5}{-1} = \dfrac{4}{-1} \neq \dfrac{1}{6}$

(D) $\dfrac{-6+5}{-6} = \dfrac{-1}{-6} = \dfrac{1}{6}$

Answer choice D is correct.

Keep in mind that a variable is not always a letter or written as "a number". It is any quantity that we do not know the value of, whether it is x or something like the number of bunnies.

- Keep in mind that a variable is not always a letter – it is any quantity that we do not know the value of

Here is an example of a question where they are asking for the value of a variable but not using a letter to represent the variable:

3. Jack has 12 coins. Some of them are nickels and some of them are dimes. If his nickels were dimes and his dimes were nickels, the value of his coins would be 20 cents less than it is now. How many nickels does Jack currently have? (Note: 1 nickel = $.05; 1 dime = $.10)

   (A) 3
   (B) 4
   (C) 5
   (D) 6

The easiest way to answer this question is to plug in answer choices. Remember that we have a total of 12 coins, so nickels plus dimes must add up to 12 coins.

(A) Before switch: 3 *nickels* + 9 *dimes* = $.15 + $.90 = $1.05
    After switch: 9 *nickels* + 3 *dimes* = $.45 + $.30 = $.75
    Difference = $1.05 − $.75 = 30 *cents less*
(B) Before switch: 4 *nickels* + 8 *dimes* = $.20 + $.80 = $1.00
    After switch: 8 *nickels* + 4 *dimes* = $.40 + $.40 = $.80
    Difference = $1.00 − $.80 = 20 *cents less*

We have our right answer (choice B), so we can stop there and choose answer B. When we are plugging in answer choices, we can stop once we get an answer that works since there cannot be more than one correct answer choice.

For the following drill, try plugging in answer choices to see what works. Even if you know how to solve another way, you need to practice this strategy because there may be a time when you need it to bail you out.

1. Which of the following could be the value of y in the equation $2 = \dfrac{7y + 7}{7}$?

(A) 1
(B) 0
(C) −1
(D) −2

2. In the equation $3 \times (\blacksquare + 5) = 18$, what number could replace $\blacksquare$?

(A) 1
(B) 2
(C) 3
(D) 4

3. A pet store divided their mice into cages. If each cage had the same number of mice in it and there were 6 cages, which could be the total number of mice that the pet store has?

(A) 11
(B) 15
(C) 21
(D) 24

Continued on the next page

Drill #3 (continued)

4. Harold has 8 coins. He has only nickels and quarters. If his nickels were quarters and his quarters were nickels, he would have 40 cents more total. How many quarters does Harold have right now?

    (A) 2
    (B) 3
    (C) 4
    (D) 5

5. Use the rectangle below to answer the question.

    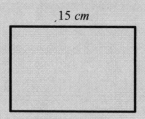

    15 cm

    If the rectangle above has a perimeter of 52 cm, what is its width?
    (Note: $P = 2l + 2w$)

    (A) 30
    (B) 15
    (C) 11
    (D) 10

(Answers to this drill are found on page 174)

Applying these strategies to Quantitative Comparison questions

On the Quantitative Reasoning section of the ISEE you will be given questions that ask you to decide whether one quantity is greater or less than another, equal to another quantity, or if the relationship between the two cannot be determined.

Here is an example:

1.

Column A	Column B
10% of 30	25% of 20

(A) Quantity in Column A is greater.
(B) Quantity in Column B is greater.
(C) Quantities in Columns A and B are equal.
(D) Not enough information to determine relationship.

In this case, we can easily do the math. To find 10% of 30, we simply move the decimal point over one place to the left and get 3 as our answer. To find 25% of 20, we can think of 25% as being equal to $\frac{1}{4}$ and $\frac{1}{4}$ of 20 is 5. Since 5 is greater than 3, the quantity in Column B is larger and answer choice B is correct.

Estimating on Quantitative Comparison questions

Estimating is a great strategy to use on quantitative comparison questions. Since we don't need to know exact quantities, but rather which quantity is larger, we often don't need to find exact answers.

Earlier we covered using estimating for square root questions. This strategy can also be used on quantitative comparison questions that use square roots.

Here is an example for you to try:

1.

Column A	Column B
$\sqrt{0.36}$	$\sqrt{3.6}$

(A) Quantity in Column A is greater.
(B) Quantity in Column B is greater.
(C) Quantities in Columns A and B are equal.
(D) Not enough information to determine relationship.

To determine the approximate value of Column A, we can come up with a range. Since $\sqrt{0} = 0$ and $\sqrt{1} = 1$, we know that the value of $\sqrt{0.36}$ must fall between 0 and 1. In order to figure out the approximate value of $\sqrt{3.6}$ we need to come up with another range. Since $\sqrt{1} = 1$ and $\sqrt{4} = 2$, we know that $\sqrt{3.6}$ must fall between 1 and 2. Since the range for Column B is always greater than any number in the range for Column A, we know that Column B must be bigger and answer choice B is correct.

Here is another problem for you to try that mixes a whole number with a square root:

2.

Column A	Column B
7	$\sqrt{50}$

(A) Quantity in Column A is greater.
(B) Quantity in Column B is greater.
(C) Quantities in Columns A and B are equal.
(D) Not enough information to determine relationship.

To answer this question, we need to get both numbers into the same form. We can leave the 7 alone and just deal with the $\sqrt{50}$. We know that $\sqrt{49} = 7$ and that $\sqrt{64} = 8$, so $\sqrt{50}$ must be between 7 and 8. This tells us that $\sqrt{50}$ must be greater than 7, so answer choice B is correct.

We can also use estimation on geometry questions as well.

Here is an example:

3.

Triangle 1

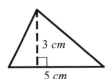

3 cm

5 cm

Triangle 2

2 cm

3 cm

<u>**Column A**</u>

The perimeter of a triangle that is similar to Triangle 1 with a scale factor of $\dfrac{1}{3}$

<u>**Column B**</u>

The perimeter of a triangle that is similar to Triangle 2 with a scale factor of $\dfrac{1}{3}$

(A) Quantity in Column A is greater.
(B) Quantity in Column B is greater.
(C) Quantities in Columns A and B are equal.
(D) Not enough information to determine relationship.

In order to answer this question, we don't need to do any real math. We can look and see that Triangle 2 is clearly smaller than Triangle 1. Therefore, since we are using the same scale factor in both cases, the triangle that is similar to Triangle 1 will be larger than the triangle that is similar to Triangle 2. Answer choice A is correct.

We can also often use estimates with problems that require us to figure out a sum.

Here is an example for you to try:

4.

<u>**Column A**</u>

<u>**Column B**</u>

$$\dfrac{1}{1+\dfrac{1}{3}}$$

$$\dfrac{1}{1+3}$$

(A) Quantity in Column A is greater.
(B) Quantity in Column B is greater.
(C) Quantities in Columns A and B are equal.
(D) Not enough information to determine relationship.

To answer this question, let's just round off. If we round off Column A, we get $\frac{1}{1}$, which is equal to just 1. If we do a little math with Column B, we get $\frac{1}{4}$. Since 1 is clearly bigger than $\frac{1}{4}$, the quantity in Column A is larger and answer choice A is correct.

Plugging in our own numbers on Quantitative Comparison questions

When there are variables in quantitative comparison questions, it is often easiest to plug in our own real numbers to see how they work.

The trick for quantitative comparison questions is that if we select choice A, then quantity A must ALWAYS be bigger than quantity B. If we select choice B, then quantity B must ALWAYS be larger than quantity A. If we choose C, then the two quantities must ALWAYS have the same value. Under any other scenario, we have to choose D.

- If we choose A it has to always be larger
- If we choose B it has to always be larger
- If we choose C the 2 quantities must always be the same
- With all other scenarios, we choose D

This tells us that when we plug in numbers, we should be looking for exceptions. We should plug in 1, 0, −1, and fractions to look for situations where the "normal" rules are not followed.

- Plug in 1, 0, −1, and fractions to look for exceptions

For example, let's say that we are comparing x and x^2. Normally we think of squaring a number as making it larger. However, what if we plug in 1 for x? Then x and x^2 would both be equal to 1, so we would have to select choice D.

Here is a basic example of a quantitative comparison question with variables for you to try:

1.

$$j > 3$$
$$k > 300$$

Column A	Column B
j	k

(A) Quantity in Column A is greater.
(B) Quantity in Column B is greater.
(C) Quantities in Columns A and B are equal.
(D) Not enough information to determine relationship.

At first glance, it might look like k has to be greater than j. However, if we start plugging in numbers we can see that isn't true. Let's say we plug in 400 for j and 301 for k. Both of these numbers fit within the rules of the problems and in this case Column A would be greater. Now let's plug in 4 for j and 301 for k. In this case, Column B would be greater. Since we can get more than one relationship to work, answer choice D is correct.

Here are a couple of questions that require you to think about different possibilities:

2.

Column A	Column B
x	$\dfrac{1}{x}$

(A) Quantity in Column A is greater.
(B) Quantity in Column B is greater.
(C) Quantities in Columns A and B are equal.
(D) Not enough information to determine relationship.

To answer this question, let's plug in numbers. If we plug in 2 for x, we get that Column A is greater. However, if we plug in 1 for x we get that Columns A and B have the same value. Since we can get more than one answer choice to work, we have to select choice D.

3.

Column A	Column B
$4(m + 2)$	$4m + (4 \times 2)$

(A) Quantity in Column A is greater.
(B) Quantity in Column B is greater.
(C) Quantities in Columns A and B are equal.
(D) Not enough information to determine relationship.

Let's start out by plugging in the number 2 for m. If we do that, we get 16 for both Column A and Column B so the quantities are equal. We need to make sure that is true for all numbers, however. Let's plug in 1 and see if the quantities are still the same. If we plug in 1 for m then we get 12 for both columns. Let's try 0 and -1 to see if we can find a situation where the quantities are not equal. If we plug in 0, we get 8 for both columns and if we plug in -1, we get 4 for both columns. Since we have tried the weird numbers and still are getting that both columns have equal value, we can select choice C.

Following is a drill for you to practice estimating and plugging in your own numbers on quantitative comparison questions.

Drill #4

1.

Column A	Column B
15% of 30	25% of 10

(A) Quantity in Column A is greater.
(B) Quantity in Column B is greater.
(C) Quantities in Columns A and B are equal.
(D) Not enough information to determine relationship.

2.

Column A	Column B
2	$2 + x$

(A) Quantity in Column A is greater.
(B) Quantity in Column B is greater.
(C) Quantities in Columns A and B are equal.
(D) Not enough information to determine relationship.

3.

$$b < 3$$

Column A	Column B
$2b + 10$	$3b + 7$

(A) Quantity in Column A is greater.
(B) Quantity in Column B is greater.
(C) Quantities in Columns A and B are equal.
(D) Not enough information to determine relationship.

Continued on the next page

4.

Column A	Column B
$\sqrt{7.9}$	$\sqrt{0.79}$

(A) Quantity in Column A is greater.
(B) Quantity in Column B is greater.
(C) Quantities in Columns A and B are equal.
(D) Not enough information to determine relationship.

5.

Triangle 1

Triangle 2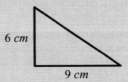

6 cm

9 cm

Triangle 1 is similar to Triangle 2 with a scale factor of $\dfrac{2}{3}$

Column A	Column B
The perimeter of Triangle 1	The perimeter of Triangle 2

(A) Quantity in Column A is greater.
(B) Quantity in Column B is greater.
(C) Quantities in Columns A and B are equal.
(D) Not enough information to determine relationship.

Continued on the next page

6.

Column A	Column B
$6g + (6 \times 3)$	$6(g + 3)$

(A) Quantity in Column A is greater.
(B) Quantity in Column B is greater.
(C) Quantities in Columns A and B are equal.
(D) Not enough information to determine relationship.

7.

Column A	Column B
6	$\sqrt{37}$

(A) Quantity in Column A is greater.
(B) Quantity in Column B is greater.
(C) Quantities in Columns A and B are equal.
(D) Not enough information to determine relationship.

8.

Column A	Column B
x	x^2

(A) Quantity in Column A is greater.
(B) Quantity in Column B is greater.
(C) Quantities in Columns A and B are equal.
(D) Not enough information to determine relationship.

Continued on the next page

9.

$$a < b < c < 0$$

Column A	Column B
$a + c$	b

(A) Quantity in Column A is greater.
(B) Quantity in Column B is greater.
(C) Quantities in Columns A and B are equal.
(D) Not enough information to determine relationship.

10.

Column A	Column B
$\dfrac{1}{1+7}$	$\dfrac{1}{1+\dfrac{1}{7}}$

(A) Quantity in Column A is greater.
(B) Quantity in Column B is greater.
(C) Quantities in Columns A and B are equal.
(D) Not enough information to determine relationship.

Answers to Math Strategies Drills

Drill #1

1. B
2. A
3. C
4. A
5. B
6. D
7. B
8. B
9. C
10. A

Drill #2

1. D
2. C
3. A
4. B
5. C

Drill #3

1. A
2. A
3. D
4. B
5. C

Drill #4

1. A
2. D
3. A
4. A
5. B
6. C
7. B
8. D
9. B
10. B

Math Content Sections

We have covered the basic strategies for the math sections. Now, we are going to take a look at some of the problem types that you will see on this test.

On the ISEE, sometimes the math to solve a problem is not that hard. However, the tough part of that problem might be recognizing what direction to go and what concept is being tested.

On the Middle Level ISEE, there are six basic categories of math questions. They are:

- Whole numbers and operations
- Fractions, decimals, and percents
- Algebraic concepts (solving for variables)
- Geometry
- Measurement
- Probability and data analysis

Doing well on the math sections is often a matter of decision-making. You need to decide what type of problem you are working on as well as what the most efficient way to solve will be.

Each lesson will:

- Teach you the facts that you need to know
- Show you how those facts are tested
- Give you plenty of practice

That is the book's side of the bargain, but you also have to keep up your end of the deal.

As you work through the content always ask yourself:

- What makes this problem unique?
- How will I recognize this problem in the future?

You are on your way to crushing the ISEE math section!

Whole Numbers and Operations

The first topic that we will cover is how whole numbers and operations are tested on the ISEE.

We will go over:

- Different types of numbers
- Basic operations
- Order of operations (PEMDAS)
- Negative numbers and number lines
- Exponents and square roots
- Multiples and factors

Different types of numbers

On the Middle Level ISEE, there are just a few types of numbers that you need to know.

They include:

- Integer/whole number
- Positive/negative
- Even/odd
- Consecutive
- Prime/composite

Integers and whole numbers are very similar. Simply put, they are numbers that do not have decimals or fractions. For example, 0, 1, 2, and 3 are all integers as well as whole numbers. The difference is that integers include negative numbers. On this test, however, they don't really require you to know the difference between integers and whole numbers. You just need to know that if they ask for an integer or a whole number, the correct answer cannot have a fraction or decimal.

- If they ask for an integer or whole number, no decimals or fractions

Positive numbers are those that are greater than zero. Negative numbers are those that are less than zero. The only tricky thing about positive and negative numbers is that zero is neither positive nor negative. The ISEE is not likely to ask you if zero is positive or negative, but they might tell you that a number must be positive, in which case you have to know that it can't equal zero.

- Zero is neither positive nor negative

Even numbers are those numbers that are evenly divisible by 2. That means that you can divide even numbers into groups of two with nothing left over. Odd numbers are those that cannot be evenly divided by 2. By this definition, zero is an even number because it can be divided by two with nothing left over. Even numbers are 0, 2 4 6, and so on. Odd numbers are 1, 3, 5, and so on.

- Zero is an even number

Consecutive numbers are simply integers that are next to each other when you count. For example, 1 and 2 are consecutive numbers. There are also consecutive even numbers and consecutive odd numbers. These are just the numbers that would be next to each other if you counted by twos. For example, 2 and 4 are consecutive even numbers and 1 and 3 are consecutive odd numbers.

- Consecutive just means in a row

Prime numbers are numbers greater than 1 that are only divisible by themselves and 1. For example, the number 7 is divisible only by itself and 1, so it is a prime number. A composite number is divisible by more than just itself and one. For example, the number 6 is divisible by 6, 1, 2, and 3, so it is a composite number. It is important to note that the only prime number that is even is 2. Also, the number 1 is neither prime nor composite.

- Prime numbers are only divisible themselves and 1
- Composite numbers are divisible by more than themselves and 1
- The only even prime number is 2
- The number 1 is neither prime nor composite

Here are some examples of questions that test these concepts:

1. On a piece of paper, Cheryl wrote down the following numbers: 2, 3, 5, 7. Which term best describes these numbers?

   (A) consecutive numbers
   (B) odd numbers
   (C) composite numbers
   (D) prime numbers

Let's use ruling out to solve this problem. Choice A might be tempting because the first two numbers in the sequence are consecutive. However, 3 and 5 are not consecutive numbers, so we can rule out choice A. We can also rule out choice B because 2 is included in the list of numbers and 2 is not an odd number. So now we just have to decide if the numbers are prime or composite. They are all only divisible by themselves and 1, so they are prime numbers. Choice D is correct.

2. Use the number set below to answer the question.

   (4, 6, 8, 10, …)

   Which of the following terms best describes the above set of numbers?

   (A) prime numbers
   (B) odd numbers
   (C) consecutive even numbers
   (D) negative numbers

If we look at choice A, it is clear that the numbers in the set are not prime, so we can rule out choice A. The numbers are also not odd, so choice B is out. We can also see that the numbers are not negative, so choice D can be ruled out. We are left with choice C, the correct answer.

3. Which of the following numbers has 1 and itself as its only factors?

   (A) 2
   (B) 4
   (C) 6
   (D) 9

This question does not use the term "prime number", but rather describes a prime number by definition. Since only a prime number has only itself and 1 as factors, we are looking for a prime number. The number 2 is the only even prime number, so answer choice A is correct.

Basic operations

There are two types of questions on the ISEE that test addition and subtraction. There are some simple questions that just require you to do a calculation. Other questions are word problems that ask you to figure out what operation would be appropriate to fit the story given.

- Some questions just require a basic calculation
- Some questions are word problems that require you to figure out what operation should be performed and then sometimes perform that operation

Here is an example of the simplest type of operation problem:

1. What is the value of the sum 4,892 + 8,953?

    (A) 12,845
    (B) 13,835
    (C) 13,845
    (D) 13,855

To answer this question, let's first look at the answer choices. We can see that our first decision is whether the answer should be almost 13,000 (choice A) or almost 14,000 (choices B-D). If we round off 4,892 to 5,000 and 8,953 to 9,000 it is easy to see that our answer should be close to 14,000 so we can rule out choice A. Now if we look at what is left, we can see that they only differ by the tens digit. If we add the units digits (2+3), we get 5 with nothing to carry over. Now we add the tens digits (9+5) and get 14, so the tens digit of our answer should be 4. Only answer choice C has a 4 in the tens place, so that is the correct answer.

You might also see a quantitative comparison question that requires you to perform basic addition or subtraction. The trick to these questions is that you can't just estimate – you have to do the actual math! You can cancel out any numbers that show up in both columns, however.

- If you get a quantitative comparison question that asks you to do a calculation, don't just estimate
- You can cancel out any numbers that show up in both columns

From this, we can see that the square root of 89 falls somewhere between 9 and 10. Answer choice B comes closest to this range, so it is the correct answer.

Here is one more for you to try:

5. Which gives the best estimate for $\sqrt{37}$?

   (A) between 3 and 4
   (B) between 4 and 5
   (C) between 5 and 6
   (D) between 6 and 7

Again, we find a range.

$$\sqrt{36} = 6$$
$$\sqrt{37} = ??$$
$$\sqrt{49} = 7$$

We can see that the square root of 37 falls in between 6 and 7. Answer choice D is correct.

Some questions can be ruled out down to one answer choice by estimating. It is best to first estimate and see what you can rule out, and then do the math if you need to.

- Estimate first – sometimes the answer choices are far enough apart that you don't need to do any actual math

Here is an example:

2.

Column A	**Column B**
237 + 513 + 750	326 + 424 + 750

(A) Quantity in Column A is greater.
(B) Quantity in Column B is greater.
(C) Quantities in Columns A and B are equal.
(D) Not enough information to determine relationship.

Our first step is to rule out any numbers that show up in both columns. The number 750 shows up in both places, so we will cross 750 out on both sides and then add what is left. If we add Column A, we get 237 + 513 = 750. Now we add Column B and get 326 + 424 = 750. Since we have done the actual calculations and not just estimated, we know that the two quantities are actually equal. Answer choice C is correct.

Sometimes addition and subtraction questions are just basic word problems.

Here is an example:

3. At the beginning of the season, Alamo Little League had 6,700 baseballs. During the season, 250 baseballs were lost and 800 new baseballs were purchased. How many baseballs did Alamo Little League have at the end of the season?

(A) 6,150
(B) 7,250
(C) 7,500
(D) 7,750

In order to answer this question, we just have to translate the words into operations. We started with 6,700, then the number was reduced by 250, but then 800 was added back in: 6,700 − 250 + 800 = 7,250. Answer choice B is correct.

More commonly, questions testing addition and subtraction will be more involved word problems or data questions. They may include information that you do not need in order to answer the question. The key to these questions is picking out what information you do need.

- Questions often include information that you do not need

Here are a couple of examples of this question type:

4. Harold kept track of the score after each inning during a baseball game.

SCORE AFTER EACH INNING		
Inning	Bluejays	Cardinals
1	0	2
2	1	4
3	3	5
4	4	6
5	4	6
6	4	6
7	6	7
8	8	8
9	10	9

During the last three innings, how many runs did the Bluejays score in each inning?

    (A) 1
    (B) 2
    (C) 4
    (D) 10

The trick to this question is that we have to ignore a lot of the data. We are looking just at the Bluejays' score and just at the last three innings. The other piece of information that we need to pay attention to is that the question asks for the change in score per inning, not the total change in score in the last three innings. After the 6th inning, the Bluejays had 4 runs but after the 7th inning, the Bluejays had 6 runs. If we find the difference, it is clear to see that they scored 2 runs in the 7th inning. This pattern continues with the 8th and 9th innings, so answer choice B is correct.

5. Lori is driving from Town A to Town D. She must drive through Town B and Town C (in that order) to get to Town D. Lori has just arrived in Town C.

MILES BETWEEN TOWNS	
Town A to Town B	43 miles
Town B to Town C	78 miles
Town C to Town D	115 miles
Town D to Town E	6 miles

Column A

The number of miles that Lori has driven.

Column B

The number of miles that Lori has left to drive.

(A) Quantity in Column A is greater.
(B) Quantity in Column B is greater.
(C) Quantities in Columns A and B are equal.
(D) Not enough information to determine relationship.

To answer this question, we have to pay attention to the details. The chart gives us the distances all the way to Town E, but Lori is only travelling to Town D. She has made it to Town C, so we add the distances from Town A to Town B and Town B to Town C. If we add 43 miles and 78 miles, we get that Lori has travelled 121 miles. She has 115 miles left to travel to Town D, so answer choice A is correct.

Other questions will ask you determine what operation to use. These questions are word problems. If you see the "equation words" from the following table, chances are good that you need to translate those words into an equation (and sometimes solve):

Here is a quick guide for what operation to use when:

Operation	Situations where you would use that operation
Addition	• The question uses the word "sum" • You are given how many items are in different groups and asked for a total (each group does not have the same number of items in it)
Subtraction	• The question uses the word "difference" • You are given a total and the number of items in all but one of the groups and the question asks for that one group (each group does not have the same number of items in it)
Multiplication	• The question uses the word "product" • The question uses the word "of" • You are given how many groups there are and how many items are in each group and asked for a total (there are the same number of items in each group)
Division	• The question uses the word "quotient" • You are given a total and either the number of groups or the number of items in each group and asked for either the number of groups or the number of items in each group (there are the same number of items in each group)

Here are some examples of questions that test these concepts:

1. Fiona is creating a display at a store. She plans to stack cans in equal rows. Which equation would help her figure out how many total cans (C) she needs in order to create her display?

    (A) c = cans per row − number of rows
    (B) c = cans per row + number of rows
    (C) c = cans per row × number of rows
    (D) c = cans per row ÷ number of rows

For this problem, let's think about what situation we have in broader terms. We are looking for the total number of items that we need. That means that we would use either addition or multiplication. We also have groups (the rows) that all have the same number of items in them. That means that we should use multiplication. Answer choice C is correct.

2. Kevin took a poll of the 31 students in his class. He asked them whether they preferred to play soccer, baseball, or lacrosse. If 15 students said they preferred to play soccer and 7 students said that they preferred to play baseball, then how many students said they preferred to play lacrosse?

   (A) 9
   (B) 10
   (C) 16
   (D) 24

Let's take a close look at this situation. We are given the total number, so we know that we should be using subtraction or division. We are also given groups that do not have equal numbers, so we can narrow it down to subtraction. Now we have to do the actual calculations. We take the total and subtract the two groups that we are given: $31 - 15 - 7 = 9$. We know that there must be 9 students in the remaining group, so answer choice A is correct.

3. Mrs. Kline is trying to figure out how many goody bags she needs to make for a birthday party. She knows how many boys will be attending and how many girls will be attending. How could she figure out how many total goody bags b she will need?

   (A) $b =$ number of girls × number of boys
   (B) $b =$ number of girls + number of boys
   (C) $b =$ number of girls − number of boys
   (D) $b =$ number of girls ÷ number of boys

In this problem, we are looking for a total, so we know that we should use either addition or multiplication. We are not dealing with groups that are all the same size, so we use addition. Answer choice B is correct.

4. Mr. Harris' class is going on a field trip and needs to divide into groups of 5. If there are 35 students in Mr. Harris' class, then how many groups should they form?

    (A) 5
    (B) 6
    (C) 7
    (D) 8

This question gives us a total and then asks for the number of individual groups. Since the groups are all the same size, we use division: $35 \div 5 = 7$. Answer choice C is correct.

5. If 50 is divided by the sum of 20 and 5, the result is

    (A) $\dfrac{25}{50}$

    (B) 2

    (C) $2\dfrac{1}{2}$

    (D) $7\dfrac{1}{2}$

Our first step is to translate the equation language into an expression:

$$\frac{50}{(20+5)}$$

The important thing to remember is that we are dividing by the sum of 20 and 5, not just 20. That means we have to add 20 and 5 and then divide 50 by that answer:

$$\frac{50}{25} = 2$$

Answer choice B is correct.

Here are examples of how these concepts could be tested on the quantitative comparison section:

6.

Column A	**Column B**
The total cost of 18 peaches at 8 cents apiece.	The total cost of 8 peaches at 18 cents apiece.

(A) Quantity in Column A is greater.
(B) Quantity in Column B is greater.
(C) Quantities in Columns A and B are equal.
(D) Not enough information to determine relationship.

Our first step is set up equations for both Column A and Column B. To find the total cost of the peaches in Column A, we would multiply 18 times 8. To find the cost of the peaches in Column B, we would multiply 8 times 18. Without even doing any math, we can see that the answer would be the same for both Column A and Column B. Answer choice C is correct.

7.

Column A	**Column B**
The sum of 13 and 16 divided by 60	$\dfrac{1}{2}$

(A) Quantity in Column A is greater.
(B) Quantity in Column B is greater.
(C) Quantities in Columns A and B are equal.
(D) Not enough information to determine relationship.

Our first step is to translate Column A into an expression and simplify:

$$\frac{13+16}{60} = \frac{29}{60}$$

From here, we could do out 29 divided by 60 to get a decimal. However, to answer quantitative comparison questions, we just need to know what quantity is larger, not the exact value of each quantity. We know that $\dfrac{30}{60}$ is equal to $\dfrac{1}{2}$, so $\dfrac{29}{60}$ must be smaller than $\dfrac{1}{2}$. Answer choice B is correct.

Order of operations (PEMDAS)

In school, you may have learned PEMDAS or Please Excuse My Dear Aunt Sally. These are both ways to remember the order of operations. Basically, the order of operations tells us which operations to do first when we are simplifying an expression.

We do anything in parentheses first (P), then exponents (E), then multiplication or division moving from left to right (MD), and finally addition or subtraction moving from left to right (AS).

For example, let's say we have the following expression:

$$4 + (3 \times 5)$$

We have to do what comes in parentheses first.

$$4 + (15) = 19$$

Notice that if we simply went from left to right, we would get a very different answer – and it would be wrong.

Generally, order of operations problems on the ISEE are testing whether or not you recognize that the operation in parentheses must be done first. The math itself tends not to be too challenging.

Here are some examples for you to try:

1. What expression is equivalent to $3 \times (2 + 1)$?

   (A) $6 + 1$
   (B) 6×1
   (C) $3 + 3$
   (D) 3×3

For this question, we need to remember to do parentheses first. If we do $2 + 1$, then we get 3, so we replace the $2 + 1$ with a 3 and are left with 3×3, or answer choice D.

2. Use the equation below to answer the question.

$$\frac{10(25+50)}{5} = q$$

What is the value of q?
(A) 75
(B) 150
(C) 300
(D) 450

First, we have to do what is in the parentheses. This gives us:

$$\frac{10(75)}{5} = q$$

Our next step is to multiply the top (there are other ways to solve – this is just one of them):

$$\frac{750}{5} = q$$

If we divide 750 by 5, we get 150 for an answer, so answer choice B is correct.

3. Which of the following expressions has a value of 10?

(A) $(2 \times 5) + 3 - 6$
(B) $(2 \times 5 + 3) - 6$
(C) $2 \times (5 + 3 - 6)$
(D) $2 \times (5 + 3) - 6$

In order to answer this question, we need to solve each answer choice and see which one gives us 10 as an answer:

(A) $(2 \times 5) + 3 - 6 = 10 + 3 - 6 = 7$
(B) $(2 \times 5 + 3) - 6 = 13 - 6 = 7$
(C) $2 \times (5 + 3 - 6) = 2 \times 2 = 4$
(D) $2 \times (5 + 3) - 6 = 2 \times 8 - 6 = 16 - 6 = 10$

We can see that only answer choice D gives us 10 as an answer, so that is the correct answer choice.

4. Which is equivalent to $4 \times (2 + 7) \div (4 + 2)$?

(A) 1
(B) 4
(C) 6
(D) 9

We have to remember to do the operations that are in parentheses first. This gives us:

$$4 \times (2 + 7) \div (4 + 2) = 4 \times 9 \div 6$$

Now we can solve from left to right:

$$4 \times 9 \div 6 = 36 \div 6 = 6$$

Answer choice C is correct.

Here is an example of how this concept could be tested as a quantitative comparison question:

5.

Column A	**Column B**
$2 \times (7 + 4) \div 2$	$(2 \times 7) + 4 \div 2$

(A) Quantity in Column A is greater.
(B) Quantity in Column B is greater.
(C) Quantities in Columns A and B are equal.
(D) Not enough information to determine relationship.

Although these two expressions look very similar, we know that location of parentheses can make a difference in the final answer. We need to solve each column in order to figure out which quantity is greater.

Column A:

$$2 \times (7 + 4) \div 2 = 2 \times 11 \div 2 = 22 \div 2 = 11$$

Column B:

$$(2 \times 7) + 4 \div 2 = 14 + 4 \div 2 = 14 + 2 = 16$$

As you can see, which operation we do first makes a difference in our final answer. Since the final answer for Column B is greater than the final answer for Column A, answer choice B is correct.

Negative numbers and number lines

On the Middle Level ISEE, you may see basic questions that ask you to apply the concepts of number lines and negative numbers.

A question may not use the word "number line" but if it is a question involving negative numbers, the easiest way to solve is generally to use a number line. The Middle Level ISEE will not give you numbers so large that a number line becomes unwieldy.

Here are a couple of examples for you to try:

1. In order for a certain river to flood, the level of water must reach 4 meters above its normal level. The river is currently 3 meters below its normal level. By how many meters must the river rise in order for it to flood?

    (A) −7 meters
    (B) −3 meters
    (C) 1 meter
    (D) 7 meters

In order to answer this question, let's make our own number line. We are going to draw a vertical number line since that makes it easier to picture the situation described in the question.

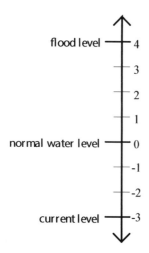

Now we just have to count how many meters the river is from flooding. We can see that the river must rise 7 meters in order to flood, so answer choice D is correct.

2. Polly's lacrosse team cannot play until the temperature reaches 24 °C. It is currently −3 °C. How many degrees must the temperature increase by before Polly's team can play?

   (A) −3 °C
   (B) 21 °C
   (C) 27 °C
   (D) 31 °C

Let's draw out our number line. It is important to note that we don't need to label every single dash, but rather need to sketch in enough information to see how the problem works.

From this basic number line, we can see that the temperature has to rise by 3 °C to get to 0 °C. Then the temperature must rise by an additional 24 °C to get to the temperature at which her team can play. If we add these two values together, we get that the temperature must rise by 27 °C in total in order for her team to play. Answer choice C is correct.

You may also see some number line problems that ask you to use two points to determine scale and then use that scale to determine another value.

- You may have to use two points to determine scale and then use that scale to find a third value

Here are a couple more examples of this problem type for you to try:

3. Use the number line below to answer the question.

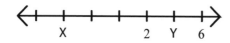

What is the approximate value of Point *M*?

(A) −25
(B) −20
(C) −10
(D) −5

First we have to use the two points given to figure out what the number line is counting by. The difference between 10 and 20 is 10, so we know that each dash is worth 10. Now we have to write in the values going down to point *M*. Our number line should now look like this:

Since *M* lies between -30 and -20, its value is approximately -25. Answer choice A is correct.

4. Use the number line below to answer the question.

What is the difference between Point *X* and Point *Y*?

(A) 4
(B) 5
(C) 8
(D) 10

Our first step in answering this question is to figure out the scale. We need to use the two points given. The difference between 2 and 6 is 4 and there is one dash between these two points on the number line. From this, we can figure out that the number line is counting by 2s. Since there are 4 segments between points X and Y, and each segment is worth 2, the difference between points X and Y is 8. Answer choice C is correct.

Exponents and square roots

Exponents tell us how many times we should multiply a number by itself. For example:

$$3^2 = 3 \times 3 = 9$$
$$2^3 = 2 \times 2 \times 2 = 8$$

Square root radicals tell us to find the number that was multiplied by itself to get the number under the radical. For example:

$$\sqrt{4} = 2$$
$$\sqrt{9} = 3$$

On the Middle Level ISEE, there are a few rules that you should know about exponents:

1. Even if two numbers have the same exponent, you cannot combine them if the numbers are added or subtracted. For example:

   $5^2 - 3^2$ does NOT equal 2^2
   $5^2 - 3^2 = 25 - 9 = 16$

2. We also cannot add two numbers just because they are both under a radical. For example:

   $\sqrt{25} + \sqrt{9}$ does NOT equal $\sqrt{25 + 9}$
   $\sqrt{25} + \sqrt{9} = 5 + 3 = 8$

3. The location of parentheses matters – particularly with negative numbers. For example:

   $(-3)^2 = -3 \times -3 = 9$
   $-(3^2) = -(3 \times 3) = -9$

4. When dealing with negative numbers, what matters is whether the exponent is even or odd (if the negative sign is inside the parentheses). For example:

$$(-2)^3 = -2 \times -2 \times -2 = -8$$
$$(-2)^4 = -2 \times -2 \times -2 \times -2 = 16$$

Notice that if the exponent is odd, the answer will be negative. If the exponent is even then the answer will be positive. Keep in mind that this rule only applies if the negative sign is within the parentheses. If the negative sign is outside the parentheses, the answer will always be negative.

We also covered square roots in the estimating section. Remember that we find a range if we need to take the square root of a number that is not a perfect square.

Exponent and square root questions are very popular in the quantitative comparison section. Remember that these questions are trying to trip you on the rules, not test your ability to do complicated calculations.

- Remember that exponent and square root questions in the quantitative comparison section are often trying to trip you up with an "obvious" answer – that is often wrong

Here are some questions for you to try:

1.

Column A	**Column B**
$\sqrt{1.6}$	$\sqrt{16}$

(A) Quantity in Column A is greater.
(B) Quantity in Column B is greater.
(C) Quantities in Columns A and B are equal.
(D) Not enough information to determine relationship.

In this case, we don't even need to do any math. Since 1.6 is smaller than 16, the square root of 1.6 is going to be smaller than the square root of 16. Answer choice B is correct.

2.

Column A   **Column B**

x x^2

(A) Quantity in Column A is greater.
(B) Quantity in Column B is greater.
(C) Quantities in Columns A and B are equal.
(D) Not enough information to determine relationship.

For this question, it might be really tempting to choose answer choice B since if we square a positive integer, the answer is larger than the original number. However, if we were to plug in 1 or 0, then the two quantities in Column A and Column B would be the same. Answer choice D is correct.

3.

Column A   **Column B**

$\sqrt{16} + \sqrt{4}$ $\sqrt{20}$

(A) Quantity in Column A is greater.
(B) Quantity in Column B is greater.
(C) Quantities in Columns A and B are equal.
(D) Not enough information to determine relationship.

It might be tempting to say that the two quantities are equal. However, if we remember our rules, we know that we cannot just add the two numbers together and put them under the same radical. Let's do a little actual math.

Column A:

$$\sqrt{16} + \sqrt{4} = 4 + 2 = 6$$

Column B:

$$\sqrt{20}$$

In this case, 20 is not a perfect square so we have to come up with a range.

$$\sqrt{16} = 4$$
$$\sqrt{20} = ??$$
$$\sqrt{25} = 5$$

We can see that $\sqrt{20}$ falls between 4 and 5. This means that Column B is always less than Column A so answer choice A is correct.

4.

Column A	Column B
-2^4	$(-2)^4$

(A) Quantity in Column A is greater.
(B) Quantity in Column B is greater.
(C) Quantities in Columns A and B are equal.
(D) Not enough information to determine relationship.

In Column A, the answer will always be negative because the negative sign is not in parentheses. In Column B, the negative sign is inside the parentheses. There is also an even exponent. These two conditions make the final answer for Column B positive. This means that Column B will always be greater than Column A, so we don't even have to do the math. Answer choice B is correct.

5.

Column A	Column B
4^2	3^3

(A) Quantity in Column A is greater.
(B) Quantity in Column B is greater.
(C) Quantities in Columns A and B are equal.
(D) Not enough information to determine relationship.

To answer this question, it is best to do the actual math. We can't just "estimate" with exponents.

Column A:

$$4^2 = 4 \times 4 = 16$$

Column B:

$$3^3 = 3 \times 3 \times 3 = 27$$

Answer choice B is correct.

6.

Column A	Column B
$6^2 - 4^2$	2^2

(A) Quantity in Column A is greater.
(B) Quantity in Column B is greater.
(C) Quantities in Columns A and B are equal.
(D) Not enough information to determine relationship.

Again, we have to do the math and not be tempted by a shortcut.

Column A:

$$6^2 - 4^2 = 36 - 16 = 20$$

Column B:

$$2^2 = 4$$

Column A is clearly a larger quantity so answer choice A is correct.

Multiples and factors

Multiples are numbers that are the result of multiplying one number by an integer.

For example, the multiples of 4 are 4, 8, 12, 16, 20, and so on.

The least common multiple is the smallest number that two or more other numbers have as a multiple. To find the least common multiple we list out the multiples of the numbers in question until we find a multiple that they all have in common.

- To find the least common multiple, list out the multiples of the numbers in question until you find a multiple that they have in common

For example, let's say we are trying to find the least common multiple of 3, 5, and 6.

> Multiples of 3: 3, 6, 9, 12, 15, 18, 21, 24, 27, <u>30</u>
> Multiples of 5: 5, 10, 15, 20, 25, <u>30</u>
> Multiples of 6: 6, 12, 18, 24, <u>30</u>

The smallest number that is a multiple of 3, 5, and 6 is 30, so 30 is our least common multiple.

Since this is a multiple-choice test, it is often easier to just start with the smallest number and then rule out numbers that are not multiples of all the given numbers.

Here is an example:

1. What is the least common multiple of 4, 6, and 8?

   (A) 2
   (B) 4
   (C) 24
   (D) 192

To answer this question, let's use ruling out. Answer choice A gives us a number that is a factor of 4, 6, and 8, but not a multiple so we can rule it out. Choice B is only a multiple of 4, but not of 6 and 8, so we can also rule out choice B. Now we have choice C to look at since it is the next biggest number. The numbers 4, 6, and 8 all go into 24 without a remainder, so we know that 24 is a multiple of all 3. Since it is the smallest answer choice that is a multiple of all 3, we can just choose choice C.

Factors are numbers that can be divided into another number with no remainder. For example, I can divide 8 by 1, 8, 2, and 4 without a remainder, so those are the factors of 8. Notice that 1 and the number itself are always factors.

- Factors are numbers that divide into another number without leaving a remainder
- 1 and the number itself are always factors of any number

The greatest common factor is the largest number that is a factor of each number in a group. Since this is a multiple-choice test, we can use ruling out again. This time we want to start with the largest answer choice and work our way down.

- Greatest common factor is the largest number that is a factor of each number in a group
- We can use ruling out – start with the largest answer choice

Here is an example for you to try:

2.   What is the greatest common factor of 50 and 60?

  (A) 5
  (B) 10
  (C) 15
  (D) 300

Let's start with the largest answer choice, D. The number 300 is a multiple of 50 and 60, but not a factor, so we can rule it out. Let's look at choice C next. The number 15 is a factor of 60, but not of 50, so we can rule out choice C. Now let's look at the next largest answer choice. The number 10 is a factor of both 50 and 60, so it is the correct answer choice. Even though the number 5, choice A, is also a factor of both 50 and 60, it is not the greatest common factor. Answer choice B is the correct answer.

Now you know what you need about whole numbers and operations. Be sure to complete the practice drill to reinforce what you have learned.

Whole numbers and operations practice set

1.

Column A	Column B
-3^3	$(-3)^3$

(A) Quantity in Column A is greater.
(B) Quantity in Column B is greater.
(C) Quantities in Columns A and B are equal.
(D) Not enough information to determine relationship.

2. Which is equivalent to $2 \times (3 + 4) \div (1 + 1)$?

(A) 5
(B) 7
(C) 14
(D) 28

3. What is the least common multiple of 5, 7, and 10?

(A) 5
(B) 7
(C) 35
(D) 70

4. Which is equivalent to 12 plus 8 summed together and then divided by 40?

(A) $\dfrac{20}{40}$

(B) $\dfrac{25}{40}$

(C) 5

(D) 20

5.

Column A	Column B
237 + 510 + 759	326 + 510 + 699

(A) Quantity in Column A is greater.
(B) Quantity in Column B is greater.
(C) Quantities in Columns A and B are equal.
(D) Not enough information to determine relationship.

6. A solution that is 10% salt and 90% water will freeze at −6°C If it is currently 18°C, by how many degrees must the temperature decrease in order for the salt solution to freeze?

(A) −6 °C
(B) 18 °C
(C) 22 °C
(D) 24 °C

7. Which of the following numbers has 1 and itself as its only factors?

(A) 4
(B) 6
(C) 13
(D) 15

8. James and Cameron are keeping track of their bank balances, as shown in the chart below.

	James' Bank Balance	Cameron's Bank Balance
Week 1	$2.30	$3.45
Week 2	$2.60	$3.90
Week 3	$2.90	$4.35
Week 4	$3.20	$4.80

After Week 1, how much did James save each week?

(A) $0.30
(B) $0.45
(C) $0.90
(D) $2.30

9.

Column A   Column B

$\sqrt{16} + \sqrt{9}$ $\sqrt{25}$

(A) Quantity in Column A is greater.
(B) Quantity in Column B is greater.
(C) Quantities in Columns A and B are equal.
(D) Not enough information to determine relationship.

10. What is the greatest common factor of 72 and 84?

(A) 2
(B) 6
(C) 12
(D) 36

11.

Column A	Column B
$(3 \times 2) + 4 \div 2$	$3 \times (2 + 4) \div 2$

(A) Quantity in Column A is greater.
(B) Quantity in Column B is greater.
(C) Quantities in Columns A and B are equal.
(D) Not enough information to determine relationship.

12. Clara is buying a t-shirt for each player on her basketball team. If there are 3 t-shirts in each package, which equation should she use to figure out how many packages (p) she should buy?

(A) p = number of players + 3
(B) p = number of players $\times$ 3
(C) p = number of players $\div$ 3
(D) p = number of players − 3

13.

Column A	Column B
x^2	x^3

(A) Quantity in Column A is greater.
(B) Quantity in Column B is greater.
(C) Quantities in Columns A and B are equal.
(D) Not enough information to determine relationship.

Answers to Whole Numbers and Operations Practice Set

1. C
2. B
3. D
4. A
5. B
6. D
7. C
8. A
9. A
10. C
11. B
12. C
13. D

Fractions, Decimals, and Percents

The fraction and decimal problems on the ISEE are pretty straightforward.

Here are some of the question types that you may see on the Middle Level ISEE:

- Determining a fraction from a picture or description
- Adding and subtracting fractions
- Multiplying and dividing with fractions
- Creating and using mixed numbers
- Converting between fractions and decimals
- Adding and subtracting decimals
- Converting between fractions and percents
- Converting between percents and actual numbers
- Percent increase and decrease
- Multiple percent discounts

An important concept to remember throughout this section is that a fraction represents part out of a whole.

$$\text{Fraction} = \frac{\text{Part}}{\text{Whole}}$$

You also need to understand the basics of equivalent fractions.

The cardinal rule for equivalent fractions is that if you multiply (or divide) the top by some number, you must also multiply (or divide) the bottom by the same number in order for the value of the fraction to remain the same. This works when you multiply or divide the top and bottom by the same number. You can NOT add or subtract the same number from both the top and the bottom and keep the same value, however.

For example:

$$\frac{1}{2} \times \frac{2}{2} = \frac{2}{4}$$ Since we multiplied the numerator (top number) and denominator (bottom number) by the same number, we know that $\frac{1}{2} = \frac{2}{4}$

$$\frac{1+2}{2+2} = \frac{3}{4}$$ Since we added the same number to the numerator and denominator, $\frac{1}{2}$ is NOT equal to $\frac{3}{4}$

Determining a fraction from a picture or description

The first type of fraction problem that we will go over is how to tell what fraction of a picture is shaded.

The basic strategy for these problem types is that you need to divide your picture into pieces.

- Divide your pictures into pieces

This is easy if it is a figure that can be divided into equally sized pieces.

For example, if we have the following picture:

We can see that there are four equally sized pieces in this picture. Two of those four pieces are shaded, so $\frac{1}{2}$ of the figure is shaded.

Here is an example of how this could be tested on the ISEE:

1. Use the shape below to answer the question.

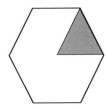

What fraction of the hexagon is shaded?

(A) $\dfrac{1}{2}$

(B) $\dfrac{1}{3}$

(C) $\dfrac{1}{4}$

(D) $\dfrac{1}{6}$

In order to solve this problem, draw in lines that divide the hexagon into equal pieces.

It should look like this:

Now we can clearly see that one part out of six is shaded in, so the correct answer is choice D.

Sometimes you will have to divide a figure into unequal pieces to see what works. This question type always asks you to identify which figures have one-half shaded in. It would be possible to write this question without using $\dfrac{1}{2}$ as the fraction that is shaded, but that would be a much harder problem type so the Middle Level ISEE is not likely to do that.

Here is an example of a figure that has one-half shaded in but isn't easily divisible into pieces that are all the same size.

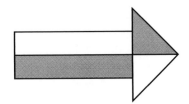

The key to these questions is just to match up parts that would be the same and then make sure that half of those parts are shaded.

Here is one for you to try:

2. Which of the following figures is NOT shaded in one-half of its region?

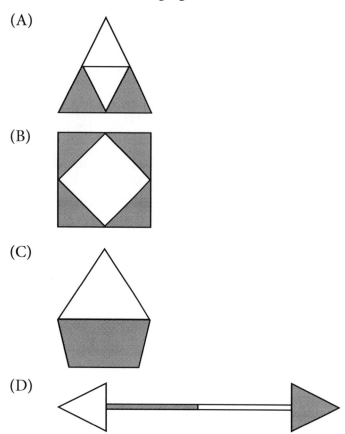

(A)

(B)

(C)

(D)

To answer this question, simply match up the shaded regions to identical non-shaded regions. If that doesn't work, then you have your correct answer. Choice C is the correct answer.

Sometimes the ISEE will give you a description of a situation and then ask what fraction a group is. To answer these questions, we have to keep in mind that a fraction is a part out of a whole. With these questions, we will sometimes have to do a little math to find the whole.

- Fraction = $\dfrac{\text{Part}}{\text{Whole}}$

- You may need to calculate the whole from the information given

Here are a couple of examples for you to try:

1. In a box of chocolates there are only cream and almond chocolates. There are 6 more almond chocolates than cream chocolates. If there are 8 cream chocolates, what fraction of the chocolates are cream chocolates?

   (A) $\dfrac{4}{11}$

   (B) $\dfrac{1}{2}$

   (C) $\dfrac{4}{7}$

   (D) $\dfrac{3}{4}$

The trick to this question is that we first have to figure out what the total number of chocolates is. We have 8 cream chocolates. The problem tells us that there are 6 more almond chocolates than cream chocolates. This means that there must be 14 almond chocolates. We aren't done yet, we have to add 14 and 8 to get the total number of chocolates. There are 22 total chocolates, so the fraction that are cream chocolates is $\dfrac{8}{22}$, which reduces to $\dfrac{4}{11}$, or answer choice A. By the way, if you chose answer choice C, then you probably forgot to include the cream chocolates in your total number of chocolates.

2. There are fifth and sixth graders on a bus. There are 15 more fifth graders than sixth graders. If there are 30 fifth graders on the bus, what fraction of the students on the bus are sixth graders?

   (A) $\dfrac{1}{5}$

   (B) $\dfrac{1}{3}$

   (C) $\dfrac{1}{2}$

   (D) $\dfrac{2}{3}$

Our first step is to figure out how many students we have in each group. The problem tells us that there are 30 fifth graders and that there are 15 more fifth graders than sixth graders. From this, we can figure out that there are 15 sixth graders. Now we have to figure out how many total students are on the bus. If we add the number of fifth graders (30) and the number of sixth graders (15), we get that there are a total of 45 students on the bus. Now we have to remember that they are asking about sixth graders and put the number of sixth graders over the total. This gives us $\frac{15}{45}$, which reduces to $\frac{1}{3}$. Answer choice B is correct. If you chose answer choice D, you answered what fraction of the students are fifth graders, not sixth graders. If you chose answer choice C, you probably forgot to add the number of sixth graders into the total.

Adding and subtracting fractions

When we add or subtract fractions, we use equivalent fractions to get the same bottom number, otherwise known as a common denominator. We then add (or subtract) across the top and keep the common denominator as the denominator in our answer.

For example, let's say our problem looks like this:

$$\frac{1}{2} + \frac{2}{3} = ?$$

We are looking for a number that both denominators go into, or are factors of. The numbers 2 and 3 both go into 6, so 6 will be our common denominator. We use this to create equivalent fractions with a common denominator.

$$\frac{1}{2} \times \frac{3}{3} = \frac{3}{6}$$
$$\frac{2}{3} \times \frac{2}{2} = \frac{4}{6}$$

We now add the equivalent fractions by adding across the top but keeping the common denominator.

$$\frac{3}{6} + \frac{4}{6} = \frac{7}{6}$$

We aren't quite done yet. We now have a fraction where the top number is bigger than the bottom number (an improper fraction). To fix this, we can break apart the fraction.

$$\frac{7}{6} = \frac{6}{6} + \frac{1}{6}$$

We broke the fraction apart so that we can see how many "ones" we have and what fraction is left. Finally, we can create a mixed number as an answer.

$$\frac{6}{6} + \frac{1}{6} = 1 + \frac{1}{6} = 1\frac{1}{6}$$

Here are a couple of examples of basic addition and subtraction questions:

1. What is the value of the expression $\frac{1}{3}+\frac{2}{5}$?

    (A) $\frac{1}{3}$

    (B) $\frac{3}{5}$

    (C) $\frac{11}{15}$

    (D) $\frac{4}{5}$

To answer this question, we first have to get a common denominator. The smallest number that both 3 and 5 go into is 15. This means that 15 will be our common denominator. Now we have to use the principles of equivalent fractions.

$$\frac{1}{3}\times\frac{5}{5}=\frac{5}{15}$$
$$\frac{2}{5}\times\frac{3}{3}=\frac{6}{15}$$

Now we just have to add the fractions with common denominators together.

$$\frac{5}{15}+\frac{6}{15}=\frac{11}{15}$$

We can see that answer choice C is correct.

2. What is the value of the expression $\frac{3}{4}-\frac{2}{3}$?

    (A) $\frac{1}{12}$

    (B) $\frac{1}{6}$

    (C) $\frac{1}{3}$

    (D) $\frac{1}{2}$

To answer this question, we first need to create a common denominator.

$$\frac{3}{4} = \frac{3 \times 3}{4 \times 3} = \frac{9}{12}$$

$$\frac{2}{3} = \frac{2 \times 4}{3 \times 4} = \frac{8}{12}$$

Now we can do the actual subtraction.

$$\frac{9}{12} - \frac{8}{12} = \frac{1}{12}$$

We can see that answer choice A is the correct answer choice.

3.

Column A	**Column B**
$\dfrac{3}{5} - \dfrac{1}{3}$	$\dfrac{3}{5} + \dfrac{1}{3}$

(A) Quantity in Column A is greater.
(B) Quantity in Column B is greater.
(C) Quantities in Columns A and B are equal.
(D) Not enough information to determine relationship.

For this question, we don't have to do any actual math. If we are dealing with two positive numbers, adding them together will always be greater than finding the difference. Answer choice B is correct.

You may very well also see word problems that require you to apply the concept of adding and subtracting fractions.

Here are some examples for you to try:

4. Katie has two jars of mayonnaise. One jar has $\frac{1}{4}$ cup of mayonnaise left in it and the other jar has $\frac{2}{5}$ cup of mayonnaise left in it. How many total cups of mayonnaise does Katie have?

(A) $\frac{1}{3}$

(B) $\frac{1}{2}$

(C) $\frac{13}{20}$

(D) $\frac{3}{5}$

First, we need to figure out what operation to use. We are given two parts and asked for the total, so we use addition. In order to add two fractions, we have to first find the common denominator.

$$\frac{1 \times 5}{4 \times 5} = \frac{5}{20}$$

$$\frac{2 \times 4}{5 \times 4} = \frac{8}{20}$$

Now we add the two fractions with common denominators together.

$$\frac{5}{20} + \frac{8}{20} = \frac{13}{20}$$

We can see that answer choice C is correct.

4. Taylor had $2\frac{1}{2}$ cups of sugar. She gave $\frac{3}{4}$ cup of sugar to her neighbor. How much sugar did Taylor have left?

(A) $1\frac{1}{2}$

(B) $1\frac{3}{4}$

(C) 2

(D) $2\frac{1}{2}$

To answer this question, we first have to decide what operation to use. Since Taylor is giving away some sugar, we use subtraction. To subtract a fraction, we have to have a common denominator.

$$2\frac{1}{2} = 2\frac{1\times2}{2\times2} = 2\frac{2}{4}$$

Now our problem looks like this:

$$2\frac{2}{4} - \frac{3}{4}$$

Our issue now is that we can't subtract $\frac{3}{4}$ from $\frac{2}{4}$. We will have to borrow from the 2.

$$2\frac{2}{4} = 1+1+\frac{2}{4} = 1+\frac{4}{4}+\frac{2}{4} = 1\frac{6}{4}$$

We now have an improper fraction with a numerator that is bigger than the denominator. This is what we need in order to do the subtraction.

$$1\frac{6}{4} - \frac{3}{4} = 1\frac{3}{4}$$

We can see that the correct answer is choice B.

Multiplying and dividing with fractions

On the Middle Level ISEE, multiplying and dividing with fractions will be tested primarily with word problems.

In general, to multiply fractions, we simply multiply across the top and multiply across the bottom. For example:

$$\frac{1}{2} \times \frac{2}{3} = \frac{2}{6}$$

We then have to reduce the fraction since there is a number that goes into both the numerator and denominator. We use our rule of equivalent fractions (do the same to the top and bottom), only this time we are dividing.

$$\frac{2\div2}{6\div2} = \frac{1}{3}$$

Our final answer is $\frac{1}{3}$.

On the ISEE, you may also be asked to multiply a fraction by a whole number. To do this, we just put the whole number over one.

Here is an example:

$$450 \times \frac{1}{3} = \frac{450}{1} \times \frac{1}{3} = \frac{450}{3}$$

For our next step, we have to understand that a fraction bar essentially means to divide.

$$\frac{450}{3} = 450 \div 3 = 150$$

To divide fractions, we flip the second fraction and then multiply. For example, let's say our problem is:

$$\frac{2}{3} \div \frac{4}{5}$$

In order to find our answer, we flip the second fraction and multiply, so our problem becomes:

$$\frac{2}{3} \times \frac{5}{4} = \frac{2 \times 5}{3 \times 4} = \frac{10}{12}$$

We aren't quite done yet, we still have to reduce. Since 10 and 12 are both divisible by 2, we divide the top and the bottom by 2.

$$\frac{10 \div 2}{12 \div 2} = \frac{5}{6}$$

Our final answer is $\frac{5}{6}$.

If we have division with a fraction and a whole number, we have to remember to put the whole number over 1.

For example, let's say that we want to divide $\frac{1}{3}$ into 3 parts. The math would look like this:

$$\frac{1}{3} \div 3 = \frac{1}{3} \div \frac{3}{1} = \frac{1}{3} \times \frac{1}{3} = \frac{1}{9}$$

Here are some for you to try:

1. Lee has $\frac{3}{4}$ gallon of chocolate milk. He wants to divide it evenly among four cups. How much chocolate milk should go in each cup?

   (A) $\frac{3}{16}$ gallon

   (B) $\frac{1}{4}$ gallon

   (C) $\frac{1}{3}$ gallon

   (D) $\frac{2}{3}$ gallon

Since the problem uses the word "divide", we know that division is in order. We have to divide $\frac{3}{4}$ into 4 parts, so we divide $\frac{3}{4} \div 4$. The math would look like this:

$$\frac{3}{4} \div 4 = \frac{3}{4} \div \frac{4}{1} = \frac{3}{4} \times \frac{1}{4} = \frac{3}{16}$$

Answer choice A is correct.

2. The distance from Chicago to Los Angeles is roughly 2,015 miles. Marni is driving from Chicago to Los Angeles and wants to stay overnight when she has driven about $\frac{1}{4}$ of the distance from Chicago to Los Angeles. Where should she stay?

   (A) Des Moines, Iowa, which is 332 miles from Chicago
   (B) Lincoln, Nebraska, which is 522 miles from Chicago
   (C) Denver, Colorado, which is 1,004 miles from Chicago
   (D) Las Vegas, Nevada, which is 1,751 miles from Chicago

To find the distance, we need to find $\frac{1}{4}$ of 2,015 miles. The word "of" tells us to multiply.

$$2,015 \times \frac{1}{4} = \frac{2,015}{1} \times \frac{1}{4} = \frac{2,015}{4}$$

From here, we can estimate since this is a multiple-choice test. 2,015 is about 2,000.

$$\frac{2,000}{4} = 500$$

We are looking for the answer choice that is close to 500 miles. Answer choice B comes the closest.

Here are a couple of problems that ask you to combine a couple of different concepts.

3. There are six equally sized cups that are filled with sugar that will be used for baking cookies. Hilary used $\frac{1}{2}$ of each cup and Thomas used $\frac{1}{3}$ of each cup. How many total cups of sugar remain?

   (A) 1 cup
   (B) 1.5 cups
   (C) 3 cups
   (D) 5 cups

We can begin this problem by figuring out how much total sugar was used from each cup. In order to do that we need to add together the $\frac{1}{2}$ cup that Hilary used and the $\frac{1}{3}$ cup that Thomas used. We must first find a common denominator. This is what the math looks like:

$$\frac{1}{2} + \frac{1}{3} = \frac{3}{6} + \frac{2}{6} = \frac{5}{6}$$

Now, we can figure out how much of the total sugar was used. They used $\frac{5}{6}$ of 6 cups and the word "of" tells us to multiply.

$$\frac{5}{6} \times 6 \text{ cups} = \frac{5}{6} \times \frac{6}{1} = \frac{30}{6} = 5 \text{ cups}$$

If 5 cups were used, then only 1 cup would remain. Answer choice A is correct.

4.

<u>Column A</u>	<u>Column B</u>
$\frac{3}{5} \div \frac{1}{3}$	$\frac{3}{5} \times \frac{1}{3}$

   (A) Quantity in Column A is greater.
   (B) Quantity in Column B is greater.
   (C) Quantities in Columns A and B are equal.
   (D) Not enough information to determine relationship.

It would be easy to choose B on this question if we don't do the math since when we deal with whole numbers, multiplication gives us a larger number for an answer than division does. However, fractions work differently. Let's go ahead and do the math:

Column A:

$$\frac{3}{5} \div \frac{1}{3} = \frac{3}{5} \times \frac{3}{1} = \frac{9}{5}$$

Column B:

$$\frac{3}{5} \times \frac{1}{3} = \frac{3}{15}$$

Answer choice A is the correct answer.

Some of the more challenging questions ask you to combine several operations. There is often more than one way to solve these problems, so if you get the right answer but used a different method, that is fine.

Here are some more challenging problems for you to try:

5. Tailor spent $\frac{2}{3}$ of her allowance on a movie and spent the remaining $7 on candy. What was her total allowance?

    (A) $3.50
    (B) $7.00
    (C) $14.00
    (D) $21.00

Our first step is to figure out what fraction of her allowance was $7. Since the other part of her allowance was $\frac{2}{3}$, then the fraction that she spent on candy was $\frac{1}{3}$ of her allowance. Now we know that $7 was $\frac{1}{3}$ of her total allowance. That means that the remaining $\frac{2}{3}$ of her allowance is $14. Now we have to add the two parts together to get the total. Since $7 plus $14 gives us $21, answer choice D is correct.

6. If $\dfrac{2}{5}$ of a cup can be filled in one minute, how many minutes would it take to fill the whole cup?

(A) $\dfrac{2}{5}$

(B) $\dfrac{3}{5}$

(C) $1\dfrac{1}{2}$

(D) $2\dfrac{1}{2}$

The first step in answering this question is to figure out how long it would take to fill $\dfrac{1}{5}$ of the cup. We can divide $\dfrac{2}{5}$ by 2 to get $\dfrac{1}{5}$, we can also divide the time it takes to fill $\dfrac{2}{5}$ of the cup by 2 in order to figure out how long it would take to fill $\dfrac{1}{5}$ of the cup. Since 1 minute divided by 2 gives us $\dfrac{1}{2}$ a minute, we now know that it would take $\dfrac{1}{2}$ a minute to fill $\dfrac{1}{5}$ of the cup. To find how long it would take to fill the entire cup, we would multiply this number by 5 since there are 5 fifths in a whole.

$$\dfrac{1}{2} \times 5 = \dfrac{1}{2} \times \dfrac{5}{1} = \dfrac{5}{2} = 2\dfrac{1}{2}$$

Answer choice D is correct. (If you are confused about how we turned $\dfrac{5}{2}$ into $2\dfrac{1}{2}$, keep reading – we will cover that next!)

Creating and using mixed numbers

Mixed numbers are numbers that have a whole number part and a fraction part.

For example, $2\dfrac{1}{2}$ is a mixed number. Mixed numbers can also be converted into improper fractions, or fractions where the top number is greater than the bottom number.

On the ISEE, the numbers that you have to convert generally are not that big. There are multiple methods to convert between mixed numbers and improper fractions, but we will show you just one that works well with smaller numbers.

Let's say we want to change $2\frac{1}{2}$ into an improper fraction. We can start by breaking down the whole number into ones.

$$2\frac{1}{2} = 1 + 1 + \frac{1}{2}$$

Our next step is to convert the ones into fractions that have the same denominator as the fraction in the mixed number.

$$2\frac{1}{2} = 1 + 1 + \frac{1}{2} = \frac{2}{2} + \frac{2}{2} + \frac{1}{2}$$

Now we just add the fractions together.

$$\frac{2}{2} + \frac{2}{2} + \frac{1}{2} = \frac{5}{2}$$

We are left with the improper fraction $\frac{5}{2}$ that is equal to the mixed number $2\frac{1}{2}$.

We can use the same process in reverse to turn an improper fraction into a mixed number. For example, let's say we want to convert $\frac{11}{4}$ into a mixed number. First, we have to break down $\frac{11}{4}$.

$$\frac{11}{4} = \frac{4}{4} + \frac{4}{4} + \frac{3}{4}$$

Now we just turn the $\frac{4}{4}$s into ones.

$$\frac{4}{4} + \frac{4}{4} + \frac{3}{4} = 1 + 1 + \frac{3}{4} = 2\frac{3}{4}$$

We now know that $\frac{11}{4}$ is equal to $2\frac{3}{4}$.

Here is a basic problem that tests these concepts:

1. $1 + \dfrac{2}{3} =$

    (A) $\dfrac{1}{3}$

    (B) $\dfrac{2}{3}$

    (C) $\dfrac{4}{3}$

    (D) $\dfrac{5}{3}$

The simple answer to this problem would be $1\dfrac{2}{3}$, but if we look at the answer choices we can see that isn't an option. Some of the answer choices are improper fractions, however, so we should convert $1\dfrac{2}{3}$ into an improper fraction.

$$1\frac{2}{3} = \frac{3}{3} + \frac{2}{3} = \frac{5}{3}$$

Answer choice D is correct.

On the ISEE, these concepts are often tested as word problems. Here are some examples for you to try:

2. Paul is putting together bags of mixed nuts. He combined the nuts in the recipe below and then divided the nuts equally into 6 bags.

MIXED NUTS
8 cups peanuts
4 cups brazil nuts
3 cups cashews
5 cups walnuts

About how many cups of nuts were in each bag?

(A) $2\dfrac{1}{2}$

(B) $2\dfrac{2}{3}$

(C) $3\dfrac{1}{6}$

(D) $3\dfrac{1}{3}$

To answer this question, first we have to figure out how many total cups of nuts we are dividing. If we add up the amounts from the recipe (8 + 4 + 3 + 5 = 20), we find that there are a total of twenty cups of nuts. Now we have to divide the total (20) by the number of bags (6) in order to figure out how many cups of nuts are in each bag.

$$\dfrac{20}{6} = \dfrac{6}{6} + \dfrac{6}{6} + \dfrac{6}{6} + \dfrac{2}{6} = 1+1+1+\dfrac{2}{6} = 3\dfrac{1}{3}$$

Answer choice D is correct.

3. Nora is making fruit punch. She combines $2\dfrac{1}{2}$ cups pineapple juice with $3\dfrac{3}{4}$ cups cranberry juice. How many cups of fruit punch will she have?

(A) $5\dfrac{3}{4}$

(B) $6\dfrac{1}{4}$

(C) $6\dfrac{1}{2}$

(D) $6\dfrac{3}{4}$

In order to answer this question, we first have to get a common denominator for the fractions. Both 2 and 4 go into 4, so we will make that our common denominator. The number $3\frac{3}{4}$ already has a denominator of 4, so we can leave that number alone. We need to convert $2\frac{1}{2}$, however.

$$2\frac{1}{2} = 2\frac{1 \times 2}{2 \times 2} = 2\frac{2}{4}$$

Now we break apart our mixed numbers and use the commutative property to group the whole numbers and the fractions.

$$2\frac{2}{4} + 3\frac{3}{4} = 2 + \frac{2}{4} + 3 + \frac{3}{4} = 5 + \frac{5}{4} = 5\frac{5}{4}$$

Our problem now is that the fraction part of our mixed number needs to be reduced.

$$5\frac{5}{4} = 5 + \frac{4}{4} + \frac{1}{4} = 5 + 1 + \frac{1}{4} = 6\frac{1}{4}$$

Answer choice B is correct.

Sometimes, when we are subtracting mixed numbers, we need to borrow in order to subtract. For example, let's say we have the following problem:

$$2\frac{1}{2} - \frac{3}{4} =$$

The issue here is that we cannot take $\frac{3}{4}$ away from $\frac{1}{2}$. We have to borrow from the 2.

$$2\frac{1}{2} = 1 + 1 + \frac{1}{2} = 1 + \frac{2}{2} + \frac{1}{2} = 1\frac{3}{2}$$

Now we just need to get a common denominator in order to subtract $\frac{3}{4}$ from $1\frac{3}{2}$.

$$1\frac{3}{2} = 1\frac{3 \times 2}{2 \times 2} = 1\frac{6}{4}$$

Now we can subtract.

$$1\frac{6}{4} - \frac{3}{4} = 1\frac{3}{4}$$

By borrowing and then finding a common denominator, we can see that $2\frac{1}{2} - \frac{3}{4} = 1\frac{3}{4}$.

Here are a couple of questions for you to try:

4. Peter had $3\frac{1}{4}$ feet of rope. He gave Tom $1\frac{3}{4}$ feet of that rope. How many feet of rope did Peter have left?

(A) $1\frac{1}{2}$

(B) $2\frac{1}{4}$

(C) $2\frac{1}{2}$

(D) $3\frac{1}{4}$

We need to subtract $1\frac{3}{4}$ from $3\frac{1}{4}$. In order to do this, we have to borrow a 1 from the 3 in the first fraction.

$$3\frac{1}{4} = 2 + 1 + \frac{1}{4} = 2 + \frac{4}{4} + \frac{1}{4} = 2\frac{5}{4}$$

We can now do the subtraction problem.

$$2\frac{5}{4} - 1\frac{3}{4} = 1\frac{2}{4}$$

Now we just have to reduce the $\frac{2}{4}$.

$$1\frac{2}{4} = 1\frac{2 \div 2}{4 \div 2} = 1\frac{1}{2}$$

The correct answer is choice A.

5. Steve had $4\frac{1}{2}$ cups of sugar. He used some of that sugar in a recipe. He now has $2\frac{7}{8}$ cups of sugar left. How many cups of sugar did he use in his recipe?

(A) $\frac{1}{2}$

(B) $\frac{5}{8}$

(C) $1\frac{3}{8}$

(D) $1\frac{5}{8}$

In order to find how much sugar he used, we have to subtract how much sugar Steve had left from how much sugar he started with.

$$4\frac{1}{2} - 2\frac{7}{8}$$

We need to borrow from the 4 and then get a common denominator.

$$4\frac{1}{2} = 4 + \frac{1}{2} = 3 + 1 + \frac{1}{2} = 3 + \frac{2}{2} + \frac{1}{2} = 3\frac{3}{2} = 3\frac{3 \times 4}{2 \times 4} = 3\frac{12}{8}$$

Now we can subtract.

$$3\frac{12}{8} - 2\frac{7}{8} = 1\frac{5}{8}$$

Answer choice D is correct.

On the Middle Level ISEE, you are also likely to see multiplication or division problems that require you to use mixed numbers. Just remember to convert the mixed number into an improper fraction before you multiply or divide.

- Convert mixed numbers into improper fractions before multiplying or dividing

Here are a couple of examples for you to try:

6. What is the result of $2\frac{3}{5} \times 3\frac{1}{3}$?

   (A) $8\frac{7}{15}$

   (B) $8\frac{2}{3}$

   (C) $9\frac{2}{15}$

   (D) $9\frac{1}{3}$

Our first step is to turn the mixed numbers into improper fractions.

$$2\frac{3}{5} = \frac{5}{5} + \frac{5}{5} + \frac{3}{5} = \frac{13}{5}$$

$$3\frac{1}{3} = \frac{3}{3} + \frac{3}{3} + \frac{3}{3} + \frac{1}{3} = \frac{10}{3}$$

Now we can multiply the improper fractions.

$$\frac{13}{5} \times \frac{10}{3} = \frac{130}{15} = \frac{15}{15} + \frac{15}{15} + \frac{15}{15} + \frac{15}{15} + \frac{15}{15} + \frac{15}{15} + \frac{15}{15} + \frac{15}{15} + \frac{10}{15} = 8\frac{10}{15}$$

Now we just have to reduce $8\frac{10}{15}$ to see which answer choice is correct.

$$8\frac{10 \div 5}{15 \div 5} = 8\frac{2}{3}$$

Answer choice B is correct.

7. What is q equal to in the equation $2\frac{1}{3} \div 3\frac{3}{4} = q$?

   (A) $\frac{28}{45}$

   (B) $1\frac{2}{5}$

   (C) $1\frac{2}{3}$

   (D) $4\frac{5}{12}$

Let's start out by converting each mixed number into an improper fraction.

$$2\frac{1}{3} = \frac{3}{3} + \frac{3}{3} + \frac{1}{3} = \frac{7}{3}$$

$$3\frac{3}{4} = \frac{4}{4} + \frac{4}{4} + \frac{4}{4} + \frac{3}{4} = \frac{15}{4}$$

Now we can rewrite our division problem:

$$\frac{7}{3} \div \frac{15}{4}$$

Remember that when we divide by a fraction, we flip that fraction and then multiply.

$$\frac{7}{3} \div \frac{15}{4} = \frac{7}{3} \times \frac{4}{15} = \frac{28}{45}$$

Answer choice A is correct.

Converting between fractions and decimals

You may see a question on the ISEE that asks you to convert between a fraction and decimal. A decimal is simply another way to express a fraction, or a part of a number.

To convert between fractions and decimals, you need to keep in mind place value.

For example, let's take a look at the number 4.723.

4	.	7	2	3
Ones	Decimal Point	Tenths	Hundredths	Thousandths

The 4 is in the ones place, so its value is just 4. The 7, however, is in the tenths place. This means that the value of the 7 is really $\frac{7}{10}$. The 2 is in the hundredths place so its value is really $\frac{2}{100}$.

Here are a few questions that test this concept:

1. Which is equivalent to $\dfrac{6}{100}$?

    (A) 0.006
    (B) 0.06
    (C) 0.6
    (D) 6.0

In the number $\dfrac{6}{100}$ we have 6 hundredths. Let's think back to our place value chart and plug 6 into the hundredths place:

0	.	0	6	0
Ones	Decimal Point	Tenths	Hundredths	Thousandths

Answer choice B is correct.

2. $0.7 =$

    (A) $\dfrac{1}{70}$
    (B) $\dfrac{1}{7}$
    (C) $\dfrac{7}{100}$
    (D) $\dfrac{7}{10}$

Let's plug this number into our chart:

Ones	Decimal Point	Tenths	Hundredths	Thousandths
0	.	7	0	0

We can see that the 7 is in the tenths place, so its value is $\dfrac{7}{10}$. Answer choice D is correct.

3.

Column A	Column B
0.65	$\dfrac{3}{5}$

- (A) Quantity in Column A is greater.
- (B) Quantity in Column B is greater.
- (C) Quantities in Columns A and B are equal.
- (D) Not enough information to determine relationship.

In order to compare these two quantities, we need them to both be fractions or both be decimals. To make Column A into a fraction is one way to solve.

$$0.65 = \frac{65}{100}$$

The problem now is that we can't compare $\dfrac{65}{100}$ to $\dfrac{3}{5}$ because they have different denominators. We can see that 5 goes evenly into 100, so it is easier to convert $\dfrac{3}{5}$ into a fraction with 100 as a denominator.

$$\frac{3 \times 20}{5 \times 20} = \frac{60}{100}$$

Now we can clearly see that 0.65 is greater than $\dfrac{3}{5}$. Answer choice A is correct.

Adding and subtracting decimals

On the Middle Level ISEE, you may see a question that asks you to add or subtract numbers that have decimals in them. The trick to these questions is just to line up the decimal points and add or subtract like you normally would.

- Just remember to line up decimal points

Here are some problems for you to try:

1. What is the value of the expression $0.23 + 0.6 + 2.5 + 3.12$?

   (A) 5.72
   (B) 5.98
   (C) 6.19
   (D) 6.45

To answer this question, let's line up the decimals and perform addition.

$$
\begin{array}{r}
1 \\
0.23 \\
0.6 \\
2.5 \\
+\ 3.12 \\
\hline
6.45
\end{array}
$$

(Note: the 1 in italics in the first column is carried from the column to the right)

We can see that answer choice D is correct.

2. $1.35 + 0.45 + 2.3 + 0.8 =$

   (A) $3\dfrac{7}{10}$

   (B) $4\dfrac{9}{100}$

   (C) $4\dfrac{9}{10}$

   (D) $5\dfrac{1}{10}$

When we add decimals, we first have to line up the decimal points and add the numbers.

$$
\begin{array}{r}
\textit{1} \quad \textit{1} \quad \\
1 \ . \ 3 \ 5 \\
0 \ . \ 4 \ 5 \\
2 \ . \ 3 \quad \\
+ \ 0 \ . \ 8 \quad \\
\hline
4 \ . \ 9 \ 0
\end{array}
$$

(Note: numbers in italics are carried over)

If we look at our answer choices, we can see that there are no decimals. In order to find the correct answer choice, we have to take the decimal part of 4.9 and convert it into a fraction. The 9 is in the tenths place, so we know its value is $\frac{9}{10}$. If we combine that with the units digit (4), we get $4\frac{9}{10}$. Answer choice C is the correct answer.

3. John had 3.6 mL of water in a graduated cylinder. He poured out 2.2 mL of water. How much water did he have left in his graduated cylinder?

(A) $1\frac{2}{5}$ mL

(B) $1\frac{4}{5}$ mL

(C) $2\frac{1}{5}$ mL

(D) $3\frac{3}{5}$ mL

Since this is a word problem, we first need to figure out which operation would be appropriate. Since John starts with 3.6 mL and then decreases the amount of water by 2.2 mL, we are going to use subtraction. Let's line up the decimal points and subtract.

$$
\begin{array}{r}
3 \ . \ 6 \\
- \ 2 \ . \ 2 \\
\hline
1 \ . \ 4
\end{array}
$$

We found that he would have 1.4 mL left. The answer choices are given in mixed numbers and not decimals, however. We need to convert 1.4 into a mixed number. We can take the decimal part (.4) and use place value to turn it into a fraction. The 4 is in the tenths place, so its value is $\frac{4}{10}$. If we add back in the 1 in the ones place, we get $1\frac{4}{10}$. We still need to reduce that to get one of the answer choices, however.

$$1\frac{4 \div 2}{10 \div 2} = 1\frac{2}{5}$$

Answer choice A is correct.

Converting between fractions and percents

A percent is just a special kind of fraction that has 100 as the denominator. To convert between a fraction and a percent, we simply use the rules of equivalent fractions. For example, let's say that we need to know what percent $\frac{1}{4}$ is equal to.

Our first step is to set up two equal fractions (or a proportion).

$$\frac{1}{4} = \frac{p}{100}$$

Now we can use cross-multiplying to solve for p.

$$1 \times 100 = 4 \times p$$
$$100 = 4p$$
$$\div 4 \quad \div 4$$
$$25 = p$$

Since $\frac{1}{4} = \frac{25}{100}$, $\frac{1}{4}$ is equal to 25%.

Here is a basic question that tests this concept:

1. Which is equivalent to 35%?

    (A) $\dfrac{1}{35}$

    (B) $\dfrac{7}{20}$

    (C) $\dfrac{7}{10}$

    (D) $\dfrac{100}{35}$

This question is basically asking us to reduce a fraction. Another way to write 35% is $\dfrac{35}{100}$. Now we have to find the answer choice that is equal to $\dfrac{35}{100}$.

$$\frac{35 \div 5}{100 \div 5} = \frac{7}{20}$$

Answer choice B is correct.

Most likely you will see more challenging questions that test this concept. Here are a couple of examples for you to try:

2. In Arnold's class, 40% of the students play soccer. Of the students who play soccer, $\dfrac{2}{5}$ of them also play tennis. What fraction of Arnold's class plays both soccer and tennis?

   (A) $\dfrac{4}{100}$

   (B) $\dfrac{8}{100}$

   (C) $\dfrac{4}{25}$

   (D) $\dfrac{1}{4}$

This question is essentially asking us to find $\dfrac{2}{5}$ of 40%. The word "of" tells us to multiply. In order to multiply $\dfrac{2}{5}$ by 40%, we must turn 40% into a fraction, however.

$$\frac{2}{5} \times 40\% = \frac{2}{5} \times \frac{40}{100} = \frac{80}{500}$$

Now we just have to reduce $\dfrac{80}{500}$ in order to see which answer choice is correct.

$$\frac{80 \div 20}{500 \div 20} = \frac{4}{25}$$

Answer choice C is correct.

3. Sarah noticed that in her family, $\frac{2}{3}$ of her family members have brown hair. Of her family members that have brown hair, 60% of them also have brown eyes. What percent of her family members have both brown hair and brown eyes?

(A) 40%
(B) 45%
(C) 50%
(D) 60%

In this question, we are being asked to find $\frac{2}{3}$ of 60%. The word "of" means to multiply and we need to convert 60% into a fraction.

$$\frac{2}{3} \times \frac{60}{100} = \frac{120}{300}$$

Now we need to convert $\frac{120}{300}$ into a fraction that has 100 as a denominator since we are looking for a percent.

$$\frac{120 \div 3}{300 \div 3} = \frac{40}{100}$$

Answer choice A is correct.

Converting between percents and actual numbers

On the ISEE, you may see questions that ask you what a certain percent of a number is or what percent of another number a certain number is.

These questions all come back to our basic definition of what a fraction and percent are:

$$\frac{\text{part}}{\text{whole}} = \frac{\text{percent}}{100}$$

To answer these questions, you need to plug in what you are given and then cross-multiply to solve for the missing quantity. For example, let's say that we need to find 15% of 60. Here is how we would set up the equation:

$$\frac{\text{part}}{\text{whole}} = \frac{\text{percent}}{100}$$

$$\frac{n}{60} = \frac{15}{100}$$

We are looking for what part of 60 is 15%, so we put in a variable for "part" in our equation. Now we can cross-multiply to solve.

$$100 \times n = 15 \times 60$$
$$100n = 900$$
$$n = 9$$

9 is 15% of 60.

There are other methods to solve these types of questions. You are not likely to see a lot of these questions, though, so we are not going to go through multiple methods of solving.

Here are a couple of basic percent questions for you to try:

1.   What is 30% of 40?

    (A) 3
    (B) 6
    (C) 8
    (D) 12

Let's start by setting up our equation. We are given the percent and the whole number and they are asking us for a part of that number.

$$\frac{n}{40} = \frac{30}{100}$$

Now we cross-multiply.

$$100 \times n = 30 \times 40$$
$$100n = 1200$$
$$n = 12$$

Answer choice D is correct.

2. 40 is 50 percent of

(A) 20
(B) 40
(C) 80
(D) 200

Let's set up our equation. We are given the part and the percent and are asked for the whole number.

$$\frac{40}{n} = \frac{50}{100}$$

Now we cross-multiply.

$$n \times 50 = 40 \times 100$$
$$50n = 4{,}000$$
$$n = 80$$

Answer choice C is correct.

Percents are also a popular concept to test in the quantitative comparison section. Here are a couple of quantitative comparison questions for you to try:

3.

Column A	Column B
40% of 80	50% of 64

(A) Quantity in Column A is greater.
(B) Quantity in Column B is greater.
(C) Quantities in Columns A and B are equal.
(D) Not enough information to determine relationship.

To answer this question, we have to calculate the quantities in Column A and Column B.

Column A:

$$40\% \text{ of } 80 = \frac{40}{100} \times 80 = \frac{3200}{100} = 32$$

Column B:

$$50\% \text{ of } 64 = \frac{50}{100} \times 64 = \frac{1}{2} \times 64 = 32$$

Notice that the calculations are done two different ways. In the calculation for Column A, it was easy to multiply out the numbers so we used that method. For Column B, the math was more complicated so we reduced the percent first since that was the easier calculation. Since you do not have a calculator on this test, you have to be smart about how to do calculations with the least amount of work.

We can see that the quantities in Column A and Column B are equal so answer choice C is correct.

4.

Column A	Column B
10% of 625	50% of 150

(A) Quantity in Column A is greater.
(B) Quantity in Column B is greater.
(C) Quantities in Columns A and B are equal.
(D) Not enough information to determine relationship.

For this question we are going to use a couple of shortcuts. For Column A, we are going to use the fact that 10% can be found by moving the decimal point one place to the left. Therefore, 10% of 625 is 62.5. For Column B, we are going to use the fact that 50% is equal to one-half. One-half of 150 is 75, so 50% of 150 is also 75. Column B has the larger quantity so answer choice B is correct.

You will also see percent problems on the ISEE that require multiple steps. These are generally word problems. Like other multi-step problems the trick is to follow the details carefully.

Here are a few examples for you to try:

5. Luke has a jar with red and green candies in it. The green candies make up 30% of the candies and the rest are red. If the jar has 12 green candies, how many red candies does the jar contain?

    (A) 6
    (B) 12
    (C) 28
    (D) 40

Let's start with the information that we have about the green candies to figure out how many total candies we have.

$$\frac{12}{total} = \frac{30}{100}$$

$$total \times 30 = 12 \times 100$$

$$total \times 30 = 1200$$

$$\div 30 \quad \div 30$$

$$total = 40$$

Now that we know that there are 40 total candies, we can just subtract the number of green candies to get the number of red candies. Since $40 - 12 = 28$, there must be 28 red candies. Choice C is correct.

6. To predict the outcome of an election, a polling company polled a random selection of citizens in two different towns. The results are shown below.

	Town 1	Town 2
Percent of Voters Surveyed	50%	25%
Number of votes for Candidate A	16	22
Number of votes for Candidate B	8	25

These results were then used to predict how many people will vote for each candidate when all the voters go to the polls.

Column A	**Column B**
The number of predicted votes for Candidate A in Town 1	The number of predicted votes for Candidate A in Town 2

(A) Quantity in Column A is greater.
(B) Quantity in Column B is greater.
(C) Quantities in Columns A and B are equal.
(D) Not enough information to determine relationship.

This question asks us to work from a part back to the whole. We can use our percent equation, we just have to remember to deal with each group separately. We are not trying to find the total number of voters; we are just trying to find the number of voters for Candidate A.

Column A:

$$\frac{16}{\text{votes for Candidate A}} = \frac{50}{100}$$

$$16 \times 100 = \text{votes} \times 50$$

$$1600 = \text{votes} \times 50$$

$$32 = \text{votes for Candidate A in Town 1}$$

Column B:

$$\frac{22}{\text{votes for Candidate A}} = \frac{25}{100}$$

$$22 \times 100 = \text{votes} \times 25$$

$$2200 = \text{votes} \times 25$$

$$88 = \text{votes for Candidate A in Town 2}$$

Answer choice B is correct.

7. Of the 200 people surveyed about a proposal, 86 said they would vote for the proposal, 78 said they would vote against the proposal, and the rest were undecided. What percent of the people surveyed were undecided?

(A) 18%
(B) 36%
(C) 53%
(D) 72%

Our first step is to figure out how many people were undecided. If we add together the two decided groups, 86 + 78 = 164, we can see that 164 were decided. Now we just subtract that from the total number of people surveyed, 200 − 164 = 36, and find that there were 36 people undecided. Now we just need to figure out what percent of 200 is 36.

$$\frac{36}{200} = \frac{x}{100}$$

$$200x = 3600$$

$$x = 18\%$$

Answer choice A is correct.

Percent increase and decrease

On the ISEE, you may see a question that asks you to find a percent increase or decrease.

The general equation for percent increase is:

$$\text{percent increase} = \frac{\text{final} - \text{initial}}{\text{initial}} \times 100$$

For example, let's say that we had 10 lollipops and then someone gave us 5 more lollipops. Our first step is to remember that the final number of lollipops is not 5, it is 15. We were given five more so we know have a total of 15 lollipops. Now we can plug into the equation.

$$\text{percent increase} = \frac{\text{final} - \text{initial}}{\text{initial}} \times 100 = \frac{15 - 10}{10} \times 100 = 50\%$$

We say that our number of lollipops has increased by 50%.

To find a percent decrease, the equation is:

$$\text{percent decrease} = \frac{\text{initial} - \text{final}}{\text{initial}} \times 100$$

Let's say that we had 10 pencils and we gave away 5 of them. If we want to figure out by what percent our number of pencils decreased, we can just plug into the equation:

$$\text{percent decrease} = \frac{\text{initial} - \text{final}}{\text{initial}} \times 100 = \frac{10 - 5}{10} \times 100 = 50\%$$

In this case, we would say that our number of pencils decreased by 50%.

If it makes it easier to remember, the general form for percent increase/decrease is:

$$\text{percent increase/decrease} = \frac{\text{change}}{\text{initial}} \times 100$$

Here are a couple of questions for you to try:

1. Erin had 10 pages of a report written as of yesterday. Today she wrote four more pages. By what percent did the number of pages she had written increase today?

    (A) 20%
    (B) 40%
    (C) 50%
    (D) 60%

In order to answer this question, we first have to figure out what the final number of pages written is. She wrote four more pages, so she now has a total of 14 pages written. Now we can plug into the equation:

$$\text{percent increase} = \frac{\text{final} - \text{initial}}{\text{initial}} \times 100 = \frac{14 - 10}{10} \times 100 = 40\%$$

Answer choice B is correct.

2. The library had 20 books. Five books were checked out. By what percent did the number of books in the library decrease?

(A) 10%
(B) 15%
(C) 20%
(D) 25%

Let's first figure out our final number of books. Since the library started with 20 but five books were checked out, we do 20 − 5 = 15 and get that there were 15 books left.

Now we can plug into our equation.

$$\text{percent decrease} = \frac{\text{initial} - \text{final}}{\text{initial}} \times 100 = \frac{20 - 15}{20} \times 100 = 25\%$$

Answer choice D is correct.

You may also see questions that give you the percent increase and ask for the final number. The trick to these types of questions is that you have to remember to add back in the original number. For example, let's say that we have 100 cats and the number of cats increases by 150%. Our first step is to find 150% of 100. In this case, it would be 150 cats. The problem tells us that number of cats *increased* by that amount. So we do NOT now have 150 cats. We have 150 cats plus the original 100 cats. We now have 250 cats.

• If you are given a percent increase or decrease, remember to add back in the number that you started with

Let's take a closer look at another example. Let's say we start with 62 mice and the population increases by 150 % and we want to find the new number of mice.

62 mice = 100% of mice
31 mice = 50% of mice
_____

93 mice = 150% of mice

We aren't done yet, we still need to add back in the number of mice that we started with. The question does not ask us for how much the number of mice was increased by, but rather it asks us for the new *total* number.

62 = *original number of mice*
93 = *number of mice added*

155 = *new total number of mice*

On the Middle Level ISEE, they generally give you easy percent increases or decreases to work with. Here is a cheat sheet for you:

If the question says...	And asks for...	You should....
Increased by 50%	By how many did it increase	Take half of original number
Increased by 50%	New total number	Take half of original number and add it to original number
Increased by 100%	By how many did it increase	Choose the original number as your answer
Increased by 100%	New total number	Double your original number
Increased by 150%	By how many did it increase	Take half of original number and add that to original number
Increased by 150%	New total number	Take half original number and add it to twice original number
Increased by 200%	By how many did it increase	Choose the answer that is twice the original number
Increased by 200%	New total number	Choose the answer that is three times the original number

Here are a few questions for you to try:

3. The number of students in a school has increased by 150%. If the school started with 36 students, how many students does it now have?

    (A) 50
    (B) 54
    (C) 84
    (D) 90

The question tells us that the number of students increased by 150%, so our first step is to figure out how many new students were added.

36 students = 100% of students
18 students = 50% of students

---

54 students = 150% of students

We now know that 54 students were added. Now we need to add 54 + 36 in order to include the students that were already at the school. There are now 90 students at the school so answer choice D is correct.

4. A population of 52 tadpoles has increased by 200%. What is the total number of tadpoles after this increase?

    (A) 52
    (B) 104
    (C) 130
    (D) 156

To find 200% of a number, we simply double the number. Therefore, 200% of 52 is 104. The population has increased by 104 tadpoles, but we need to add back in the starting number of tadpoles in order to get the new total. Since 104 + 52 = 156, answer choice D is correct.

5. Clark had 64 toy cars. His collection increased by 150%. How many new cars did he get?

    (A) 32
    (B) 64
    (C) 96
    (D) 160

Our first step is to find 150% of 64.

$$64 \; cars = 100\% \; of \; cars$$
$$32 \; cars = 50\% \; of \; cars$$
_____

$$96 \; cars = 150\% \; of \; cars$$

The question only asks for the number of new cars, and not the new total, so 96 is the correct answer. Answer choice C is correct.

6. The number of cars on the road today increased by one and a half times over the number of cars on the road yesterday. By what percent did the number of cars increase?

(A) 50%
(B) 100%
(C) 150%
(D) 250%

The question tells us that the increase itself was one and a half times. To increase by one time is a 100% increase. Therefore, to increase by one and a half times is a 150% increase. Answer choice C is correct

7. The number of soccer games that Kline played this year increased by one and half times over the number of games that he played last year. What percent of the number of games that he played last year did he play this year?

(A) 50%
(B) 100%
(C) 150%
(D) 250%

This problem is very similar to the problem before it, only this time the question is asking for the new total, not simply the increase. To increase by one and a half times means that the number of games increased by 150%. But now we have to add back in 100% of the original number of games he played. That means that his new total number of games is 250% of the games that he played last year. Answer choice D is the correct answer choice.

Multiple percent discounts

You may see questions on the ISEE that ask you to take multiple discounts off of an item. The trick to these questions is that you can NOT just add the percents together. The reason that we cannot do that is that the second discount is taken off of the new price and not off of the original price. You need to take the first discount, find the new price, and then take the second discount off of that new price.

- Do NOT add percents together if more than one discount is taken
- Take first discount, find new price, then take second discount off of this new price

For example, let's say a lamp costs $100. First, the price was lowered by 20%. The new price of the lamp is now $80. Then the price was lowered by another 10%. The trick here is that the 10% discount is 10% of $80, not 10% of $100. 10% of 80 is $8, so we take an additional $8 off of $80 and get that the final price is $72.

Here are a few examples for you to try:

1. A hat was originally priced at $20. It was on sale for 20% off of the original price. Laura then had a coupon for an additional 10% off of the sale price. How much did Laura pay for the hat?

   (A) $14
   (B) $14.40
   (C) $16
   (D) $18

Our first step to answering this question is to take the first discount. Let's find 20% of $20:

$$\frac{x}{20} = \frac{20}{100}$$
$$100x = 400$$
$$x = 4$$

We can see that 20% of $20 is $4, so we take $4 from $20 and get that the new price is $16. Now we have to take the additional 10% discount. We will use our trick of moving the decimal point one place to the left in order to find 10%. This tells us that 10% of $16 is $1.60. Now we just subtract $1.60 from $16 and get that the final price of the hat was $14.40. Answer choice B is correct.

2. Martin bought a table that was originally priced at $50. The table was marked down 10% for a storewide sale. An additional 20% was then taken off of the sale price. What did Martin pay for the table?

(A) $32
(B) $35
(C) $36
(D) $40

We need to first take the 10% discount. We can use our trick of moving the decimal point one place to the left to find 10% of a number. That tells us that 10% of 50 is $5. If we take that off of the original price, we find that the sale price is $45. Now we need to take 20% off of that number. We could set up an equation to find 20%, or we can adapt our 10% trick. If we move the decimal over one place, we find that 10% of $45 is $4.50. If we double that, we get that 20% of $45 is $9.00. If we subtract $9 from $45, we get that the final price that Martin paid was $36. Answer choice C is correct.

3.

Column A	**Column B**
The final price after two separate discounts are taken of 10% and 10%	The final price after one 20% discount is taken

(A) Quantity in Column A is greater.
(B) Quantity in Column B is greater.
(C) Quantities in Columns A and B are equal.
(D) Not enough information to determine relationship.

This question is easier to answer if we make up a starting price for an item and see how each scenario works. We are going to choose $100 as the starting price since that makes it easier to find percents. For Column A, if we take one 10% discount, then the new price is $90. We then take another 10%, or $9, off of that to get a final price of $81. Now we need do the math to figure out what the final price would be after one 20% discount. Since $100 was our starting price, it is very easy to find that a 20% discount would just be $20. If we take $20 from $100, we get a final price of $80. We can see that the scenario in Column A gave us a higher final value than the scenario in Column B, so answer choice A is correct.

4.

Column A	Column B
The amount saved when two separate discounts of 10% and then 20% are taken	The amount saved when two separate discounts of 20% and then 10% are taken

(A) Quantity in Column A is greater.
(B) Quantity in Column B is greater.
(C) Quantities in Columns A and B are equal.
(D) Not enough information to determine relationship.

Let's use the same trick of using an imaginary $100 item. Under the scenario in Column A, we would first take off 10%, which would give us a new price of $90. Now we would take 20% off of the new price. Since 20% of 90 is $18, the final price for Column A would be $72. Now let's look at Column B. We will first take 20% off of $100, which give us a new price of $80. Now we will take 10%, or $8, off of this new price. This gives us a final price of $72. Since the final values for both Column A and Column B are the same, answer choice C is correct.

Those are the basics that you need to know about fractions, decimals, and percents on the ISEE. Be sure to complete the practice set to reinforce what you have learned.

Fractions, decimals, and percents practice set

1.

Column A	**Column B**
$2.4 + 0.31 + 5.46 + 0.4$	$5.46 + 2.3 + 0.8 + 0.31$

(A) Quantity in Column A is greater.
(B) Quantity in Column B is greater.
(C) Quantities in Columns A and B are equal.
(D) Not enough information to determine relationship.

2. A bike store had bikes on sale for 20% off of the regular price. The store then had a special where they took an additional 10% off of the sale price. If a bike was originally priced at $150, what is the final price of that bike?

(A) $90
(B) $100
(C) $105
(D) $108

3. If $\dfrac{2}{3}$ of a glass can be filled in one minute, how many minutes would it take to fill the rest of the glass at the same rate?

(A) 0.30
(B) 0.33
(C) 0.50
(D) 0.66

4. What fraction of the rectangle is shaded?

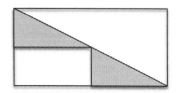

(A) $\frac{1}{4}$

(B) $\frac{1}{3}$

(C) $\frac{2}{5}$

(D) $\frac{1}{2}$

5. A poll was taken to predict whether or not a proposal would be approved by voters in two different groups. Samples of each group were asked how they would vote. The table below shows what percent of each group was surveyed and the number of YES and NO votes from each group.

	Group 1	Group 2
Percent of Group polled	50%	20%
NO votes	8	12
YES votes	19	9

The results in the table were used to predict how many voters would vote for the proposal and how many voters would vote against the proposal.

Column A

The number of YES votes predicted from Group 1

Column B

The number of YES votes predicted from Group 2

(A) Quantity in Column A is greater.
(B) Quantity in Column B is greater.
(C) Quantities in Columns A and B are equal.
(D) Not enough information to determine relationship.

6.

Column A	Column B
50% of 130	10% of 625

(A) Quantity in Column A is greater.
(B) Quantity in Column B is greater.
(C) Quantities in Columns A and B are equal.
(D) Not enough information to determine relationship.

7. Of the 60% of the students in a class that have a brother, $\frac{2}{3}$ of them also have a sister. What fraction of the class has both a brother and a sister?

(A) $\frac{1}{5}$

(B) $\frac{1}{3}$

(C) $\frac{2}{5}$

(D) $\frac{2}{3}$

8. When Ms. Holder's class counted their fruit flies on Monday they had 72 fruit flies. When they counted them again on Tuesday, they found that the population had increased by 150%. How many total fruit flies did Ms. Holder's class count on Tuesday?

(A) 36
(B) 108
(C) 144
(D) 180

9. The expression $3.8 + 0.01 + 23$ is equal to

(A) 26.81
(B) 26.9
(C) 27.01
(D) 27.81

10. $0.75 =$

    (A) $\dfrac{1}{75}$

    (B) $\dfrac{75}{1,000}$

    (C) $\dfrac{75}{100}$

    (D) $\dfrac{75}{10}$

11. The expression $1 + \dfrac{1}{4}$ is equivalent to

    (A) $\dfrac{3}{4}$

    (B) $\dfrac{5}{4}$

    (C) $\dfrac{6}{4}$

    (D) $\dfrac{7}{4}$

12.

Column A	Column B
40% of 80	80% of 40

    (A) Quantity in Column A is greater.
    (B) Quantity in Column B is greater.
    (C) Quantities in Columns A and B are equal.
    (D) Not enough information to determine relationship.

13. Which is equivalent to the expression $3\frac{2}{3} \div 2\frac{1}{2}$?

    (A) $\frac{8}{15}$

    (B) $\frac{5}{16}$

    (C) $1\frac{1}{6}$

    (D) $1\frac{7}{15}$

14. There are 5 equally sized cups of flour. Larry used $\frac{1}{3}$ of each cup and Sam used $\frac{1}{2}$ of each cup. About how many cups of flour remain?

    (A)   0.83 cups
    (B)   1.33 cups
    (C)   1.50 cups
    (D)   1.67 cups

15. Manny has a bag of lemons and limes. If 60% of the fruit are lemons and there are 9 lemons, how many limes does the bag contain?

    (A)   5
    (B)   6
    (C)   9
    (D)   15

Answers to Fractions, Decimals, and Percents Practice Set

1. B
2. D
3. C
4. A
5. B
6. A
7. C
8. D
9. A
10. C
11. B
12. C
13. D
14. A
15. B

Algebraic Concepts (solving for variables)

On the Middle Level ISEE, there are questions that test the principles of algebra. These questions require you to set up equations, solve, use the equations to find another value, etc.

The types of algebra questions you will see include:

- Setting up an equation to fit a story
- Solving for a variable
- Plugging in for a variable
- Rearranging an equation using properties
- Setting up an equation and then solving
- Using proportion and scale
- Patterns
- Input/output tables

Setting up an equation to fit a story

On the Middle Level ISEE, you may be asked to translate a story into an equation. These problems are really just testing your ability to identify which operation fits various situations.

- These questions are mainly testing which operation we use in different situations

These are a lot like the problems that we had in the whole numbers section only they now have variables in them. Variables are simply letters that stand in for some unknown quantity. They may also put in a shape instead of a letter for a variable.

- Variables are simply letters or shapes that stand in for some unknown number

Since we covered the basics of operations in the whole numbers section, we will focus here on a couple of different types of problems that you may see on the Middle Level ISEE.

The first type of problem will we go over is problems that ask you to figure out a total when two types of items are purchased. The basic equation that we need to use to answer this type of problem is:

$$\text{total cost} = (\text{\# of item \#1} \times \text{price of item \#1}) + (\text{\# of item \#2} \times \text{price of item \#2})$$

Here is a basic example of a question that tests this equation:

1. At a restaurant, Lori bought a hamburger and two orders of French fries that cost $3 each. Her total before tax was $7. Which equation would find the cost of the hamburger (h)?

   (A) $2 + h = 7$
   (B) $2 + 3h = 7$
   (C) $2(3) + 2h = 7$
   (D) $2(3) + h = 7$

To answer this question, first think about how you would figure out the total if you did know the price of the hamburger. You would first take the cost of the French fries ($3) and multiply it by the number of orders of fries (2). Then you would add in the cost of the hamburger to get the total cost. Answer choice D correctly represents this, so it is the correct answer.

On the Middle Level ISEE, this problem is often more involved. Here are a couple of examples of more challenging questions:

2. Jane bought five pens and five pencils at the store. Each pencil costs ten cents less than each pen. Her total before tax was $2.40. Which equation would find the cost of each pen (P)?

   (A) $5P + 5P - 0.10 = 2.40$
   (B) $5(P - 0.10) = 2.40$
   (C) $5P + 5(P - 0.10) = 2.40$
   (D) $10(P - 0.10) = 2.40$

This problem is a little more involved. If we keep in mind plugging into our equation, however, it isn't so bad. Here is what we know:

$5 = \text{number of item \#1}$
$5 = \text{number of item \#2}$
$P = \text{cost of item \#1 (pens)}$
$P - 0.10 = \text{cost of item \#2 (pencils)}$
$\text{total cost} = 2.40$

Now we can just put the pieces together:

$$\text{total cost} = (\text{\# of item \#1} \times \text{price of item \#1}) + (\text{\# of item \#2} \times \text{price of item \#2})$$
$$2.40 = 5 \times P + 5\,(P - 0.10)$$

If we rearrange this equation we get answer choice C, which is the correct answer.

3. Maria bought lollipops and candy bars at the general store. Both the lollipops and the candy bars cost 50 cents each. She bought 5 more lollipops than candy bars. If her total before tax was \$9.50, which equation would find the number of lollipops (L) that she bought?

(A) $0.50L + 0.50(L - 5) = 9.50$
(B) $0.50 + 0.50L = 9.50$
(C) $0.50 + 0.50(L - 5) = 9.50$
(D) $1.00(L - 5) = 9.50$

Let's use the same method of listing out the information that the question gives us:

L = number of item #1 (lollipops)
0.50 = cost of item #1
$L - 5$ = number of item #2 (candy bars)
0.50 = cost of item #2
9.50 = total cost

Now we will just plug into our equation:

$$\text{total cost} = (\text{\# of item \#1} \times \text{price of item \#1}) + (\text{\# of item \#2} \times \text{price of item \#2})$$
$$9.50 = 0.50 \times L + 0.50(L - 5)$$

If we rearrange this equation we get answer choice A, which is the correct answer.

The next type of problem we will work on is rate questions. The important equation to know for rate problems is:

$$\text{rate} \times \text{time} = \text{distance}$$

Here is an example of a basic rate question:

4. Trevor is travelling to New Orleans, which is 240 miles away. If he travels at an average speed of 50 miles per hour, which equation will help him figure out how many hours it will take him to get to New Orleans?

    (A) $240 \times h = 50$
    (B) $50 \times 240 = h$
    (C) $\dfrac{50}{240} = h$
    (D) $\dfrac{240}{50} = h$

To answer this question, we just have to plug into the rate equation and then rearrange.

$$\text{rate} \times \text{time} = \text{distance}$$
$$50 \times h = 240$$
$$\div 50 \quad \div 50$$
$$h = \frac{240}{50}$$

Answer choice D is correct.

You will also see rate questions that are much more involved. Here are a couple of examples of rate questions that are more challenging:

5. Carly and Marge started walking along a straight path at the same time and place. After 20 minutes, Marge is 500 feet ahead of Carly. If Marge's speed was twice as fast as Carly's, then which equation could be used to find Carly's speed *(C)* in feet per minute?

    (A) $40C - 500 = 20C$
    (B) $40C + 500 = 20C$
    (C) $40C = 20C - 500$
    (D) $40C + 20C = 500$

Our first step for this question is to write equations that represent the distance that each person has walked. We will go back to our equation for rate:

distance = rate × time
Carly's distance = $C \times 20$
Marge's distance = $2C \times 20$

Now we can use the fact that they were 500 feet apart to relate Marge's distance to Carly's distance.

Marge's distance − 500 = Carly's distance

Now we can substitute the equations that we set up for each girl's distance.

$(2C \times 20) - 500 = C \times 20$

If we simplify this, we are left with $40C - 500 = 20C$, or answer choice A.

6. Lawrence and Clara are driving along a straight path. After 30 minutes, Lawrence is 10 miles behind Clara. If Clara's speed is three times as fast as Lawrence's speed, then which equation could be used to find Clara's speed (C) in miles per hour?

(A) $30C - C = 10$

(B) $\dfrac{1}{2}C + \dfrac{1}{3}C = 10$

(C) $\dfrac{1}{2}\left(C + \dfrac{1}{3}\right) = 10$

(D) $\dfrac{1}{2}C = \dfrac{1}{6}C + 10$

We will begin by coming back to the distance = rate × time equation. First we will set up an equation for Clara's distance. The trick to this is remembering that the speed is given in miles per hour. That means we have to convert 30 minutes into $\dfrac{1}{2}$ hour in order to create an equation.

Clara's distance $= \dfrac{1}{2}C$

Now we need to set up an equation for Lawrence's rate and then distance (remember that our time has to be $\dfrac{1}{2}$ hour and NOT 30 minutes).

Lawrence's rate = one third of Clara's rate $= \dfrac{1}{3}C$

Lawrence's distance $= \dfrac{1}{2}\left(\dfrac{1}{3}C\right)$

Now we put all the pieces together, remember that we need to add 10 to Lawrence's distance in order to get Clara's distance:

$$\frac{1}{2}C = \frac{1}{6}C + 10$$

Answer choice D is correct.

The next type of question that we will work on is fixed cost + variable rate problems. These questions give you a fixed cost for a certain first number of items and then a cost per item for additional items. The general form of the equation for these types of questions is:

Total cost = fixed cost + variable cost (total # of items – # of items included in fixed cost)

For example, let's say that it costs $2 for the first 20 minutes of a phone call and $0.05 for each minute after the first 20 minutes. Let's set up an equation that would tell us the total cost for a call that was w minutes long.

First, we will list what the problem gives us:

Total cost = ?
Fixed cost = $2
Variable cost = $0.05
Total # of minutes = w
# of minutes included in fixed cost = 20

Now we will put it all together:

Total cost = 2 + 0.05(w – 20)

The reason that we subtract 20 from w is that we already paid for the first 20 minutes in the $2 part of the equation.

Here are a couple of sample problems for you to try:

7. A store is having a sale on shirts. The first shirt costs $20 and each additional shirt costs $15. Which equation would give the total cost (T) for purchasing v shirts, where v must be greater than 0?

    (A) $T = 20 + 15v$
    (B) $T = 20 + 15(v – 1)$
    (C) $T = 20v + 15$
    (D) $T = 15 + 20(v – 1)$

Let's start out by identifying the parts that the question gives us:

Total cost = T
Fixed cost = $20
Variable cost = $15
Total # of shirts = v
# of shirts included in fixed cost = 1

Now we can just plug into our equation and we get:

$$T = 20 + 15(v - 1)$$

Answer choice B is correct.

8. A taxicab charges $4 for the first 3 miles and $1.50 per mile for each additional mile or fraction of mile after the first 3 miles. Which equation would give the total cost (T) of a taxi ride that was m miles long?

(A) $T = 4m + 1.50m$
(B) $T = 4m + 1.50$
(C) $T = 4 + 1.50(m - 3)$
(D) $T = 4 + 3(m - 1.50)$

We will use the same method of first listing out the information given in the question.

Total cost = T
Fixed cost = $4
Variable cost = $1.50
Total # miles = m
# of miles included in fixed cost = 3

Now we can plug into our equation:

$$T = 4 + 1.50(m - 3)$$

Answer choice C is correct.

Solving for a variable

The basic goal of solving for a variable is to get a variable by itself – or to isolate it.

There are two basic rules for isolating a variable:

1. Use PEMDAS (order of operations), but in reverse
2. Do the opposite operation in each step

What does this mean to reverse the order of PEMDAS?

Here is a basic example:

$x + 2 = 4$ Using our reverse order of operations, first we look for addition or subtraction.

(In each step, notice that we do the *opposite* operation in order to simplify the equation.)

$$x + 2 = 4$$ The left side has addition, so we must subtract.
$$\underline{-2 \quad -2}$$
$$x = 2$$ The problem is solved, the value of x is 2.

Here is another example:

$$3 \times w = 9$$ The left side is multiplied by 3 so we must divide by 3.
$$\underline{\div 3 \quad \div 3}$$
$$w = 3$$ The problem is solved, the value of w is 3.

On the ISEE, you may also see equations that are more than one step to solve. Just remember to follow the order of operations in reverse. Here is an example:

$$3 \times (b + 5) = 15$$ Because we are doing PEMDAS in reverse order, we are going to save the parentheses for LAST. We are going to do the opposite of
$$\underline{\div 3 \quad \div 3}$$ multiplying by 3, which is dividing by 3.

$$(b + 5) = 5$$ Now we have to do the opposite of adding 5, which is to subtract 5
$$\underline{-5 \quad -5}$$ from both sides.

$$b = 0$$ We can see that b is equal to 0.

Here is an example of how this type of question could look on the ISEE:

1. If $16 = 4v + 4$, then v is equal to

    (A) 1
    (B) 2
    (C) 3
    (D) 4

In this question, we want to get v by itself. First we look for anything that is added or subtracted on the side of the equation that has v. There is a 4 added to the right side of the equation, so we have to subtract 4 from both sides. We are left with $12 = 4v$. Now we look for anything that is multiplied or divided. Currently, the v is multiplied by 4, so we have to divide both sides by 4. We are left with $v = 3$. Answer choice C is correct.

2. If $(8 \times \boxdot) + 2 = 5$, then what number could replace the $\boxdot$?

    (A) $\dfrac{3}{8}$

    (B) $\dfrac{6}{8}$

    (C) 2
    (D) 8

To solve, first we have to see if there is anything added or subtracted. There is a 2 added to the side with the variable, so we subtract that from both sides and get $8 \times \boxdot = 3$. Now we have an 8 that is multiplied by the variable, so we divide both sides by 8 and get $\boxdot = \dfrac{3}{8}$, so answer choice A is correct.

3.

$$\frac{x}{3} + 4 = 25$$

$$8y + 12 = 108$$

Column A   **Column B**

x y

(A) Quantity in Column A is greater.
(B) Quantity in Column B is greater.
(C) Quantities in Columns A and B are equal.
(D) Not enough information to determine relationship.

In order to answer this question, we simply need to solve for both x and y. Let's start with solving for x:

$$\frac{x}{3} + 4 = 25$$
$$ -4 \quad -4$$
$$\frac{x}{3} = 21$$
$$\times 3 \quad \times 3$$
$$x = 63$$

Now we will solve for y:

$$8y + 12 = 108$$
$$-12 \quad -12$$
$$8y = 96$$
$$\div 8 \quad \div 8$$
$$y = 12$$

Since the value of x is greater than the value of y, answer choice A is correct.

Some questions also require you to solve for more than one variable. Just remember to circle what the question is asking for since this is a multi-step problem.

Here is one for you to try:

4. Use the equations below to answer the question.

$$8 + m = 10$$
$$6 + n = 10$$

What is the value of $m + n$?

(A) 2
(B) 4
(C) 5
(D) 6

To answer this question we first have to solve for m and n. If $8 + m = 10$, then we know that m must be equal to 2 in order for the equation to be true. If $6 + n = 10$, then we can see that n must be equal to 4. Now we need to remember to add the values of m and n together in order to get our final answer. Since $2 + 4 = 6$, the correct answer is choice D.

Plugging in for a variable

You will probably see at least one question on the ISEE that asks you to plug in for one variable and then solve for a different variable. These problems are very straightforward – you just need to substitute in the value. We will just do a few sample problems since these problems are not too complicated.

1. If $A = \frac{b_1 + b_2}{2} \times h$, then what is A when b_1 is 10 inches, b_2 is 14 inches, and h is 4 inches?

(A) 24 inches
(B) 28 inches
(C) 36 inches
(D) 48 inches

We are given values for b_1, b_2, and h, so we just need to substitute those values into the equation:

$$A = \frac{b_1 + b_2}{2} \times h = \frac{10 + 14}{2} \times 4 = \frac{24}{2} \times 4 = 48 \text{ inches}$$

Answer choice D is correct.

2.

$$r = 3q + 1$$

Column A	**Column B**
The value of q when $r = 16$	The value of r when $q = 5$

(A) Quantity in Column A is greater.
(B) Quantity in Column B is greater.
(C) Quantities in Columns A and B are equal.
(D) Not enough information to determine relationship.

We will use the same method of plugging in the values given. The trick to this problem is keeping straight which variable each column is asking for.

Column A:

$$r = 3q + 1 \ \ (r = 16)$$
$$16 = 3q + 1$$
$$15 = 3q$$
$$5 = q$$

Column B:

$$r = 3q + 1 \ \ (q = 5)$$
$$r = 3(5) + 1$$
$$r = 16$$

Answer choice B is correct. Don't get thrown by the fact that you get the same values for r and q in each column. The columns ask for the values of different variables so they are not equal.

3. If $6\blacksquare = 2\triangle$ and one $\triangle$ is 18, what is the value of $\blacksquare$?

(A) 2
(B) 3
(C) 6
(D) 36

Even though this question uses symbols instead of letters for variable, it is still just a simple plugging in for a variable question. We just plug in 18 for $\triangle$ and then solve for $\blacksquare$.

$$6\blacksquare = 2\triangle$$
$$6\blacksquare = 2(18)$$
$$6\blacksquare = 36$$
$$\blacksquare = 6$$

Answer choice C is correct.

Rearranging an equation and using properties

On the Middle Level ISEE, there are three basic properties that might be tested.

The first (and most likely to be tested) is the distributive. Here is the general form for the distributive property:

$$A(B + C) = AB + AC$$
$$\text{or}$$
$$A(B - C) = AB - AC$$

You can remember this one because the number or variable in front is distributed (or handed out to) the numbers in parentheses. Notice that to use the distributive property we need to have either addition or subtraction within the parentheses.

The next property that you might be tested on is the associative property. The general form of the associative property is:

$$(A + B) + C = A + (B + C)$$
$$\text{or}$$
$$(A \times B) \times C = A \times (B \times C)$$

You can remember the associative property because the associations (or groups) change. Notice that this property works with addition and multiplication – it does not work with subtraction or division.

Finally, we have the commutative property. The general form of the commutative property is:

$$A + B + C = B + A + C$$
$$\text{or}$$
$$A \times B \times C = A \times C \times B$$

To remember this property, think about what commuting is. Commuting is getting from one place to another, and the commutative property moves numbers from one place to another. Notice that it only works with addition or multiplication – it does not work with subtraction or division.

Here are some examples of how these properties could be tested on the ISEE:

1. Which picture demonstrates the commutative property?

    (A) $\Delta + \nabla = \nabla + \Delta$
    (B) $\blacksquare (\nabla + \Delta) = \blacksquare \nabla + \blacksquare \Delta$
    (C) $\blacksquare (\nabla + \Delta) = \nabla (\Delta + \blacksquare)$
    (D) $(\blacksquare + \nabla) + \Delta = \blacksquare + (\nabla + \Delta)$

We are looking for the answer choice that gives us symbols that move around since we are looking for an example of the commutative property. Answer choice A is correct.

2. Which expression uses the distributive property correctly in order to solve $21 \times (2 + 7)$?

    (A) $(21 \times 2) + 7$
    (B) $2 \times (21 + 7)$
    (C) $7 \times (21 + 2)$
    (D) $(21 \times 2) + (21 \times 7)$

We are looking for the answer choice that distributes the 21 to both the 2 and the 7. Answer choice A just moves the parentheses, and would give us an answer that wasn't even the same as the expression in the question. In answer choices B and C, the 21 is switched with another number. This is not even mathematically correct – we can only move numbers around if all the operations are addition or all the operations are multiplication. In answer choice D, the 21 is distributed to both the 2 and the 7, so it is the correct answer choice.

3. Which expression shows the associative property being used correctly?

    (A) $(X + Y) + Z = Z + (X + Y)$
    (B) $(X + Y) + Z = X + (Y + Z)$
    (C) $X + Y + Z = Z + Y + X$
    (D) $X(Y + Z) = XY + XZ$

With the associative property, groupings are changed. In answer choice A, the variables are moved around, but the groupings are not changed, so we can rule out choice A. In answer choice C, there are no groupings, so we can eliminate choice C as well. Choice D gets rid of the groupings (and shows the distributive property) but doesn't change the groupings, so it can be ruled out. Answer choice B shows the groupings change, and all the operations are addition, so it is the correct answer.

On the Middle Level ISEE, you are more likely to see questions that ask you to apply properties.

The first type of question that asks you to apply properties includes questions that give you the value of one expression and then ask for the value of a second expression. The trick to this type of question is that the second expression is generally just the first expression multiplied by a number. We don't solve for the variable in these situations, we just figure out what the first expression was multiplied by in order to get the second expression.

- When they give you a value of one expression and ask for the value of another, see if you can just multiply by a number instead of solving for the variable

Here are a couple of examples:

1. If $3z - 2 = 14$, then what does $6z - 4$ equal?

   (A) 4
   (B) 6
   (C) 28
   (D) 38

To answer this question, we are going to factor the second expression. Factoring is just like using the distributive property in reverse.

$$6z - 4 = 2 \times (3z - 2)$$

Can you now see that we just multiplied the left side of the first equation by two to get the expression that the question asks for? This means we can just multiply the right side of the equation by 2 to get our answer. Since $14 \times 2 = 28$, answer choice C is correct.

2. If $6x + 30 = 21$, then what is $2x + 10$ equal to?

   (A) 3
   (B) 7
   (C) 21
   (D) 63

In order to answer this question, we need to think about what to multiply the equation by in order to get the expression. In this case, we do not multiply by a whole number, however.

$$\frac{1}{3}(6x + 30) = 2x + 10$$

Now we just have to also multiply 21 by $\frac{1}{3}$ in order to get our answer. Since $21 \times \frac{1}{3} = 7$, answer choice B is correct.

Some questions will require you to apply the rules that you learned with isolating a variable. Just remember to combine like terms before you start moving numbers and variables around.

- When you have to rearrange terms in an equation, combine like terms first

Here are a couple of questions for you to try:

3. If $m - 5 + 3 = n$, then what must $(m - n)$ be equal to?

    (A) −8
    (B) −2
    (C) 2
    (D) 8

Our first step is to combine like terms:

$$m - 5 + 3 = n$$
$$m - 2 = n$$

Now we need to move the n to the left side of the equation. In order to do that, we remember our rule to "do the opposite". Currently the right side has a positive n, so we will subtract (or add a negative n) to each side.

$$m - 2 = n$$
$$\underline{ - n \quad -n}$$
$$m - n - 2 = 0$$

Now we just have to move the −2 to the other side. We do this by adding 2 to each side.

$$m - n - 2 = 0$$
$$\underline{ + 2 \quad + 2}$$
$$m - n = 2$$

Answer choice C is correct.

4. Which expression is equivalent to the expression below?

$$\frac{8(\sqrt{36} + 12x)}{\sqrt{4}}$$

(A) $\dfrac{\sqrt{288} + 96x}{4}$

(B) $\dfrac{8\sqrt{48x}}{\sqrt{4}}$

(C) $4(3 + 6x)$

(D) $4(6 + 12x)$

Let's start by simplifying the radicals:

$$\frac{8(\sqrt{36} + 12x)}{\sqrt{4}} = \frac{8(6 + 12x)}{2}$$

We could distribute the 8 at this point, but it is easier to break apart the expression instead:

$$\frac{8(6 + 12x)}{2} = \frac{8}{2} \times (6 + 12x) = 4(6 + 12x)$$

This matches answer choice D so we can stop there. Note that we could keep going and distribute out the 4, but then we would not get one of the answer choices.

Another way to approach this question would have been to plug in a number for x since there are variables in the answer choices.

Setting up an equation and then solving

We have worked on setting up an equation from a story. We have worked on solving for a variable when we are given an equation. Now we will work on questions that require you to use both of these skills.

Since we have covered problem types and how to solve in other sections, we will jump right to some practice problems. Here are some examples for you to try of questions that require you to apply the concept of *fixed cost + variable rate*:

1. Taxi Today charges $2 for the first mile and then $0.50 for each mile after the first mile for a taxi ride. Cab Country charges a flat fee of $1.50 per mile for all taxi rides. For what distance would Taxi Today and Cab Country charge the same amount for a ride?

   (A) 1 mile
   (B) 1.5 miles
   (C) 2 miles
   (D) 3 miles

In order to answer this question, we need to first set up an equation for each taxi company. Taxi Today uses the *fixed cost + variable rate* model that we covered earlier in this section. Cab Country uses a straight cost per unit model.

$$\text{Cost of Taxi Today ride} = 2 + 0.50(x - 1)$$
$$\text{Cost of Cab Country ride} = 1.50x$$

Now we want to know how many miles make the cost of the ride the same with both taxi companies. To find this, we simply set the equations equal to one another and then solve for x.

$$2 + 0.50(x - 1) = 1.50x$$
$$2 + 0.50x - 0.50 = 1.50x$$
$$1.50 + 0.50x = 1.50x$$
$$1.50 = 1x$$

We can see that when $x = 1.50$, the cost would be the same for both companies. Answer choice B is correct.

2.

A phone call with Company A costs $2 for the first five minutes and then $0.05 for each minute after the first five minutes. A phone call with Company B costs $0.08 a minute.

Column A	**Column B**
The cost of a 20 minute phone call with Company A.	The cost of a 20 minute phone call with Company B.

   (A) Quantity in Column A is greater.
   (B) Quantity in Column B is greater.
   (C) Quantities in Columns A and B are equal.
   (D) Not enough information to determine relationship.

Let's solve for each column separately. Column A is a *fixed cost + variable rate* problem.

Cost with Company $A = 2 + 0.05(m - 5)$

Now we can just plug in 20 for m since we are told that the call is 20 minutes long.

Cost with Company $A = 2 + 0.05(20 - 5) = 2 + 0.05(15) = 2.75$

Column B is just a straight cost per minute problem.

Cost with Company $B = 0.08m$

Now we just plug in 20 for m.

Cost with Company $B = 0.08m = 0.08(20) = 1.60$

We can see that the call with Company A costs more than the call with Company B, so answer choice A is correct.

Now we will try a few rate problems. Earlier, we learned how to set up the equations, now we just need to solve:

3. Lori and Myra walked along a straight path, starting at the same time and place. Lori walked at a speed of 40 feet per minute and Myra walked at speed of 30 feet per minute. How many feet in front of Myra was Lori after 20 minutes?

    (A) 100 feet
    (B) 200 feet
    (C) 600 feet
    (D) 800 feet

In order to answer this question, we simply need to use the equation *distance = rate × time*.

Lori's distance $= 40 \times 20 = 800$ feet
Myra's distance $= 30 \times 20 = 600$ feet

Now we have to pay attention to what the question is asking for. The question wants to know how far apart they are, so we subtract 600 from 800 and get that they are 200 feet apart. Answer choice B is correct.

4.

> When Ms. Brown goes from her home to Middletown, she can either drive on Mountain Road or Valley Lane. If she travels on Mountain Road the trip is 30 miles long and she can travel at an average speed of 40 miles per hour. If she takes Valley Lane, the trip is 45 miles long and she can travel at an average speed of 60 miles per hour.

Column A	**Column B**
Average time the trip takes if Ms. Brown drives on Mountain Road	Average time the trip takes if Ms. Brown drives on Valley Lane

(A) Quantity in Column A is greater.
(B) Quantity in Column B is greater.
(C) Quantities in Columns A and B are equal.
(D) Not enough information to determine relationship.

In order to compare the two times, we first have to find how long each trip took. The easiest way to do this is to rearrange our equation. If we divide both sides by rate, we get:

$$\frac{distance}{rate} = time$$

Now we can just plug into this equation to get how long each trip would take:

$$Mountain\ Road = \frac{distance}{rate} = \frac{30\ miles}{40\ miles\ per\ hour} = \frac{3}{4}\ hour$$

$$Valley\ Lane = \frac{distance}{rate} = \frac{45\ miles}{60\ miles\ per\ hour} = \frac{3}{4}\ hour$$

We can see that when we reduce the fractions, we get that each trip took the same amount of time. Answer choice C is correct.

Another popular problem type on the ISEE is questions that ask you to find a total cost or revenue. These problems often use situations that involve tickets sales, but not always. These questions always come down to the basic equation:

total cost or revenue = cost per item × number of items

Just like other multi-step problems, we need to make sure that we follow the details of the problem. Here are a few for you to try:

5.

At a performance, box seats cost $60 each and floor seats cost $35 each.

Column A	**Column B**
The total cost of 7 box seats	The total cost of 12 floor seats

(A) Quantity in Column A is greater.
(B) Quantity in Column B is greater.
(C) Quantities in Columns A and B are equal.
(D) Not enough information to determine relationship.

To figure out the total cost, we are just going to apply our basic equation:

total cost = cost per ticket × number of tickets

Cost for Column A:
total cost = cost per ticket × number of tickets = 60 × 7 = $420

Cost for Column B:
total cost = cost per ticket × number of tickets = 35 × 12 = $420

We can see that the cost is the same for both Column A and Column B. Answer choice C is correct.

6. Tickets for a performance were sold for $5 in advance and $6 at the door. If a total of $1,365 worth of tickets were sold and the value of the tickets sold in advance was $675, how many tickets were sold on the day of the show?

(A) 30
(B) 65
(C) 90
(D) 115

This is a multi-step problem, so we need to break down each part of the problem. First we have to figure out the total cost of the tickets that were sold on the day of the show. We will subtract the value of the tickets sold in advance ($675) from the total ($1365) and get that $690 worth of tickets were sold on the day of the show.

Now we can use our basic equation:

$$\text{total for show day tickets} = \text{cost per ticket} \times \text{number of tickets}$$
$$690 = 6 \times \text{number of tickets}$$
$$115 = \text{number of tickets}$$

Answer choice D is correct.

7. Kalamazoo Playhouse wants to make a $10,000 profit off of their summer production. Profit is equal to revenue minus costs. If the play will cost approximately $2,000 and each ticket will cost $16, how many tickets will they have to sell?

(A) 125
(B) 625
(C) 750
(D) 1,200

For this question, we first have to use the equation that they give us in words.

$$\text{profit} = \text{revenue} - \text{cost}$$
$$10,000 = \text{revenue} - 2,000$$
$$12,000 = \text{revenue}$$

Now that we know the revenue that is needed, we can adapt our basic equation:

$$\text{revenue} = \text{cost of ticket} \times \text{number of tickets}$$

$$12,000 = 16 \times \text{number of tickets}$$
$$\frac{12,000}{16} = \text{number of tickets}$$
$$750 = \text{number of tickets}$$

Answer choice C is correct.

Using proportion and scale

A special kind of word problem on the ISEE requires you to use a proportion, which is basically two fractions that are equivalent. We can use cross-multiplying to answer these questions.

- Use cross-multiplying to solve proportions or equivalent fractions

For example, let's say we are given the following problem and asked to solve for *x:*

$$\frac{4}{15} = \frac{12}{x}$$

Cross-multiplying means that we can multiply the numerator of one fraction by the denominator of the other and set it equal to the denominator of the first fraction multiplied by the numerator of the second fraction.

$$4 \times x = 15 \times 12$$
$$4x = 180$$
$$\div 4 \quad \div 4$$
$$x = 45$$

We now know that $\dfrac{4}{15} = \dfrac{12}{45}$.

Here are a couple of basic proportion problems like those you see on the ISEE:

1. If $\dfrac{T}{32} = \dfrac{21}{28}$, then what is the value of *T?*

    (A) 24
    (B) 28
    (C) 32
    (D) 48

In order to answer this question we can use cross-multiplying. Looking at the numbers, however, cross-multiplying could be tough since we do not have a calculator. If we look at the right side of the equation, however, we can see that it can be reduced.

$$\frac{21 \div 7}{28 \div 7} = \frac{3}{4}$$

Now we will substitute in $\frac{3}{4}$ for $\frac{21}{28}$.

$$\frac{T}{32} = \frac{3}{4}$$

Cross-multiplying will now be a lot easier with smaller numbers.

$$T \times 4 = 32 \times 3$$
$$4T = 96$$
$$T = 24$$

Answer choice A is correct.

2. If $\frac{2}{5} = \frac{12}{\blacksquare}$ and $\frac{5}{6} = \frac{25}{\blacksquare}$, then what is the value of $\blacksquare$?

    (A) 12
    (B) 24
    (C) 25
    (D) 30

The trick to this question is that we really only need to solve one of the proportions. There is only one number that will make either proportion true, so we just need to find the value of $\blacksquare$ in one of them.

$$\frac{2}{5} = \frac{12}{\blacksquare}$$
$$2 \times \blacksquare = 5 \times 12$$
$$2 \times \blacksquare = 60$$
$$\blacksquare = 30$$

Answer choice D is correct.

3. If $\frac{t}{t+4} = \frac{6}{14}$, then what is the value of t?

    (A) 2
    (B) 3
    (C) 6
    (D) 10

Even though this question has a variable, we can still use cross-multiplying.

$$\frac{t}{t+4} = \frac{6}{14}$$
$$14 \times t = 6 \times (t+4)$$
$$14t = 6t + 24$$
$$8t = 24$$
$$t = 3$$

Answer choice B is correct. Note that we could have also plugged in answer choices to see what works.

4. If $\dfrac{m+2}{m} = \dfrac{2}{3}$ then what is the value of m?

(A) −6
(B) −2
(C) 2
(D) 4

Again, we can use cross-multiplying to solve.

$$\frac{m+2}{m} = \frac{2}{3}$$
$$3 \times (m+2) = m \times 2$$
$$3m + 6 = 2m$$
$$m + 6 = 0$$
$$m = -6$$

Answer choice A is correct. Note that we could have also plugged in answer choices to answer this question.

Another type of question that you can use proportions for is scale questions. For example, let's say the question tells us that the scale on a map is 1.2 inches per every 200 miles. If two cities are 6 inches apart on a map, then how far apart are they in reality?

$$\frac{1.2 \text{ inches}}{200 \text{ miles}} = \frac{6 \text{ inches}}{m \text{ miles}}$$
$$1.2 \times m = 200 \times 6$$
$$1.2m = 1{,}200$$
$$m = 1{,}000$$

Using a proportion, we were able to figure out that the two cities are 1,000 miles apart in reality. One habit that is good to develop is labeling the numerator and denominator in your first proportion. This makes it much easier to see where the variable goes in the second proportion.

- When you set up the scale proportion, label the numerator and the denominator

A term that you may see is "scale factor". The scale factor is simply the number that you multiply by to get one from one object to another. For example, let's say that we have two squares and the scale factor is 1.2. That means that if a side of one square is 4 inches, we would multiply 4 in. × 1.2 to figure out that one side of the other square is 4.8 inches.

- A scale factor is simply what we multiply a piece of one figure by to get the size of another figure that is to scale

Here are a few questions for you to try:

5. A scale for a model airplane is 2 centimeters on the model is equal to 3 meters on the actual airplane. If the actual airplane is 48 meters long, how long should the model airplane be?

  (A) 6 cm
  (B) 8 cm
  (C) 16 cm
  (D) 32 cm

Let's start by setting up our proportion. We will remember to label the numerator and denominator in order to keep it all straight.

$$\frac{2 \text{ cm}}{3 \text{ m}} = \frac{c \text{ cm}}{48 \text{ m}}$$
$$2 \times 48 = 3 \times c$$
$$96 = 3c$$
$$32 = c$$

Answer choice D is correct.

6. Two triangles are similar. If the side of one triangle is 3 cm long and the scale factor is 2.5, what is the length of the corresponding side of the larger triangle?

  (A) 2.5 cm
  (B) 3 cm
  (C) 5 cm
  (D) 7.5 cm

This problem is more straightforward. We simply have to multiply the side length (3 cm) by the scale factor (2.5). Since $3 \times 2.5 = 7.5$, answer choice D is correct.

7. On a certain map, 3 centimeters is equal to 150 kilometers. If two buildings are 10 centimeters apart on the map, how far apart are they actually?

(A) 50 km
(B) 500 km
(C) 650 km
(D) 900 km

This question is easy to answer as long as we set up our proportion and remember to label the numerator and denominator.

$$\frac{3 \text{ cm}}{150 \text{ km}} = \frac{10 \text{ cm}}{k \text{ km}}$$

$$3 \times k = 150 \times 10$$

$$3k = 1500$$

$$k = 500 \text{ km}$$

Answer choice B is correct.

Patterns

On the ISEE, you may be asked to identify patterns. For these questions, you have to find the rule that will help you predict a future number in the sequence.

- The trick to these questions is to find a rule.

There are no hard and fast rules about how to determine what a pattern is on the ISEE. Is the same number added each time? Is one term multiplied by the same number each time to get the next term? Is it a multi-step pattern?

Here are some examples of how this could be tested on the ISEE:

1. Use the set of numbers below to answer the question.

$$\left\{ \frac{1}{5}, \frac{2}{6}, \frac{3}{7}, ... \right\}$$

What would be the next fraction in this pattern?

(A) $\frac{1}{8}$

(B) $\frac{2}{8}$

(C) $\frac{3}{8}$

(D) $\frac{4}{8}$

Look at the numerators (top numbers). Their pattern is to increase by 1 each time. The next numerator would be 4. Now look at the denominators (bottom numbers). They also get bigger by 1 each time, so the next denominator would be 8. Thus, the answer is $\frac{4}{8}$ or answer choice D.

2. A number is 3 more than twice the previous number. The first number in the pattern is one. What is the 3rd number in the pattern?

(A) 3
(B) 5
(C) 7
(D) 13

You start with the number 1. The directions say to take twice the number 1 and then add 3 to it. Twice the number 1 is 2, and then when you add 3 to it, you get 5. So 5 is the second number in the pattern. Now repeat the directions to find the next number, but start with the number 5. Take twice 5 and add 3. This gives us 10 + 3, which is 13, so answer choice D is correct.

3. A number is said to be a square number if that number of objects can be arranged in rows such that a square can be built from the number of objects. Here is a diagram for the first three square numbers:

What are the next 2 square numbers?

(A) 10 and 12
(B) 16 and 20
(C) 16 and 25
(D) 25 and 36

To find this pattern, it is helpful to list out the parts of the pattern that we already have and look for the rule:

$$1st\ perfect\ square = 1 = 1 \times 1$$
$$2nd\ perfect\ square = 4 = 2 \times 2$$
$$3rd\ perfect\ square = 9 = 3 \times 3$$

Now it is easy to see how we would find the 4th perfect square – we would just multiply 4×4 and get 16. To find the fifth perfect square, we would just follow this pattern and multiply 5×5 to get 25. Answer choice C is correct.

4. Use the set below to answer the question.

(4, 5, 7, 10, 14, 19, ...)

What number would come next in this sequence?

(A) 20
(B) 25
(C) 31
(D) 39

First we to determine the pattern to the sequence. The difference between 4 and 5 is 1. To get from 5 to 7, we had to add 2. Then to get from 7 to 10, we had to add 3. We can see that the pattern is to add one more between each term. To get from 14 to 19, we had to add 5, so we will have to add 6 to get to the next term. Since $19 + 6 = 25$, answer choice B is the correct answer.

5.   Use the pattern below to answer the question.

$$
\begin{array}{rcl}
4^1 & = & 4 \\
4^2 & = & 16 \\
4^3 & = & 64 \\
4^4 & = & 256 \\
4^5 & = & 1{,}024 \\
4^6 & = & 4{,}096 \\
4^7 & = & 16{,}384
\end{array}
$$

According to the pattern above, what would be the units digit for 4^{35}?

(A) 1
(B) 3
(C) 4
(D) 6

If we look at the table, we can see that if there is an even exponent, the units digit is a 6 and if there is an odd exponent the units digit is a 4. Since 35 is an odd number, the units digit would be a 4. Answer choice C is correct.

Input/output tables

Another question type that you may see on the ISEE asks you to use "input/output" machines. These questions are testing your ability to determine the rule used to get from one number to another. It may be a one-step machine, where you add/subtract/multiply/divide just once to get from one number to another. Keep in mind that there may be more than one step in the process, though. For example, the rule might be to multiply by 3 and then add 4. The trick is that the rule must work for all the input/output pairs.

- The rule may have one step, but it could also have two steps
- The rule must work for ALL input/output pairs

Here is an example of a basic input/output question:

1. Use the table below to answer the question.

Input Δ	Output ⊠
2	6
3	7
4	8
5	9

What is the rule that this function follows?

(A) $Δ \times 3 = ⊠$
(B) $(Δ \times 4) - 2 = ⊠$
(C) $(Δ \times 2) + 2 = ⊠$
(D) $Δ + 4 = ⊠$

The easiest way to approach this question is to plug in the inputs and outputs to the rules and see which one works. The trick is that if we plug in the first set of inputs and outputs, all the rules work. However, if we plug in the second set of inputs/outputs, then the only rule that works is answer choice D.

The next two questions are a little harder. You have to determine the rule on your own and then apply the rule to figure out the answer.

2. A number machine takes in an input number, performs the same operation on each number, and then prints an output number. The results are shown below.

Input	Output
21	7
18	6
15	5
9	3

Which input number would cause the machine to print 9?

(A) 3
(B) 9
(C) 27
(D) 36

Our first step is to figure out the operation that the machine is performing. If we look at just our first output, we might say that the machine subtracts 14 because $21 - 14 = 7$. However, if we look at our second output, we can see that rule does not work for all of the outputs. If we go back to the first output we could also say that the rule is to divide by 3. This works for all the inputs and outputs so we know that our rule is to divide by 3. Now we have to work backwards since the question gives us the output and asks for the input. To get from the output to the input, we would have to do the opposite operation, or multiply by 3 instead of dividing by 3. If we multiply 9 by 3, we get 27 as our answer. Choice C is the correct answer choice.

3. A number machine takes in an input number, performs the same operation on each number, and then prints an output number. The results are shown below.

Input	Output
20	9
18	8
16	7
14	6

If the number 10 was entered into the machine, what number would the machine print?

(A) 4
(B) 5
(C) 6
(D) 7

First we need to determine the rule. This question is a little harder because the input/output machine has a two-step rule. You have to play around with the numbers to see what works. For example, maybe you notice that to get from 20 to 9, you have to subtract 11. However, if you subtract 11 from 18, you do not get 8, so that cannot be the rule. Maybe you notice that all of the inputs are even, so you try to divide by 2. If you divide 20 by 2, you get 10. You would then have to subtract 1 to get the output of 9. Then you can try that same rule on the next input and output. If you divide 18 by 2, you get 9. You would then have to subtract 1 to get the output of 8. If you keep trying the rule of divide by 2, subtract 1, you will see that it works for all of the inputs and outputs. We now have to apply this rule to the number 10. If we divide 10 by 2 and then subtract 1, we get 4 as an answer. Answer choice A is the correct answer.

Now you have the basics for algebra questions on the ISEE. Be sure to complete the Algebraic Concepts Practice Set to reinforce what you have learned.

Algebraic concepts practice set

1. If $\dfrac{m+6}{m} = \dfrac{1}{4}$, what is the value of m?

   (A) −8
   (B) −6
   (C) 4
   (D) 6

2. If $W = 3 \times (X + Y)$, what is W when X is equal to 4 and Y is equal to 5?

   (A) 9
   (B) 12
   (C) 17
   (D) 27

3. The figure below displays the first four elements of a dot pattern.

   What is the fifth element in this pattern?

   (A) (B)

   (C) (D)

4. Peter is building a scale model airplane. 5 feet on the actual airplane is equal to 2 inches on the scale model. If the wingspan of the actual airplane is 150 feet, how long is the wingspan on the scale model?

   (A) 30 inches
   (B) 60 inches
   (C) 75 inches
   (D) 100 inches

5. A concert series costs between $3,000 and $3,500 to produce. The series will consist of 12 concerts in total. They expect between 150 and 250 people each night and tickets cost $9 each. If profit is equal to revenue minus cost, what will be the approximate profit for this concert series?

   (A) $13,000
   (B) $18,000
   (C) $24,000
   (D) $27,000

6.

$$\frac{m}{3} + 4 = 22$$
$$2n + 5 = 113$$

Column A	**Column B**
m	n

   (A) Quantity in Column A is greater.
   (B) Quantity in Column B is greater.
   (C) Quantities in Columns A and B are equal.
   (D) Not enough information to determine relationship.

7. If $b + 5 - 9 = c$, then what is the value of $b - c$?

   (A) −4
   (B) −2
   (C) 2
   (D) 4

8.

In	Out
2	3
3	5
4	7
5	9

Column A

The output when the input is 7

Column B

The input when output is 15

(A) Quantity in Column A is greater.
(B) Quantity in Column B is greater.
(C) Quantities in Columns A and B are equal.
(D) Not enough information to determine relationship.

9. If $\dfrac{k+2}{k} = \dfrac{2}{6}$, then what does k equal?

(A) –3
(B) –1
(C) 1
(D) 3

10. If $\dfrac{1}{3}n + 4 = 15$, then what is the value of n?

(A) 11
(B) 19
(C) 33
(D) 45

11. If $3x + 7 = 6$, then what is the value of $6x + 14$?

(A) 2
(B) 12
(C) 24
(D) 30

12. In a quiz game, points are awarded based on the pattern in the table below.

Number of Correct Answers	Points
1	3
2	9
3	27

If a player scored 243 points, how many questions did they answer correctly?

(A) 4
(B) 5
(C) 18
(D) 39

13. James and Erik ran along a straight path, starting at the same time and place. James ran twice as fast as Erik. After 5 minutes, James was 200 feet in front of Erik. What equation could be solved to find Erik's speed (E)?

(A) $2E - E = 200$
(B) $2(E + 2E) = 200$
(C) $200 - 5E = 10E$
(D) $5E + 200 = 10E$

14. The following currency system was developed:

1 button = 3 snaps
4 zippers = 2 buttons

How many snaps is 16 zippers worth?

(A) 12
(B) 16
(C) 24
(D) 36

15. Use the following expression to answer the question.

$$\frac{4\left(\sqrt{49}+22x\right)}{\sqrt{4}}$$

(A) $2(7 + 22x)$

(B) $4(7 + 22x)$

(C) $\dfrac{\sqrt{196}+22x}{2}$

(D) $\dfrac{\sqrt{196}+88x}{2}$

Answers to Algebraic Concepts Practice Set

1. A
2. D
3. C
4. B
5. B
6. C
7. D
8. A
9. A
10. C
11. B
12. B
13. D
14. C
15. A

Geometry

On the Middle Level ISEE, the geometry questions are pretty basic.

Geometry problem types that you will see on the Middle Level ISEE include:

- Basic network questions
- Definitions of various shapes
- Nets
- Symmetry, congruency, and similarity
- Coordinate geometry
- Slope and equations of lines
- Transformations

Basic network questions

You may see a question on the ISEE that references networks or routes. These questions are not hard. Just don't be confused the by word "network" if you haven't heard it before. It simply means paths taken.

- A network is just a group of paths taken

The best way to answer this question is simply to use your pen to trace paths and use ruling out.

Here are a couple of examples of network questions that you could see:

1. Which network shows routes from K to M, K to L, K to N, L to N, and L to M and NOT any other routes?

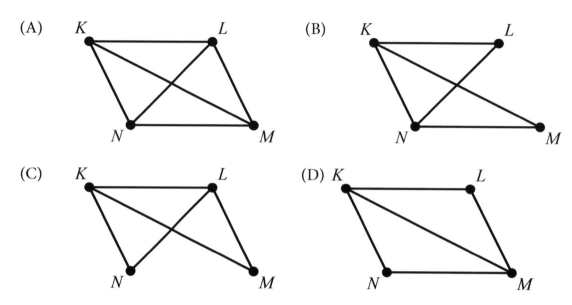

(A) K L

(B) K L

(C) K L

(D) K L

To answer this question, simply use your pencil to draw out each route named. If you do this you can see that only answer choice C has the routes listed but NOT any other routes.

2. Use the picture below to answer the question.

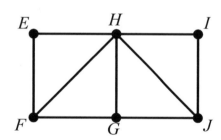

If EFGH and HIJG are both squares, which path would be the longest?

(A) E to F to G to J
(B) E to F to H to I
(C) E to H to I to J
(D) E to F to H to J

All of the paths have three segments. However, not all of the segments are the same length. The segments that lie along the edges of the squares are all the same length. However, FH and HJ are both hypotenuses of right triangles that cut each square in half, so they have to be longer than the other sides. Answer choice D includes both of these hypotenuses, so its path is the longest.

Definitions of various shapes

On the Middle Level ISEE, you will need to know the definitions of various shapes. In general, we can divide the shapes into quadrilaterals and not quadrilaterals.

Quadrilaterals are simply shapes that have four sides. A shape can be described by more than one name. For example, a square is also a rectangle, a parallelogram, and a quadrilateral. The least specific name for a square is a quadrilateral since that just tells us that has four sides. A more specific is the name parallelogram, which tells us that it has two pairs of parallel sides. Even more specific is the term rectangle. Now we know that not only does the figure have two pairs of parallel sides, but also that all of the figures' angles are right angles. Finally, the most specific name is square – telling us that the figure has four sides, all the angles are right angles, and all the sides are of the same length.

- Quadrilaterals are shapes with four sides
- A shape can have more than one name

The quadrilaterals that you will need to know for the Middle Level ISEE include:

- Parallelogram
- Rectangle
- Square
- Kite
- Rhombus
- Diamond
- Trapezoid

A parallelogram is a shape with two pairs of parallel lines and opposite sides that are the same length.

Here is an example of a parallelogram:

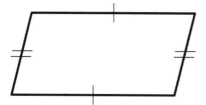

A rectangle is a parallelogram that has four right angles. Here is an example of a rectangle:

A square is a rectangle that has four sides of the same length. Here is an example of a square:

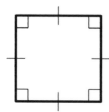

Another type of quadrilateral is a kite. A kite is a four-sided shape that has two pairs of adjacent sides that are the same length – adjacent means that the sides are next to each other. Here is an example of a kite:

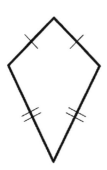

A special kind of kite is a rhombus. A rhombus has four sides that are all the same length. A rhombus can also be called a diamond. Here is an example of a rhombus or diamond:

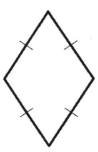

A rhombus can also have four right angles – in this case the more specific name for that shape would be square.

The final type of quadrilateral that you may see is a trapezoid. A trapezoid has one set of opposite, parallel sides, one set of adjacent acute angles (less than 90 degrees) and one set of adjacent obtuse angles (more than 90 degrees). Here is an example of a trapezoid:

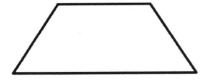

You will also need to know some shapes that are not quadrilaterals. These shapes include:

- Triangles
- Pentagons
- Hexagons

Triangles are simply shapes that have three sides. Here is an example:

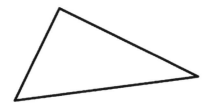

A pentagon is a shape that has five sides. Here is an example of a pentagon:

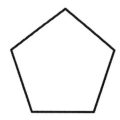

Finally, you need to know that a hexagon has six sides. Here is an example of a hexagon:

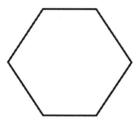

Following are some sample questions that test these definitions. On the ISEE, you are more likely to see a coordinate geometry question that also tests the definitions of shapes, so we will have more of those in the coordinate geometry section.

Here are some questions for you to try:

1. What is the name of a shape that has six sides?

   (A) pentagon
   (B) hexagon
   (C) trapezoid
   (D) triangle

A shape that has six sides is a hexagon. The prefix "hex" means six, so any shape with six sides is a hexagon. Answer choice B is correct.

2. What name best describes a rhombus with four right angles?

   (A) square
   (B) diamond
   (C) trapezoid
   (D) pentagon

If we go to the answer choices, we can rule out choices C and D right away because neither a trapezoid nor a pentagon has four right angles. Now we are left with choices A and B. This is tricky because a rhombus can also be a diamond or a square. However, while a diamond can have right angles, it does not have to. A square must have right angles, however, so answer choice A is correct.

Nets

Nets are simply patterns that could be folded to create three-dimensional shapes, or polyhedrons. The key to this type of question is to visualize what shape would be formed if the sides were folded up.

Here are a couple of questions that test your ability to visualize polyhedrons:

1. The pattern below is going to be folded to create a polyhedron.

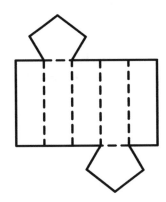

Which polyhedron could be the result if the pattern was folded along the dotted lines?

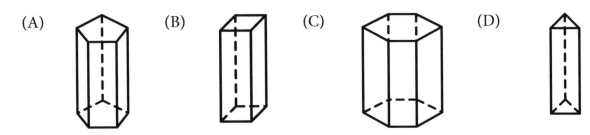

To answer this question, we can first identify the bases. We can see that there are five rectangle sides and two pentagons that would act as bases. Answer choice A has pentagons as bases.

2. The pattern below can be folded into a cube.

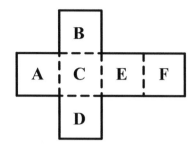

If the net is folded into a cube and side A is on the bottom, what side would be on the top?

(A) B
(B) D
(C) E
(D) F

This problem is a little tricky because you probably visualized the cube with C on the bottom. However, the question states that A is on the bottom. That means that C would be on the side and E would be on the top. Answer choice C is correct.

Symmetry, congruency, and similarity

On the Middle Level ISEE, you will need to know what the terms symmetric, congruent, and similar mean.

Symmetric

A shape is symmetric if you could draw a line down the middle and the two halves would be flipped versions of each other.

Here is an example:

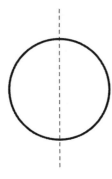
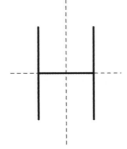

A circle is symmetric because if we folded it along the dotted line, the two sides awould match up. A circle has many lines of symmetry since we could draw that dotted line in many places and still have the two halves match up.

The letter H above has two lines of symmetry. The two dashed lines show the lines of symmetry.

The letter Z above doesn't have any lines of symmetry. We cannot draw any lines that make the two sides match up exactly.

Congruent

Two objects are congruent if they are the same length/size/shape.

Here is an example:

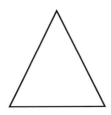

The two triangles above are congruent because they are exactly the same size and shape.

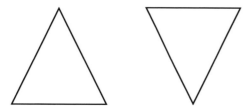

The two triangles above are also congruent. Even though one triangle has been flipped, they are still the same size and shape so they are congruent.

Similar

Two shapes are similar if they have the same angles and side lengths that are in proportion to one another.

Here is an example:

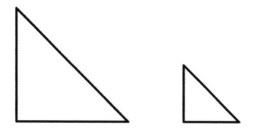

The two triangles above are similar because they have the same angle measures and each side of the smaller triangle is half the length of the corresponding side of the larger triangle.

Here are some examples of questions that test these concepts:

1. Which figure below has exactly two lines of symmetry?

(A)

(B)

(C)

(D)

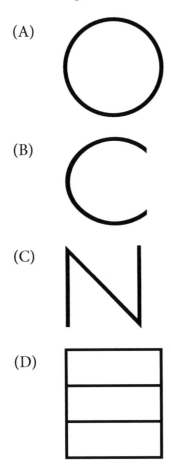

We are looking for a figure that we could fold in two different ways and have the sides match up. The figure in answer A has infinite lines of symmetry since you could draw many lines and have the sides match up. We can rule out choice A. Answer choice B has only one line of symmetry. We could draw a line across the letter C and have the top and bottom halves match up, but there isn't a second line of symmetry. Answer choice B can be eliminated. In answer choice C, the letter N has no lines of symmetry. Answer choice C can be ruled out. Finally, we have answer choice D. We could draw a line across the middle of the figure and the top and bottom halves would match up. We could also draw a line up and down on the figure and the right and left halves would match up. Answer choice D is correct.

2. The figure below could be folded along the dotted lines.

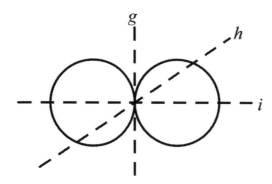

Which line (or pair of lines), when folded, would allow the two halves of the figure to match up exactly?

(A) line *g* only
(B) line *h* only
(C) lines *g* and *h*
(D) lines *g* and *i*

This question doesn't use the word "symmetric", but that is what the question is really testing. We are looking for which lines are lines of symmetry for the figure. Only lines *g* and *i* would cause the two halves to match up, so answer choice D is the correct answer.

3. Which pair of figures below is congruent?

(A)

(B)

(C)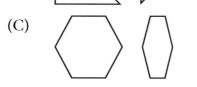

(D)

We are looking for two figures that are exactly the same. In choice A, the two figures are similar, but not congruent. Choice A can be ruled out. Choice B has two figures that are exactly the same. One figure is rotated, but the two triangles still have the same angles and the same side lengths, so they are congruent. Answer choice B is the correct choice.

4. Use the figure below to answer the question.

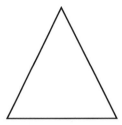

Which figure is similar to the triangle above?

(A)
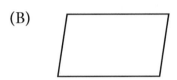

(B)
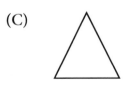

(C)

(D)
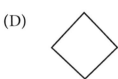

We are looking for a figure that is a triangle with the same angle measures as the given triangle. Answer choices B and D aren't even triangles, so we can eliminate those answer choices. Answer choice A is a triangle, but we don't want a right triangle so choice A can be eliminated. Choice C is the correct answer.

Coordinate geometry

Coordinate geometry uses a grid. The important thing to remember about points on a coordinate grid is that the x-coordinate is given first and then the y-coordinate. Ordered pairs are written (x, y). If you have trouble remembering what comes first, just think "first you run, then you jump".

Here is an example:

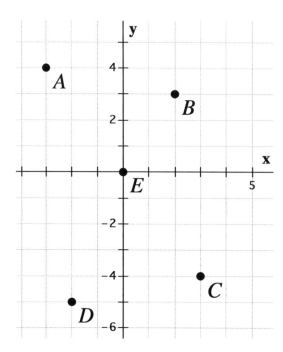

In the coordinate grid above, there are several points plotted.

On this grid, we would call point E the origin. The coordinates of point E are $(0, 0)$.

The coordinates of point B are $(2, 3)$ because we go over 2 and up 3 to get to point B from the origin.

If we have to go to the left of the origin, then the x-coordinate becomes a negative number. If we have to go down (instead of up), then the y-coordinate is negative.

Therefore, the coordinates of point A are $(-3, 4)$.

What are the coordinates of point D?

We have to go to the left two spots to get from the origin to point *D*, so the *x*-coordinate is −2. We then have to go down 5 places, so the *y*-coordinate of point *D* is −5. We write the coordinates of point *D* as (−2, −5).

What about point *C*?

Let's remember to run then jump. To get from the origin to point *C*, we have to go 3 places to the right in the positive direction and then go down 4 places in the negative direction. The coordinates of point *C* are (3, −4).

Here is an example of a question type that tests the coordinate grid on the Middle Level ISEE:

1. Use the coordinate grid below to answer the question.

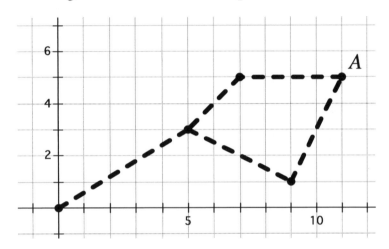

What are the (*x*, *y*) coordinates of point *A* in the figure above?

(A) (9, 5)
(B) (11, 5)
(C) (5, 11)
(D) (5, 9)

To get from the origin to point *A*, we have to go over 11 spaces and then up 5 spaces. This means the coordinates of point *A* are (11, 5). Answer choice B is correct.

Some of the questions on the ISEE that test coordinate geometry also test the definition of shapes. Here are a couple of examples for you to try:

2. Jackie plots the points $(1, 2)$, $(2, 3)$, $(4, 3)$, and $(5, 2)$. She then connects these points to make a quadrilateral. Which term could describe that quadrilateral?

(A) square
(B) diamond
(C) hexagon
(D) trapezoid

The best way to answer this question is to draw our own grid. It does not have to be exact since we are just looking for a rough idea of where the points are in relation to one another.

Your grid should look something like this:

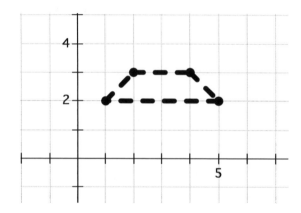

We can see that the shape is clearly not a square or a diamond, so we can rule out choices A and B. Choice C, a hexagon, is not even a quadrilateral so it can be eliminated. Answer choice D is the correct answer.

3. The vertices of a quadrilateral are $(2, 2)$, $(4, 0)$, $(6, 2)$, and $(4, 4)$. Which term best describes this quadrilateral?

(A) pentagon
(B) square
(C) trapezoid
(D) hexagon

Again, let's plot the points and see what we have. Our grid looks something like this when we plot the points and then connect them:

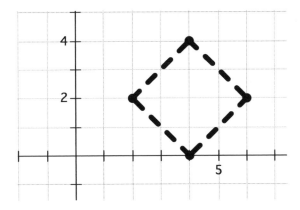

Even though the shape is turned diagonally on the axes, it is still definitely a square. It has four sides that are the same length and four right angles. Answer choice B is correct.

Slope and equations of lines

On the ISEE, you will need to know the following about equations of lines:

- The basic equation of a line ($y = mx + b$)
- What slope is and what it really means
- Rearranging an equation to find slope
- Finding slope using two points
- How the slopes of perpendicular and parallel lines are related
- How to come up with an equation when you are given point(s) and/or slope
- What the y-intercept is and what it really means

The basic equation of a line ($y = mx + b$)

There are different ways that you can write the equation of a line. The most useful way to write the equation of a line on the ISEE is to use slope-intercept form. The basic form for slope-intercept is:

$y = mx + b$, where m is equal to the slope and b is equal to the y-intercept

The y-intercept is the point on the y-axis that the line crosses, or where the line intersects the y-axis.

What slope is and what it really means

Slope tells us how *y*-values change as *x*-values change. You can think of slope as telling us how "steep" a line is. You can also say that slope describes the rate of change. Another description of slope is rise over run.

For example:

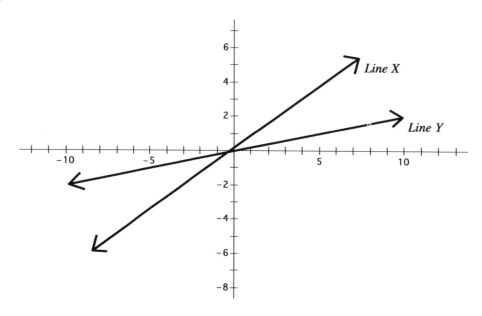

In the above diagram, Line X has a greater slope than Line Y. This means that the rate of change is greater for Line X than for Line Y.

Slope can also be positive or negative. If slope is positive, that means that as the *x*-values increase, the *y*-values also increase. If the slope is negative, that means that as the *x*-values increase, the *y*-values decrease.

For example:

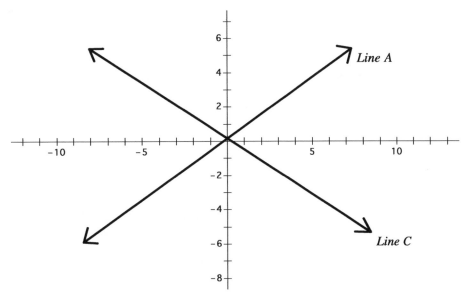

On the above coordinate graph, Line A has a positive slope and Line C has a negative slope.

Here is an example of how slope could be tested on the ISEE:

1. For which of the following functions do the *y*-values decrease at the greatest rate as *x*-values increase?

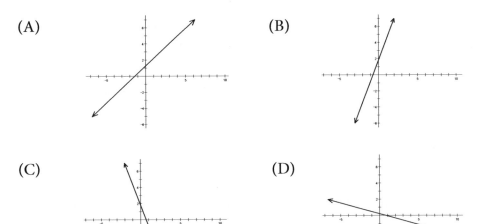

First we need to decide whether the slope is positive or negative. Since the question says that the *y*-values decrease as the *x*-values increase, we know that the slope must be negative. That means that choices A and B cannot be the correct answer because they both show a function with a positive slope. We are down to choices C and D. Now we are looking for the function that changes at the greatest rate. Another way to say that is we are looking for the line that is steepest. Answer choice C is correct.

Here is another one for you to try:

2. For which of the following functions do the *y*-values increase at the least rate as *x*-values increase?

(A)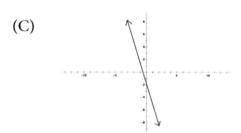

(B)

(C)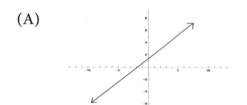

(D)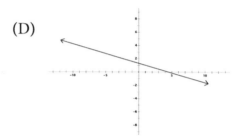

The question says that as the *y*-values increase, the *x*-values also increase, which means that we are looking for a positive slope. That means we can rule out C and D.

Now we are looking at choice A and B and want to choose the one that increases at the least rate, or has the smaller slope. Answer choice A is the correct answer.

Rearranging an equation to find slope

Some questions on the ISEE will ask you rearrange an equation in order to find the slope. The easiest way to do this is to use the rules of isolating a variable to get the equation into the form:

$$y = mx + b$$

Think of it like any other equation where you are trying to get *y* by itself.

Here is an example of a question that asks you to find slope:

3. What is the slope of the line with the equation $2x + 7y = 1$?

(A) $\dfrac{2}{7}$

(B) 2

(C) $-\dfrac{2}{7}$

(D) -2

To find the slope, we have to get the equation in the form $y = mx + b$, where m is the slope. This basically means that we get y by itself.

$$2x + 7y = 1$$
$$\underline{-2x \quad -2x}$$
$$7y = -2x + 1$$
$$\underline{\div 7 \quad \div 7}$$
$$y = -\dfrac{2}{7}x + \dfrac{1}{7}$$

Now that we have the equation in the form $y = mx + b$, we can easily see that the slope is $-\dfrac{2}{7}$ and answer choice C is correct.

Here is another one for you to try:

4. What is the slope of the line with the equation $5x - 2y = 15$?

(A) $\dfrac{2}{5}$

(B) $\dfrac{5}{2}$

(C) 2

(D) 5

Again, we have to get the equation in the form $y = mx + b$

$$5x - 2y = 15$$
$$\underline{-5x \quad -5x}$$
$$-2y = -5x + 15$$
$$\div -2 \quad \div -2$$
$$y = \frac{5}{2}x - \frac{15}{2}$$

The slope is $\frac{5}{2}$, so answer choice B is correct.

Finding slope using two points

Another way to find slope is to use two points. Slope can be described as:

$$\text{slope} = \frac{\text{rise}}{\text{run}}$$

This basically means that slope is equal to how much the line goes up over how far it moves to the side.

Here is an example:

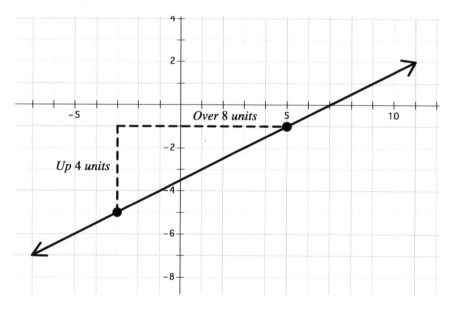

If you look at the line above, you can see that to go from one chosen point to another chosen point, we have to go up 4 units and over 8 units. Remember that slope is equal to:

$$\frac{\text{rise}}{\text{run}} = \frac{4}{8} = \frac{1}{2}$$

From this, we can see that the slope is $\frac{1}{2}$.

If we are given two points not on a graph, we can turn rise over run into a usable equation:

$$\frac{\text{rise}}{\text{run}} = \frac{\text{difference in } y\text{-coordinates}}{\text{difference in } x\text{-coordinates}} = \frac{y_1 - y_2}{x_1 - x_2}$$

Here is an example of how you may have to apply this on the ISEE:

5.   What is the slope between the points (5, 4) and (3, 7)?

(A) $-\dfrac{3}{2}$

(B) $\dfrac{3}{2}$

(C) $-\dfrac{2}{3}$

(D) $\dfrac{2}{3}$

To find the answer, we just need to plug into our equation:

$$\frac{y_1 - y_2}{x_1 - x_2} = \frac{4 - 7}{5 - 3} = -\frac{3}{2}$$

Answer choice A is correct.

Now here is an example of a question that combines what you have learned about finding slope:

6.

Column A	Column B
The slope of $3x - 5y = 7$	The slope between $(6, 2)$ and $(1, 5)$

(A) The quantity in Column A is greater
(B) The quantity in Column B is greater
(C) The two quantities are equal
(D) The relationship cannot be determined from the information given

Our first step is to find the slope of the line in Column A. In order to do that, we need to get it in the form $y = mx + b$. Here is what the math would look like:

$$3x - 5y = 7$$
$$-3x \quad -3x$$
$$-5y = -3x + 7$$
$$\div -5 \quad \div -5$$
$$y = \frac{3}{5}x - \frac{7}{5}$$

From this we can see that the slope of the line in Column A is $\frac{3}{5}$.

Now we have to use the two points in Column B to find the slope between them. Here is what the math looks like:

$$\frac{y_1 - y_2}{x_1 - x_2} = \frac{2 - 5}{6 - 1} = -\frac{3}{5}$$

We can now see that the slope in Column A is $\frac{3}{5}$ and the slope in Column B is $-\frac{3}{5}$. The correct answer is A.

How the slopes of perpendicular and parallel lines are related

If two lines are parallel, then they have the same slope. Here is how this could be tested on the ISEE:

7. The graph below shows $\overline{BC}$.

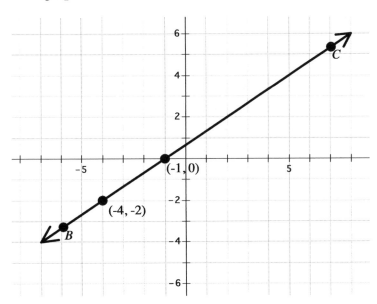

Which line is parallel to $\overline{BC}$?

(A) $y = -\dfrac{2}{3}x + 4$

(B) $y = -\dfrac{2}{5}x - 5$

(C) $y = \dfrac{2}{3}x + 2$

(D) $y = \dfrac{2}{5}x + 3$

Our first step is to figure out the slope of $\overline{BC}$. We are given two points that are on that segment. Since we have a picture, we can count rise over run:

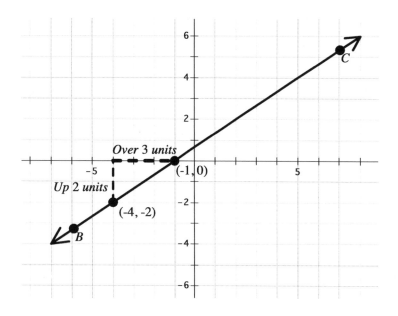

From this, we can see that the slope of $\overline{BC}$ is $\dfrac{2}{3}$. Now we just have to look at the answer choices and see which one has a slope of $\dfrac{2}{3}$. Answer choice C is correct.

If two lines are perpendicular then their slopes are negative reciprocals. Basically, this means that if you take the slope of a line, flip the numerator and denominator, and then add a negative sign, you will have the slope of a line that is perpendicular to the first line.

Here are some examples:

If $m = \dfrac{2}{3}$, then a perpendicular line would have $m = -\dfrac{3}{2}$

If $m = 2$, then a perpendicular line would have $m = -\dfrac{1}{2}$

If $m = -\dfrac{1}{3}$, then a perpendicular line would have $m = 3$

Here is an example of a question that tests the concept of perpendicular lines:

8. The graph below shows $\overline{PQ}$.

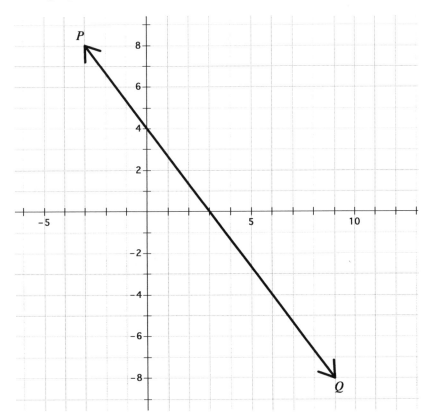

Which of the following could be the equation of a line that is perpendicular to $\overline{PQ}$?

(A) $y = -\dfrac{4}{3}x + 3$

(B) $y = -\dfrac{3}{4}x + 7$

(C) $y = \dfrac{4}{3}x + 6$

(D) $y = \dfrac{3}{4}x + 5$

First, we calculate the slope of $\overline{PQ}$. By looking at the x- and y-axes, we can see that the points $(3, 0)$ and $(0, 4)$ are on the segment. Using these two points to determine the slope, we get:

$$\frac{\text{rise}}{\text{run}} = \frac{0-4}{3-0} = -\frac{4}{3}$$

The slope of a perpendicular line will be the negative reciprocal of $-\frac{4}{3}$, which is $\frac{3}{4}$. Answer choice D is correct.

How to come up with an equation when you are given point(s) and/or slope

You may be given two points or a point and the slope and be asked to find the equation of a line.

Here are the basic steps:

1. Solve for slope (if it is not given)
2. Set up the equation $y = mx + b$
3. Plug in the x and y values from one point for x and y in the equation and also plug in the slope for m
4. Use this equation to solve for b
5. Rewrite $y = mx + b$ plugging in the values you found for m (slope) and b (y-intercept) – your final equation should have x and y in it

Here is an example of how this question could be asked on the ISEE:

9. Line m has a slope of $\frac{3}{2}$ and goes through the point $(4, 6)$. What is the equation of line m?

(A) $y = \frac{3}{2}x$

(B) $y = \frac{3}{2}x + 6$

(C) $y = 4x + \frac{3}{2}$

(D) $y = 3x + \frac{3}{2}$

We are given slope, so we can jump right to setting up our equation.

$y = mx + b$

Now we substitute in the values were given for slope, x, and y.

$6 = \frac{3}{2} \times 4 + b$

Now we solve for b.

$$6 = 6 + b$$
$$0 = b$$

Since $b = 0$, we now know that the equation of the line is $y = \dfrac{3}{2}x$ and answer choice A is correct.

Here is an example of a problem where you first have to solve for slope.

10. Line q runs through the points $(-2, 3)$ and $(2, 7)$. What is the equation of line q?

(A) $y = 4x + 5$

(B) $y = x + 5$

(C) $y = \dfrac{1}{4}x + 5$

(D) $y = \dfrac{2}{3}x + 4$

In this question, we are not given slope, so we must first solve for slope.

$$\text{slope} = \frac{y_1 - y_2}{x_1 - x_2} = \frac{3 - 7}{-2 - 2} = \frac{-4}{-4} = 1$$

Now that we have found that the slope is 1, we can plug into $y = mx + b$ and then solve for b. When we are given two points, we can just pick one to plug into the equation. It does not matter which one we pick.

$$y = mx + b$$
$$7 = 1 \times 2 + b$$
$$7 = 2 + b$$
$$5 = b$$

If we plug back into $y = mx + b$, we can see that the equation of our line is $y = x + 5$, so answer choice B is correct.

Now here is a problem that combines a lot of what you have learned about slope:

11. The graph below shows $\overline{XY}$.

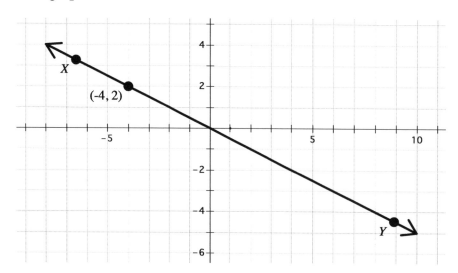

Line f is perpendicular to $\overline{XY}$ at the point $(8, -4)$. What is the equation of line f?

(A) $y = -\dfrac{1}{2}x + 12$

(B) $y = -\dfrac{1}{2}x - 20$

(C) $y = 2x + 12$

(D) $y = 2x - 20$

First, we have to find the slope from the picture. We can see that the line goes through the point $(-4, 2)$ and the origin $(0, 0)$. If we count down and then over, we get that the slope of $\overline{XY}$ is $-\dfrac{1}{2}$. This means that the slope for line f is 2. That means that answer choice C or D must be correct. Now, we just have to decide if the y-intercept should be positive or negative. If we sketch in a line that is perpendicular to $\overline{XY}$ at the point $(8, -4)$, we can clearly see that the y-intercept has to be negative. Answer choice D is correct.

What the y-intercept is and what it really means

In literal terms, the y-intercept is where a line crosses the y-axis. What it represents, however, is the non-variable part of an equation. It can also represent the starting point if the graph is showing how something changes as time progresses.

Here are some examples:

- The cost of printing books is a $500 set up fee plus $2 per book. If we were to graph this, the y-intercept would be 500 since that is the fixed cost. The slope would then be 2 since that is the variable cost.

- If we were plotting the temperature throughout the day, starting at 12 AM, then the y-intercept would represent the temperature at 12 AM.

Here is an example of how this could be tested on the ISEE:

12. The cost (in dollars) for renting a truck, c, depends upon how many miles, m, the renter drives the truck. To figure out the total cost, the formula $c = 2.5m + 100$ can be used. What is the meaning of 100 in this formula?

(A) For every 100 miles driven, it costs one dollar.
(B) For every 1 mile driven, it costs $100.
(C) When the truck is driven 0 miles, the cost is $100.
(D) When 100 miles are driven the cost is $2.50.

Since the y-intercept represents the fixed cost, choices A, B, and D can be eliminated. Choice C is correct.

Transformations

A transformation is basically just moving or flipping a figure. In order for it to be a transformation, the side lengths and angles must remain unchanged.

- A transformation moves a figure but does not change the figure itself

There are three main types of transformations:

1. Rotation or turn – in this transformation, a figure is just turned. Here is an example:

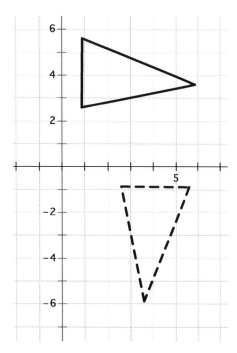

The solid figure is just rotated, or turned, but notice that it is still the same figure.

2. Reflection or flip – with this transformation, a figure is flipped across a line. The line that the figure is flipped across is often the *x*-axis or the *y*-axis. Here is an example:

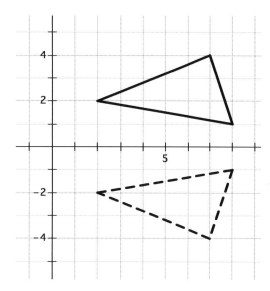

The figure with solid lines has been reflected across the *x*-axis to create the figure with dashed lines.

3. Translation or slide – in this transformation the figure is not turned or reflected, but rather just slid to a new location. Here is an example:

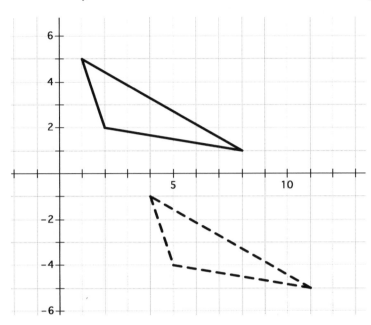

In the above figure, the solid line triangle has just been slid down and to the right to create the dashed line triangle.

Here are two examples of questions that test transformations:

1.   Use the coordinate grid below to answer the question.

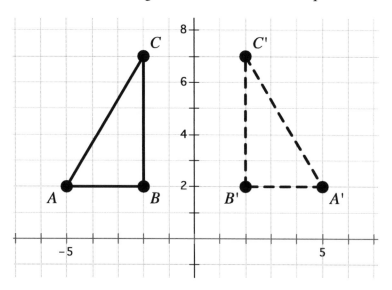

Which transformation(s) took place with triangle *ABC* to get triangle *A'B'C'*?

(A)   a slide
(B)   a flip
(C)   a flip and then another flip
(D)   a turn

Triangle *ABC* is the mirror image of triangle *A'B'C'*. This means that a flip, or reflection, must have occurred. This allows us to rule out answer choices A and D. Triangle *ABC* was only flipped once to get *A'B'C'*, so answer choice B is correct.

2. Use the coordinate grid below to answer the question.

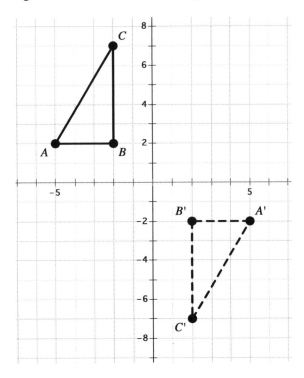

What transformation(s) must have been applied to triangle *ABC* in order to get triangle *A'B'C'*?

(A) a flip only
(B) a slide only
(C) a flip and then another flip
(D) a slide and then a flip

Let's use ruling out on this question. If only a flip was applied, then triangle *A'B'C'* would be in either the top right or bottom left quadrant. This is not the case, so we can rule out choice A. If only a slide was applied to triangle *ABC* then point C would still be at the top of the figure. It is not, so we can rule out choice B. If triangle *ABC* was flipped over the *y*-axis and then flipped over the *x*-axis, triangle *A'B'C'* would be the result. Answer choice C is correct.

Those are the basics that you need to know for geometry questions on the Middle Level ISEE. Be sure to complete the geometry practice set to reinforce what you have learned.

Geometry practice set

1.

Column A	Column B
The slope of $4y - 3x = 10$	The slope between $(1, 2)$ and $(5, 5)$

(A) The quantity in Column A is greater
(B) The quantity in Column B is greater
(C) The two quantities are equal
(D) The relationship cannot be determined from the information given

2. The pattern below can be folded to create a prism.

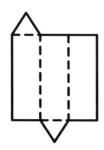

Which prism could result from the above figure being folded?

(A)    (B)    (C) 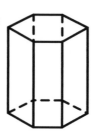   (D)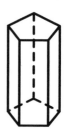

3. What is the slope of the line $7x + 2y = 8$?

(A) $-\dfrac{7}{2}$

(B) $\dfrac{7}{2}$

(C) $-\dfrac{2}{7}$

(D) $\dfrac{2}{7}$

4. Which figure always has sides that are all the same length?

    (A) rhombus
    (B) pentagon
    (C) hexagon
    (D) rectangle

5. The graph below shows $\overline{MN}$.

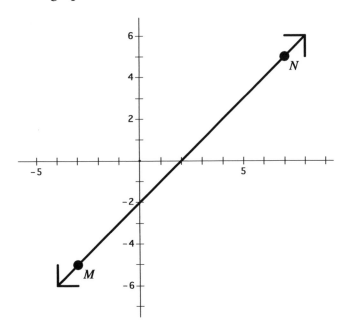

    What is the equation of the line that is perpendicular to $\overline{MN}$ at (4, 2)?

    (A) $y = x - 6$
    (B) $y = x + 6$
    (C) $y = -x - 6$
    (D) $y = -x + 6$

6. Which network shows the routes from M to P, M to O, N to P, N to O, N to M, and P to O, and no other routes?

(A)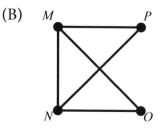

(B)

(C)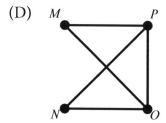

(D)

7. The cost (in dollars), c, of getting groceries delivered is given by the formula $c = 0.2p + 10$, where p is pounds of food. Which of the following statements correctly describes how much it costs to get groceries delivered?

(A) For every 10 pounds of food delivered, it costs $0.20.
(B) The fixed cost for a delivery is $10 plus $0.20 per pound of food.
(C) It costs $10 to have any amount of food delivered.
(D) It costs $10.20 to have 20 pounds of food delivered.

8. The coordinate points (2, 6), (3, 8), (4, 6), and (3, 1) are connected to form a quadrilateral. What term would best describe this quadrilateral?

(A) square
(B) kite
(C) trapezoid
(D) rhombus

9. Which equation shows the greatest increase in *y*-values as *x*-values increase?

(A) $y = 2x + 5$

(B) $y = \dfrac{1}{2}x + 5$

(C) $y = -\dfrac{1}{2}x + 5$

(D) $y = -2x + 5$

10. Use the coordinate grid below to answer the question.

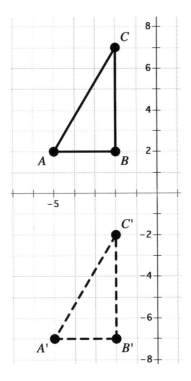

Which transformation(s) could be applied to triangle *ABC* to get triangle *A'B'C'*?

(A) a flip only
(B) a flip and then a slide
(C) a slide only
(D) a turn

Answers to Geometry Practice Set

1. C
2. B
3. A
4. A
5. D
6. C
7. B
8. B
9. A
10. C

Measurement

On the Middle Level ISEE, there are just a few types of measurement questions that you need to know. They include:

- Perimeter
- Area (including shaded region problems)
- Volume and surface area of rectangular solids
- Solving for side lengths with similar triangles

Perimeter

Perimeter is defined as the distance around a figure. To find the perimeter of a figure, just add up the side lengths.

Perimeter = side + side + side...

Some questions are very straightforward and just ask you to add up the sides to find the perimeter. Here is a very basic example of a perimeter question:

1. Tara is going to build a rectangular garden as shown below.

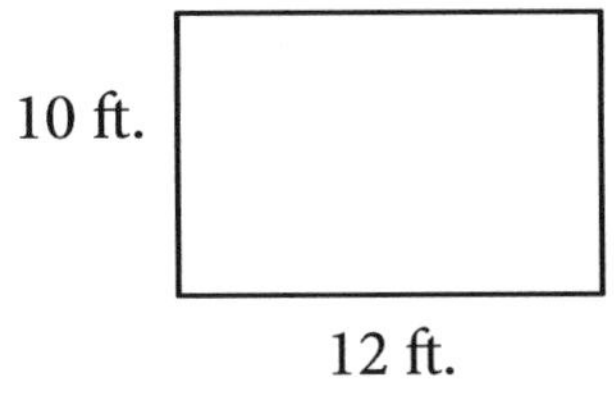

10 ft. ⬚

12 ft.

She wants to run a string around the perimeter of the garden. How many feet of string will she need to go all the way around her garden?

(A) 20 ft.
(B) 22 ft.
(C) 42 ft.
(D) 44 ft.

In order to figure out how much string Tara will need, we need to find the perimeter of the garden. To do that, we add up the lengths of all of the sides. The key is to remember to add two lengths and two widths. If we add 10 + 10 + 12 + 12, we get that the perimeter of Tara's garden is 44 ft., so she will need 44 ft. of string. Answer choice D is correct.

It is more likely that you will see questions that give you the perimeter and then ask you to work backwards to solve for a side length. Here are a couple of examples:

2. Use the triangle below to answer the question.

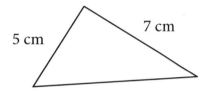

If the perimeter of the triangle is 22 cm, then what is the length of the third side?

(A) 10 cm
(B) 12 cm
(C) 22 cm
(D) 34 cm

For this question, we need to first add up the lengths of the sides that we do have: 5 cm + 7 cm = 12 cm. Now we subtract that sum from the total perimeter to figure out the length of the third side: 22 cm − 12 cm = 10 cm. Answer choice A is correct.

3. If the perimeter of a square is 12w, then what is the length of one side?

(A) 3
(B) 4
(C) 3w
(D) 4w

The trick to this question is to not forget the w. Since perimeter of a square is equal to 4 × *side length*, we know that we must divide the perimeter by 4 in order to get the side length. If we divide 12w by 4, we get 3w. Answer choice C is correct.

Some problems will ask you to find segment lengths before adding them together to find a perimeter. The trick to this type of question is to remember to figure out the missing side lengths instead of adding together just the side lengths given.

Here's a problem for you to try:

4. All angles in the figure below are right angles. What is the perimeter of the figure?

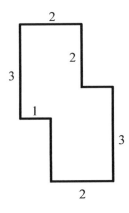

    (A) 11
    (B) 12
    (C) 13
    (D) 16

To find the perimeter of the figure, we first have to figure out some of the side lengths. From the bottom segments, we can see that the width of the figure is 1 + 2 = 3. That means that the unlabeled segment on the right has to be 1 unit long. From the right side of the figure, we can determine that the height of the figure is 3 + 2 = 5, so we can see that the unlabeled segment on the left must be 2 units long. Now we just add all of our segment lengths together to get 16, or choice D.

Area

Area is the surface that a figure takes up or the amount of space inside a figure.

On the Middle Level ISEE, you will need know how to find the area of a rectangle and the area of a triangle.

> *Area of a rectangle = length × width*
>
> *Area of a triangle = $\dfrac{1}{2}$ × base × height*

For example, let's say we have to find the area of the rectangle below:

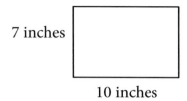

7 inches

10 inches

Area of a rectangle = length × width = 7 in. × 10 in. = 70 in.²

Notice that the units that describe area are squared.

Keep in mind that a square is also a rectangle. This means that the area of a square is also length × width. Since length and width are the same with a square, you will generally just be given one side length.

For example, let's say we need to find the area of the square below:

5

We still do length × width, we just plug in the number 5 for both the length and the width.

Area of a rectangle = length × width = 5 in. × 5 in. = 25 in.²

The area of a triangle is found by using the formula:

$$Area\ of\ a\ triangle = \frac{1}{2} \times base \times height$$

For example, let's say that you want to find the area of the following triangle:

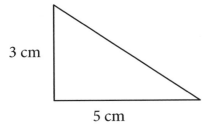

3 cm

5 cm

We just need to plug into the formula:

$$Area\ of\ a\ triangle = \frac{1}{2} \times base \times height = \frac{1}{2} \times 3\ cm \times 5\ cm = 7\frac{1}{2}\ cm^2$$

Notice that since we found an area, the units are squared.

On the Middle Level ISEE, you may see area problems that require you to divide a figure into pieces, find the area of each piece, and then add those areas together.

For example, let's say that we have to find the area of the figure below:

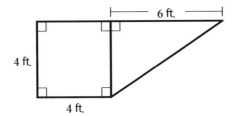

6 ft.

4 ft.

4 ft.

To find the area of the entire figure, we first have to divide it into pieces. We have a square on the left side and a triangle on the right side.

The area of the square is: $4 \times 4 = 16$ sq. ft.

The area of the triangle is: $\frac{1}{2}(4 \times 6) = 12$ sq. ft. (Note: We had to use the fact that all sides of a square are the same length in order to get the height of the triangle.)

Now we add the areas of those two regions together in order to get the area of the entire figure:

Area = 16 sq. ft. + 12 sq. ft. = 28 sq. ft.

Here are a couple of examples of questions that test this concept:

1. Hillside elementary is planning to build a new garden. The garden plan is shown below.

    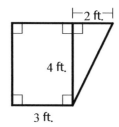

    According to the garden plan, what is the area of the garden?

    (A) 4 sq. ft.
    (B) 10 sq. ft.
    (C) 12 sq. ft.
    (D) 16 sq. ft.

First, we have to find the area of the rectangle:

Area of a rectangle $= l \times w = 4 \times 3 = 12$ sq. ft.

Now we have to find the area of the triangle:

$$\frac{1}{2}(b \times h) = \frac{1}{2}(2 \times 4) = \frac{1}{2}(8) = 4 \text{ sq. ft.}$$

To find the total area, we just have to add the area of the rectangle and the area of the triangle:

Total area $= 4$ sq. ft.$+12$ sq. ft. $= 16$ sq. ft.

Answer choice D is the correct answer.

2. The figure below was created by combining a square with two congruent triangles.

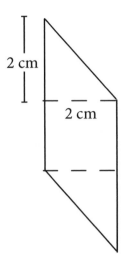

What is the total area of the figure?

(A) 2 cm²
(B) 4 cm²
(C) 8 cm²
(D) 12 cm²

The question tells us that the figure is made up of a square and two triangles. That is a good indicator that we should find the area of a square and two triangles!

Area of a square = side × side = 2 × 2 = 4 cm²

Area of one triangle = $\frac{1}{2}(b \times h) = \frac{1}{2}(2 \times 2) = \frac{1}{2}(4) = 2$ cm²

Area of two triangles = 2 × 2 cm² = 4 cm²

Total area = area of square + area of triangles = 4 + 4 = 8 cm²

Answer choice C is correct.

You may also be asked to find the area of a triangle that is not a right triangle. In order to find the area of a non-right triangle, you just need to keep in mind that the height will not be a side of the triangle.

3. Use the figure below to answer the question.

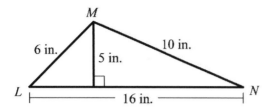

To find the area of a triangle we use the equation $A = \dfrac{1}{2}bh$, where b is the length of the base and h is the height. What is the area of triangle *LMN*?

(A) 16 sq. in.
(B) 20 sq. in.
(C) 40 sq. in.
(D) 48 sq. in.

This question is not hard – we just need to plug into the equation given. The only tricky part is that we need to recognize that the height of the triangle is not a leg of the triangle. The height is always perpendicular to the base, so the height of this triangle is 5 in.

$$A = \frac{1}{2}bh = \frac{1}{2}(16)(5) = 40 \text{ sq. in.}$$

Answer choice C is correct.

Another type of area question requires you to find the area of a portion of a figure (usually you are looking for the area of a shaded region). The trick to these questions is that you have to first find the area of the bigger figure and then subtract off smaller shapes.

- For these "shaded portion" questions, you have to find the area of a bigger figure and then subtract to find the shaded area

Here are a few examples:

4. Figure 1 below is a rectangle. Four congruent triangles are removed from the corners of Figure 1 in order to create Figure 2, as shown below.

Figure 1

Figure 2

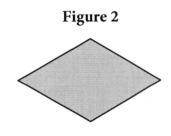

What is the area of Figure 2?

(A) 2 in²
(B) 4 in²
(C) 6 in²
(D) 8 in²

Our first step is to find the area of the bigger figure:

Area of a rectangle = l × w = 4 × 2 = 8 in²

Now we have to find the area of the triangles that are cut out:

Area of one triangle = $\frac{1}{2}$(b × h) = $\frac{1}{2}$(2 × 1) = $\frac{1}{2}$(2) = 1 in²

Area of 4 triangles = 4 × 1 in² = 4 in²

Now we subtract the triangles from the bigger figure:

Area of rectangle – Area of triangles = 8 in² – 4 in² = 4 in²

The correct answer is choice B.

5. The large square shown below has four smaller squares within it. Half of each of these squares is shaded.

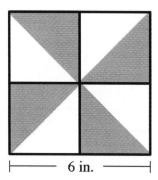

├─────── 6 in. ───────┤

What is the area of the shaded region?

(A) 18 in²
(B) 24 in²
(C) 36 in²
(D) 48 in²

First we need to find the area of the bigger square. Since each side of the bigger square is 6 in the area of the larger square is 36 in². Now, we just have to find half the area of the larger square. Even though it does not tell us that half of the square is shaded, it does tell us that half of the regions that make up the larger square are shaded. Since 36 in² ÷ 2 = 18 in² answer choice A is correct.

6. Refer to the following figure:

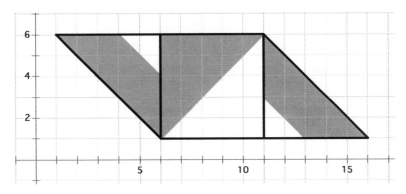

Column A

The area of the shaded
portions of the shape

Column B

The area of the unshaded
portions of the shape

Which of the following is true?

(A) The quantity in Column A is greater
(B) The quantity in Column B is greater
(C) The two quantities are equal
(D) Not enough information given to determine which quantity is greater

This a great question to use estimation. If we look at the center square, the shaded and unshaded portions are equal. However, if we look at the side triangles, we can clearly see that the shaded portion is much greater than the unshaded portion. Answer choice A is correct

Some questions may give you an area and ask you which dimensions would create that area. For these questions, you just have to try out the answer choices and see what works since there are multiple pairs of dimensions that give the same area.

- If the question gives you an area and asks for dimensions, just try out the answer choices

Here is an example of this type of question:

7. A rectangle has an area of 42 cm². What could be the dimensions of this rectangle?

(A) 2 cm × 22 cm
(B) 3 cm × 14 cm
(C) 4 cm × 16 cm
(D) 6 cm × 8 cm

Let's go ahead and figure out the area of each answer choice!

(A) 2 cm × 22 cm = 44 cm²
(B) 3 cm × 14 cm = 42 cm²
(C) 4 cm × 16 cm = 64 cm²
(D) 6 cm × 8 cm = 48 cm²

We can see that only the dimensions given in answer choice B create a rectangle with an area of 42 cm². Answer choice B is correct.

Some other questions may ask you to find the area of a shape that is placed over a coordinate grid. To answer these questions, generally you can just count up how many squares the figure covers. You will have to use estimating if you do this since some of the squares will only be partially covered. The other way to answer these questions is to divide the figure into pieces, find the area of each piece, and then add those areas together to get the total.

- If a figure is placed over a coordinate grid you can count up how many squares are covered but remember to estimate and not count partially covered squares as full squares

Here is an example of this type of question:

8. Use the coordinate grid below to answer the question.

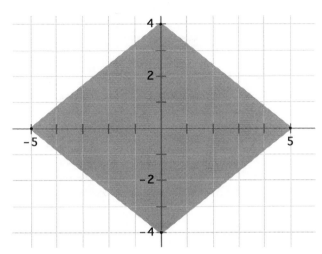

What is the area of the rhombus in the figure above?
(A) 30
(B) 35
(C) 40
(D) 45

To answer this question, we can count up how many squares are covered, estimating for squares that are not completely covered by the rhombus. Since this is a multiple-choice test, we can come close enough using this method to get the right answer. Another option, however, is to divide the figure into four smaller triangles. We can use the numbers on the axes to figure out that each triangle is 4 units high and 5 units across.

Now we can use our area formula:

$$Area\ of\ one\ triangle = \frac{1}{2}(b \times h) = \frac{1}{2}(4 \times 5) = \frac{1}{2}(20) = 10$$

$$Area\ of\ four\ triangles = 10 \times 4 = 40$$

Answer choice C is correct.

Another type of area question that you may see asks you to convert between area and perimeter.

9. The area of the square in the figure below is 36 square inches. What is the perimeter of the square?

area = 36 sq in

(A) 9 inches
(B) 12 inches
(C) 24 inches
(D) 36 inches

In a square, the area is equal to side length × side length. If the area of our square is 36 square inches, then the side length must be 6 inches. To find the perimeter, we then multiply the side length by 4: 6 × 4 = 24 inches. Answer choice C is correct.

You may also see questions that require you to use area to figure out cost.

10. Grass seed costs $16 per bag that covers 1,000 square feet of lawn. How much will it cost to buy enough seed for a lawn that is 400 feet by 75 feet?

(A) $7.60
(B) $15.20
(C) $48.00
(D) $480.00

To answer this question, we first have to find the area of the lawn. Since 400 × 75 = 30,000, we know that the area of the lawn is 30,000 sq. ft. Now we can use a proportion to solve for the total cost – the word "per" tells us to use a proportion.

$$\frac{\$16}{1{,}000 \text{ sq. ft.}} = \frac{x}{30{,}000 \text{ sq. ft.}}$$

$$\$16 \times 30{,}000 = 1{,}000x$$

$$\$480 = x$$

Answer choice D is correct.

While most of the area questions that you will see on the Middle Level ISEE ask you to find the area of rectangles/squares, you may also see questions that ask you to find the area of shapes like trapezoids and circles. If you see one of these questions, keep in mind that they will give you the formula for area with these shapes.

Here are a couple of examples:

11. The area of a trapezoid is $\frac{1}{2}(b_1 + b_2)h$.

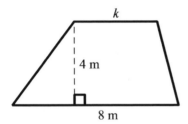

If the area of the trapezoid above is 24 square meters, what is the length of k?

(A) 4 meters
(B) 6 meters
(C) 8 meters
(D) 24 meters

To get the answer, we plug the values we know into the equation given to us. Using $b_1 = 8$, $b_2 = k$, and $h = 4$, we set up the following equation and solve:

$$area = \frac{1}{2}(b_1 + b_2)h = \frac{1}{2}(8+k) \times 4 = 2(8+k) = 16 + 2k = 24$$

$$2k = 24 - 16 = 8$$

$$k = 4$$

Answer choice A is correct.

12. In the figure below, a circle is inscribed within a square

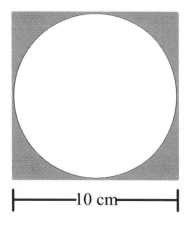

├──────10 cm──────┤

What is the area of the region that is shaded? (*area of circle = πr²*)

(A) 40 − 10π cm²
(B) 40 − 25π cm²
(C) 100 − 10π cm²
(D) 100 − 25π cm²

The area that is shaded is the difference between the area of the square and the area of the circle inscribed within the square. When a circle is inscribed within a square, its diameter is equal to the length of each side of the square. So the radius of the circle, *r*, is half the length of each side of the square, or 5. Knowing this, we can set up the following equation:

Area that is shaded = area of square − area of circle
$$= (10 \times 10) - (\pi \times 5^2) \text{ cm}^2$$
$$= 100 - 25\pi \text{ cm}^2$$

Answer choice D is correct.

Volume and surface area of rectangular solids

On the Middle Level ISEE, you will see questions that ask you about the volume of rectangular prisms. Think of a rectangular prism as being the shape of a cardboard box. A cube is just a rectangular prism that has sides that are all the same length.

- Think of a rectangular prism as being the shape of the cardboard box with the lid on
- A cube is a rectangular prism with side lengths that are all equal – picture dice

The volume of a rectangular prism (or cube) is:

volume = length × width × depth

Since a rectangular prism is a 3-D (short for three-dimensional) figure, we have to multiply all three dimensions to find the volume.

A basic question will just ask you to figure out the dimensions. It is important to remember how 3-D representations work. With a 3-D picture, you can't see all of the figure. Rectangular prism questions often ask you to divide a larger prism into smaller cubes and you have to remember that there are cubes that you cannot see.

- Remember that with a 3-D picture, we cannot see the entire figure

Here are some examples of rectangular prism questions:

1. The prism below was built by stacking one-unit cubes.

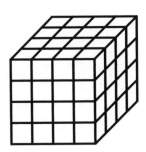

Which computation correctly shows how the volume of the larger prism could be found?

(A) $4 \times 4 \times 4 \times 2$
(B) $4 \times 4 \times 16$
(C) $4 \times 4 \times 4$
(D) $16 \times 16 \times 16$

To answer this question, we first have to figure out the dimensions. From the face of the prism, we can see that the length is 4 units and the width is also 4 units. If we count back, we can see that the depth is also 4 units (see diagram below).

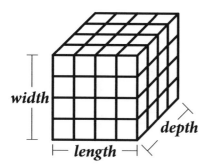

The volume of the prism would therefore be found by multiplying 4 by 4 by 4. Answer choice C is correct.

2. Use the figure below to answer the question.

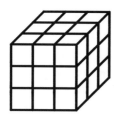

How many smaller cubes were used to build the larger cube?

(A) 9
(B) 18
(C) 27
(D) 36

This is really just a volume question event though it does not use the word "volume" at all. We can see that the front face of the larger cube has dimensions of 3 × 3. We can also see that the prism is three cubes deep. If we multiply 3 × 3 × 3, we get that there must have been 27 smaller cubes used to build the bigger cube.

The following question is a little different, but just use the same principles. If it makes it easier, you can also create your own sketch.

3. The small cube below is 1 inch on all sides. How many cubes of this size would be required to create a larger cube that is 2 inches on all sides?

(A) 2
(B) 4
(C) 8
(D) 16

One way to think of the problem is to compare the volumes of the two cubes. The volume of the small cube is $1 \times 1 \times 1 = 1$ in³. The volume of the 2-inch cube is $2 \times 2 \times 2 = 8$ in³. The larger cube has 8 times the volume of the smaller cube, so we would need 8 of the smaller cubes to create a cube that is 2 inches on each side. Answer choice C is correct.

On the Middle Level ISEE, you are more likely to see volume questions that are more challenging.

For example, you may see a question that does not ask you find volume, but rather asks you to use volume to work back to side length.

Here is an couple example:

4. The figure below has two cubes.

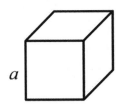

volume = 216 cu ft   volume = 27 cu ft

What is the ratio of the length of side a to the length of side b?

(A) 1:1
(B) 2:1
(C) 4:1
(D) 8:1

A cube has all sides equal, so we know that the volume of the larger cube equals $a \times a \times a$ and the volume of the smaller cube is $b \times b \times b$. We can now try plugging in different values to determine the side lengths a and b.

$2 \times 2 \times 2 = 8$
$3 \times 3 \times 3 = 27$ – side length b is 3
$4 \times 4 \times 4 = 64$
$5 \times 5 \times 5 = 125$
$6 \times 6 \times 6 = 216$ – side length a is 6

We now know that the ratio of a to b is 6:3, which can also be expressed as 2:1. Answer choice B is correct.

You may also be asked to visualize what a net would create and then find the volume of that three-dimensional shape.

Here are a couple of examples:

5. What is the volume of the cube created by cutting and folding the net below? (unit of graph is cm)

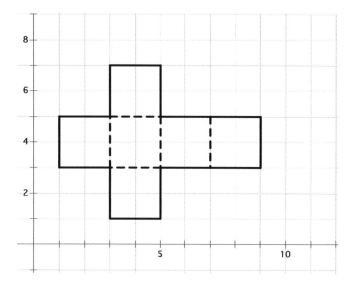

(A) 4 cm³
(B) 8 cm³
(C) 24 cm³
(D) 48 cm³

Since the question tells us that the net will form a cube when folded, we know that all sides will have equal length. We can then look at any side of the net to see that the length is 2. So the volume of the cube will be $2 \times 2 \times 2 = 8$. Answer choice B is correct.

Here is another one to try:

6. What is the volume of the rectangular prism created by cutting and folding the net below? (unit of graph is m)

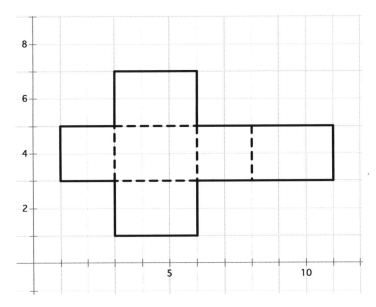

(A) $4\,\text{m}^3$
(B) $6\,\text{m}^3$
(C) $12\,\text{m}^3$
(D) $28\,\text{m}^3$

We need to use our equation for the volume of a rectangular prism in order to get the answer:

volume = length × width × depth

By examining the net, we see we can plug in $2 \times 3 \times 2 = 12\,\text{m}^3$. Answer choice C is correct.

Finally, you may see questions that ask you to use the concept of surface area.

The surface area of a rectangular solid is equal to the sum of the areas of each surface of the solid. Rectangular solids have six surfaces, as pictured in the following figure.

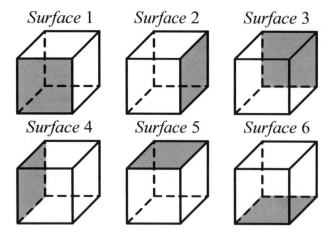

Surface 1 *Surface 2* *Surface 3*

Surface 4 *Surface 5* *Surface 6*

Here is a basic example of a question requiring you to find surface area:

7. A cube has sides that are 4 in long. What is the surface area of the cube?

(A) 16 in²
(B) 24 in²
(C) 64 in²
(D) 96 in²

Each face of the cube is 4 in by 4 in, so the area of each face is 16 in². The surface area of the cube is equal to the sum of the areas of all faces of the cube. Rectangular solids (including cubes) have 6 faces, and since we know that all faces of a cube will have the same area, we can just multiply 6 × 16 to get 96 in². Choice D is correct. Notice that the units of surface area are squared, just like the units of area.

Now let's try a harder question:

8. The surface area of a cube is 150 cm². What is the volume of the cube?

(A) 25 cm³
(B) 100 cm³
(C) 125 cm³
(D) 900 cm³

The key to figuring out this answer is to use the surface area of the cube to determine the length of a side, and then use the length of a side to determine the volume. Since we know that a cube has 6 congruent faces, we can calculate the area of each by dividing the surface area of 150 cm² by 6 to get 25 cm². Since we know that the face of a cube is a square, we know that the length of a side of this cube is $\sqrt{25}$, or 5. We can now plug the length of a side into the formula for the volume of a cube.

$$volume = length \times width \times depth = 5 \times 5 \times 5 = 125 \text{ cm}^3$$

Answer choice C is correct.

Solving for side lengths with similar triangles

In the geometry section we covered what similar triangles are. You are more likely to see questions that ask you to apply the fact that two triangles are similar rather than just identifying that they are similar.

Some questions will ask you to determine the length of the side of a triangle based on the fact that it is similar to another triangle with known dimensions. You can calculate the missing length by setting up a proportion of corresponding sides and cross-multiplying. Corresponding sides are sides that are in the same spot on two different (but similar) shapes.

The figure below shows two triangles that are similar.

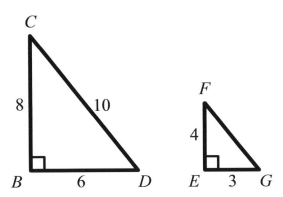

The side *BC* of the left triangle corresponds to *EF* of the triangle on the right. Similarly, *BD* corresponds to *EG* and *CD* corresponds to *FG*. Knowing the corresponding sides, we can set up the following proportion:

$$\frac{side\ 1}{side\ 2} = \frac{corresponding\ side\ 1}{corresponding\ side\ 2}$$

The proportion will work for any two sets of corresponding sides. So we will now set up the proportion for these triangles:

$$\frac{BC}{CD} = \frac{EF}{FG}$$

$$\frac{8}{10} = \frac{4}{FG}$$

Now we cross-multiply to get the answer:

$$8 \times FG = 4 \times 10$$

$$FG = 40 \div 8 = 5$$

Here is an example for you to try:

9. Triangles *HJK* and *NOP* are similar. What is the value of *y*?

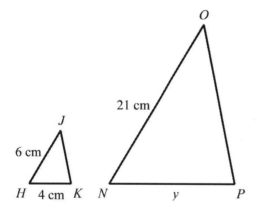

(A) 14 cm
(B) 19 cm
(C) 21 cm
(D) 32 cm

First we need to set up a proportion of the corresponding sides:

$$\frac{side\ 1}{side\ 2} = \frac{corresponding\ side\ 1}{corresponding\ side\ 2}$$

$$\frac{4}{6} = \frac{y}{21}$$

Then cross-multiply to get 6*y* = 84, or *y* = 14. Answer choice A is correct.

You may also be asked to calculate the ratio of two corresponding sides. A ratio is the relationship of one number to another. For example, if B is twice as large as A then we say the ratio of B to A is 2 to 1. If you have 5 vanilla candies and 4 chocolate, then the ratio of chocolate candies to vanilla candies is 4 to 5. If you have 4 markers and 6 pens, then the ratio of markers to pens is 4 to 6. A ratio of 4 to 6 is more commonly expressed as a ratio of 2 to 3 – you can reduce a ratio in the same manner that you can reduce a fraction, in this case by dividing both sides by 2.

Here is an example of a question that asks you to determine a ratio:

10. The triangles in the diagram below are similar.

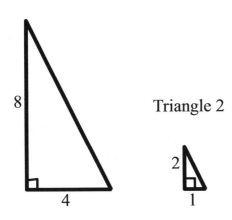

What is the ratio of a side of Triangle 1 to the corresponding side of Triangle 2?

(A) 1 to 4
(B) 2 to 1
(C) 4 to 1
(D) 8 to 1

First, make sure to identify the corresponding sides, or the sides that are in the same position on the two triangles. The side of Triangle 1 with length 8 corresponds with the side of Triangle 2 with length 2, and the side of Triangle 1 with length 4 corresponds with the side of Triangle 2 with length 1. Each set of corresponding sides will give us the same ratio, so let's choose the longer sides. Expressing the lengths as a ratio, we would say that the ratio of a side of Triangle 1 to the corresponding side of Triangle 2 is 8 to 2. This can be reduced to a ratio of 4 to 1, so answer choice C is correct.

Finally, you may be asked to perform calculations on a triangle based on a scale factor applied to another triangle. We reviewed scale factor already in the algebra section. A key point to remember is that the scale factor should be applied to length, not area. So make sure to apply the scale factor to the sides of a shape first, then calculate the area. Here is an example to try:

11. The triangles in the following figure are similar.

Triangle 1

Triangle 2

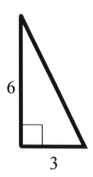

Column A

Area of a triangle similar to

Triangle 1 with a scale factor of $\frac{3}{4}$

Column B

Area of a triangle similar to

Triangle 2 with a scale factor of $\frac{4}{3}$

(A) The quantity in Column A is greater
(B) The quantity in Column B is greater
(C) The two quantities are equal
(D) Not enough information given

Column A is the area of a triangle with a scale factor of $\frac{3}{4}$ applied to a triangle with b of 4 and h of 8. We can apply the factor directly to b and h to create a triangle with b of 3 and h of 6.

Column B is the area of a triangle with a scale factor of $\frac{4}{3}$ applied to a triangle with b of 3 and h of 6. Applying the factor creates a triangle with b of 4 and h of 8.

Without even calculating the areas, we can see that Column B is the area of a larger triangle. Answer choice B is correct.

Those are the basics that you need to know for measurement questions on the Middle Level ISEE. Be sure to complete the measurement practice set to reinforce what you have learned.

Measurement practice set

1. Jim is going to build a fence around a play area, as shown in the figure below.

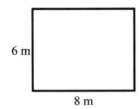

   If Jim wants the fence to go around the entire perimeter of the play area, how many meters of fence will he need to build?

   (A) 28
   (B) 48
   (C) 96
   (D) 14

2. Lincoln Junior High School is planning a community garden. Based on the figure below, what is the area of the garden?

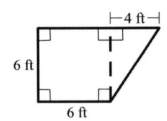

   (A) 16 ft²
   (B) 40 ft²
   (C) 48 ft²
   (D) 60 ft²

3. What is the volume of the cube that would be created by cutting out and folding the net in the figure below? (units in figure are cm)

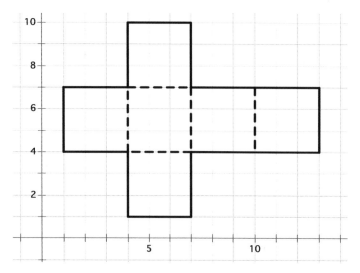

(A) 9 cm³
(B) 27 cm³
(C) 42 cm³
(D) 54 cm³

4. The two triangles in the figure below are similar.

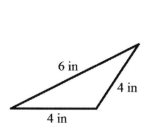 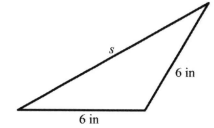

What is the value of *s*?

(A) 6 in
(B) 8 in
(C) 9 in
(D) 12 in

5. The perimeter of the triangle shown below is 17.

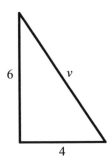

What is the value of *v*?

(A) 10
(B) 9
(C) 8
(D) 7

6. What is the area of the shaded region of the rectangle below?

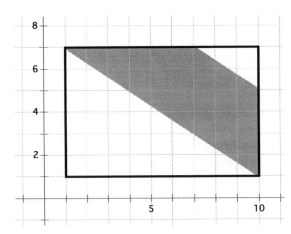

(A) 48 units²
(B) 24 units²
(C) 21 units²
(D) 3 units²

7. A rectangular prism has length, width, and depth as shown in the figure. What is the volume of the prism?

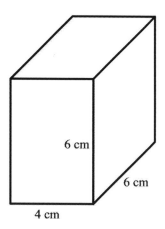

6 cm

6 cm

4 cm

(A) 24 cm³
(B) 36 cm³
(C) 60 cm³
(D) 144 cm³

8. The area of a rectangle is 56 ft². What could possibly be the dimensions of the rectangle?

(A) 20 ft by 8 ft
(B) 14 ft by 4 ft
(C) 12 ft by 16 ft
(D) 5 ft by 6 ft

9. A square has a perimeter of 44c. What is the length of one side of the square?

(A) 11c
(B) 11
(C) 4c
(D) 4

10. All angles in the following figure are right angles. What is the perimeter of the figure?

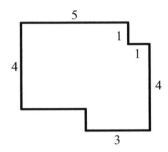

(A) 18
(B) 22
(C) 26
(D) 30

11. What is the perimeter of the square below?

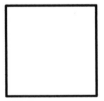

area = 64 sq m

(A) 8 m
(B) 16 m
(C) 24 m
(D) 32 m

12. The volume of the following cube is 64 cm³.

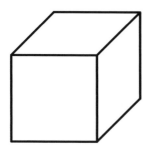

What is its surface area?

(A) 16 cm²
(B) 64 cm²
(C) 96 cm²
(D) 128 cm²

13. The triangles in the following figure are similar.

Triangle 1

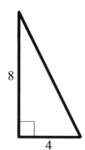

Triangle 2

Column A	Column B
Area of a triangle similar to Triangle 1 with a scale factor of 1.75	Area of a triangle similar to Triangle 2 with a scale factor of 2

(A) The quantity in Column A is greater
(B) The quantity in Column B is greater
(C) The two quantities are equal
(D) Not enough information given

14. In the figure below, a circle is inscribed within a square.

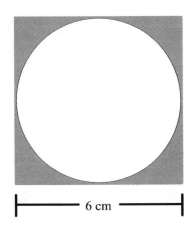

6 cm

What is the area of the region that is shaded? (*area of a circle = πr^2*)

(A) $36 - 9\pi$ cm²
(B) $36 - 6\pi$ cm²
(C) $24 - 9\pi$ cm²
(D) $24 - 6\pi$ cm²

Answers to Measurement Practice Set

1. A
2. C
3. B
4. C
5. D
6. B
7. D
8. B
9. A
10. B
11. D
12. C
13. A
14. A

Probability and Data Analysis

Some of the most challenging math problems on the Middle Level ISEE are the questions involving the interpretation of data and figuring out probabilities. The good news is that the concepts themselves are relatively straightforward. You just may not have learned all of them yet in school.

The question types we will cover here include:

- Different types of graphs
- Central tendencies in data
- Basic probability
- Probability with multiple events
- Complementary events
- Outcome tables

We will start with going over the different types of graphs that you will see on the Middle Level ISEE. You won't be asked to identify the type of a graph, but you will be asked to interpret data in various formats.

Different types of graphs

The following are the types of graphs you need to know for the Middle Level ISEE:

- Bar graph
- Histogram
- Stem and leaf plot
- Line graph
- Scatter plot
- Circle graph

Bar graph

A bar graph is great way to compare data. It allows you to easily see data taken at different times.

One important detail that you always want to look at is the scale on the left side. You may need to figure out a data value that doesn't fall exactly on a line, so you will need to know the scale in order to figure out the data value.

- Always check the scale on a bar graph before answering any questions about it

Sometimes it is also hard to tell exactly where a bar falls if it is far away from the numbers on the y-axis. If you are finding this difficult, use the side of your answer sheet to trace across a straight line to the axis.

- If you are having trouble figuring out how a bar corresponds to the numbers on the y-axis, use the side of your answer sheet to trace across

Here is an example of how you might see bar graphs on the ISEE:

1. The graph below shows how many cars a dealership sold in each month last year.

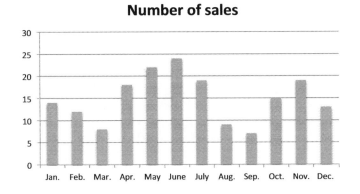

Number of sales

According to the graph, how many more cars were sold in June than in January?

(A) 2
(B) 5
(C) 10
(D) 14

The important thing to keep in mind here is the scale. The scale shows us that each line delineates 5 cars sold. The graph shows that in January, just under 15 cars were sold. In June, just under 25 cars were sold. That makes the difference around 10 cars, so answer choice C is correct.

Histogram

A histogram looks kind of like a bar graph. The difference is that a bar graph is generally used when data fits into neat categories. A histogram shows you how data is clustered, or distributed, instead. It groups numbers into ranges.

- Bar graphs are used when data is in clear categories
- Histograms group data into ranges

Here is an example of how you could see histograms on the ISEE:

2. A student took a survey of the ages of the residents on her street. The ranges of ages of the residents on her street are shown in the histogram below.

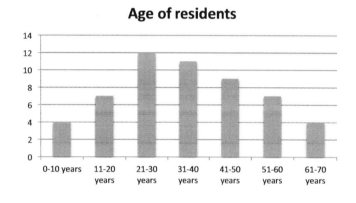

Age of residents

Which of the following age groups has the greatest number of residents?

(A) 0-20 years old
(B) 21-30 years old
(C) 31-50 years old
(D) 51-70 years old

In order to solve this question, we have to not jump on the obvious answer. Since the biggest bar on the histogram is for the age range 21-30 years old, it would be tempting to choose B. However, the other answer choices require you to combine more than one range from the histogram. For answer choice A, you have to add 4 residents in the range 0-10 years old and 7 residents in the range 11-20 years old, to get a total of 11 residents in the range of 0-20 years old. For answer choice B, there are 12 residents in the range of 21-30 years old. For answer choice C, you have to add 11 and 9 to get 20 residents in the range of 31-50 years old. For answer choice D, you have to add 7 and 4 to get that there are 11 residents in the range of 51-70 years old. Therefore, answer choice C is correct.

3. The 8th grade science classes were assigned to observe as many different types of insects as possible over a two-week period. The results for all of the students were compiled into the following histogram.

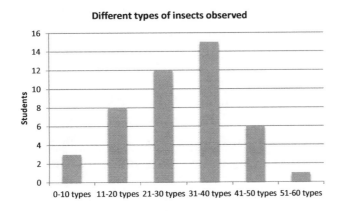

How many students could have observed exactly 45 types of insects?

(A) 4
(B) 8
(C) 15
(D) 45

The graph doesn't tell us the specific number of insects each student observed, but it does tell us that 6 students saw somewhere between 41 and 50 types of insects. Answer choice A is possible. For example, 4 students could have observed 45 types of insects while 2 other students observed 47. However, it is not possible that 8, 15, or 45 students observed 45 types of insects, so answer choice A is correct.

Stem and leaf plot

Stem and leaf plots are also used to illustrate frequency, or how often a number shows up, as well as how the data clusters. The advantage of a stem and leaf plot is that it is super easy to show where numbers cluster without a lot of work. They function a lot like histograms, but are just easier to compose. On this test, however, you don't need to compose any graphs, you just need to able to read them!

A stem and leaf plot is created by grouping numbers by their first digits.

Here is an example:

Let's say that we want to create a stem and leaf plot for the numbers 2, 2, 3, 5, 7, 9, 10, 10, 13, 14, 14, 14, 16, 16, 17, 19, 20, 21, 22, 22, 24, 25

Here is what the stem and leaf plot would look like:

0	2	2	3	5	7	9			
1	0	0	3	4	4	4	6	6	7	9
2	0	1	2	2	4	5			

From this stem and leaf plot, we can see that there are six numbers that fall between 0 and 9, there are ten numbers that fall between 10 and 19, and there are six numbers that are between 20 and 29. We can also see that the number that shows up most often is 14.

With a stem and leaf plot, each data point gets its own input, even if it repeats another input. For example, 14 shows up three times in the original data set, so it shows up three times in the stem and leaf plot.

Here is an example of a question that tests stem and leaf plots:

4. A local farmer surveyed his neighbors and asked them how many animals they had on their farms. The stem and leaf plot below reflects the results of the farmer's survey.

0	3	3	5	5	6	6	7	7	8					
1	0	0	0	2	2	3	3	3	4	4	5	7	7	8
2	0	1	1	2	5	7								

How many neighbors did the farmer survey?

(A) 3
(B) 15
(C) 29
(D) 32

In order to solve this question, you need to count up how many numbers there are on the right side of the bar. The trick here is not to count the numbers are on the left side of the bar because these are not separate numbers, but rather they are the first digit of the numbers on the right side of the bar. Answer choice C is correct.

Line graph

The next type of graph is a line graph. A line graph is best used for data where one variable affects the other.

- With a line graph one variable usually affects the other variable

For example, as time increases, the height of a plant often increases, so a line graph would be appropriate.

With a line graph, the slope tells you how one variable affects the other.

For example, here is a graph that shows a positive relationship, such as with hours worked and wages earned.

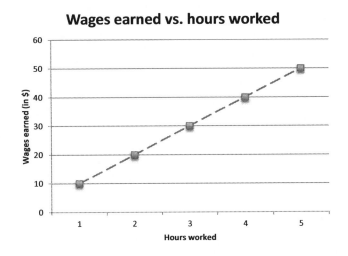

Sometimes there is a negative relationship, such as the value of a car declining the longer that it is owned, as shown below.

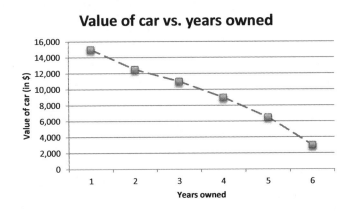

Keep in mind that the relationship can change from positive to negative, or even flatten out. For example, a child may grow continually up until age 18, so the graph would have a positive relationship. Then height might remain constant (or flat) for decades. The trick is to really take a close look at the axes and what they really mean.

- Take a close look at the axes and think about what the relationship between the axes is

Here is an example of how a line graph could be tested on the ISEE:

5. The following graph shows the distance of four different cars from the repair shop.

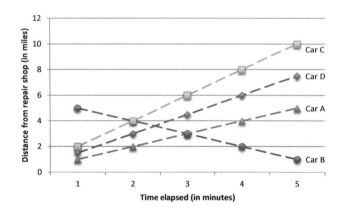

Which car is driving toward the repair shop at the greatest speed?

(A) Car A
(B) Car B
(C) Car C
(D) Car D

This is a bit of a trick question. Only one car is actually driving toward the repair shop. The distance from the repair shop is actually decreasing for Car B, so that means that Car B is getting closer to the shop. Choice B is correct.

Scatter plot

The next type of graph that we are going to cover is a scatter plot. A scatter plot simply gives you data points and you have to look for the trends.

For example, the following scatter plot gives the age of the cars sold at one dealership in a day and the amount of money that they sold for.

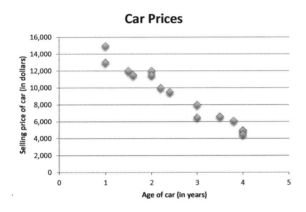

Many scatter plot questions on the ISEE ask you to use the line of best fit.

The **line of best fit** is simply a line that you draw in that goes through your data points to figure out a trend. A line of best fit is far from an exact science. You want to draw the line so that you have about the same number of points above the line as below the line.

An **outlier** is a point that is pretty far separated from the other points. Generally, we don't worry too much about taking outliers into consideration when we are drawing a line of best fit.

If we were to add a line of best fit to the above scatter plot, it would look something like this:

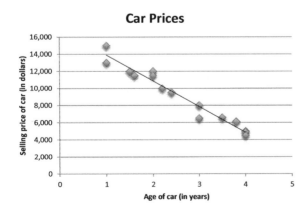

Notice that the line does not go through every single point, but rather that it captures kind of an average of all the points.

Here is an example of a question on the ISEE that uses a line of best fit:

6. The graph below shows the relationship between the cost of a single book and the number of books sold.

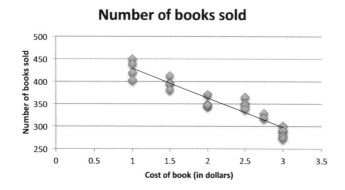

Number of books sold

Using the line of best fit, what is the average number of books sold if a book costs $1.50?

(A) 370
(B) 395
(C) 410
(D) 435

The graph provides a line of best fit for us, so we use that line to figure out average sales. If we trace up from 1.50 on the *x*-axis, we can see that the line of best fit is just below the 400 line when *x* is equal to 1.5. Only answer choice B is just below 400, so that is the correct answer.

Some problems require you to draw in your own line of best fit. You can use the side of your answer sheet to get a roughly straight line. Aim to have as many points above the line as below the line and try to run halfway in between two points if possible. Remember, this is not an exact science!

- If you have to draw in your own line of best fit, do your best and use the side of your answer sheet to approximate a straight line

Here is an example of a question that requires you to come up with your own line of best fit:

7. According to the scatter plot, what would it cost to buy a lot that is 1.1 acres?

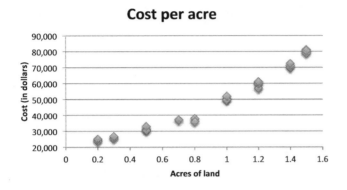

Cost per acre

(A) $45,000
(B) $50,000
(C) $55,000
(D) $70,000

We can see from the scatter plot that 1.0 acres costs about $50,000 and that 1.2 acres costs about $60,000. Since 1.1 is halfway in between 1.0 and 1.2, we would expect the cost of 1.1 acres to be halfway in between $50,000 and $60,000, so choice C is correct.

Circle graph

The next type of graph that we will talk about is a circle graph. Circle graphs give us a visual representation of how different sets of data compare to each other in terms of the entire set of data. Circle graphs show us what percent of the data fits certain categories. In other words, circle graphs give us a representation of the fractional breakdown of data (a percent is really just a fancy fraction).

- Circle graphs show us what percent (or fraction) of the total data different categories represent

Here is an example of how circle graphs are tested on the ISEE:

8. Clark conducted a survey of his classmates to find out how many of his classmates preferred chocolate ice cream, how many preferred vanilla ice cream, and how many preferred strawberry ice cream. The results are shown in the circle graph below.

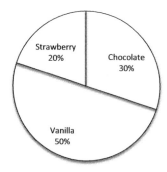

Which data could correspond to this circle graph?

(A) 15 chocolate lovers, 10 strawberry lovers, and 25 vanilla lovers
(B) 15 chocolate lovers, 15 strawberry lovers, and 30 vanilla lovers
(C) 15 chocolate lovers, 10 vanilla lovers, and 5 strawberry lovers
(D) 15 chocolate lovers, 30 vanilla lovers, and 10 strawberry lovers

The first thing that we should note is that all the answer choices begin with 15 chocolate lovers. If we look at the graph, we can see that 30% is equal to 15.

We can then set up proportions to solve for the other numbers:

$$\frac{15 \text{ chocolate lovers}}{30\%} = \frac{v \text{ vanilla lovers}}{50\%}$$

Now we can cross-multiply to solve:

$$15 \times 50 = 30 \times v$$
$$750 = 30v$$
$$\div 30 \quad \div 30$$
$$25 = v$$

This tells us that if there were 15 chocolate lovers, then there must have been 25 vanilla lovers. Only answer choice A has this combination, so it is correct.

Central tendencies in data

Central tendencies are different ways for us to interpret data and make meaning from it.

The central tendencies that you need to know are:

- Mean
- Median
- Mode
- Range

Mean

Mean tells us the average of data. To find the mean, we add up all of the data points and then divide by the number of data points.

- To find the mean, add up all of the data points and then divide by the number of data points (i.e., find the average)

This is the basic equation to find mean (or average):

$$\text{mean} = \frac{\text{sum of numbers}}{\text{number of numbers}}$$

Here is an example of a very basic mean question:

1. The average of 4, 6, 8, and 10 is

   (A) 6
   (B) 7
   (C) 8
   (D) 9

To find the answer, we simply plug into our basic equation.

$$\text{average} = \frac{\text{sum of numbers}}{\text{number of numbers}} = \frac{4 + 6 + 8 + 10}{4} = \frac{28}{4} = 7$$

Answer choice B is correct.

More likely, you will see questions that ask you to use the basic equation more than once in order to solve. You will often have to use the mean to solve for the sum and then do additional steps.

Here is an example of this type of question:

2. A set of 6 numbers has a mean of 10. One of the six numbers is 5. If this number is removed, what is the new mean?

   (A) 6
   (B) 9
   (C) 10
   (D) 11

In order to find the answer, we first have to use the mean to find the total sum of the numbers.

$$\frac{\text{sum of six numbers}}{6} = 10$$
$$\text{sum of six numbers} = 10 \times 6 = 60$$

Now we know that the number 5 has been removed. That means that our new sum will be 5 less, or 55. The number of numbers that we now have has also been reduced to 5.

$$\text{new average} = \frac{55}{5} = 11$$

Answer choice D is correct.

Here is one more for you to try:

3. A set of 5 numbers has a mean of 6. What number must be added to this set in order to create a new set that has a mean that is 2 less than the original mean?

   (A) −10
   (B) −6
   (C) −4
   (D) 4

Our first step here is to find the sum of the original set of numbers. We can use the mean and number of numbers to do that.

$$\frac{\text{sum of original set}}{5} = 6$$

sum of original set $= 30$

Now we have to use the information that we have for the second set. We know that the mean has been decreased by 2, so that the new mean is 4. We also know that there is one more number and we therefore now have 6 numbers. We can use this information to figure out the sum of the new set of the numbers.

$$\frac{\text{sum of new set}}{6} = 4$$

sum of new set $= 24$

We can see that the sum of the original set was reduced by 6 to get the sum of the new set. That means that −6 must have been added, so answer choice B is correct.

Here is an example of a question that asks you to apply the concept of mean using a graph:

4. The graph below shows the number of flights delayed at Airport X over a six-month period last year.

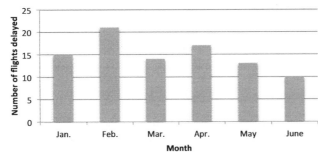

According the graph, what was the mean number of flights delayed per month?

(A) 14
(B) 15
(C) 16
(D) 17

If we add up all the delayed flights over the six-month period, we find that 90 flights were delayed. We then divide this by the number of months to get the mean monthly number of flights delayed. Since 90 divided by 6 is 15, answer choice B is correct.

Median

Median is the number that is right in the middle when you line up the data from least to greatest.

- To find the median, put the data in order from least to greatest and then find the middle number
- If there is an even number of numbers, take the average of the two middle numbers in order to find the median

Here is an example of a question that tests median:

5. The students in Mr. Zim's class made a graph of the snowfall reported by local ski areas in the month of January.

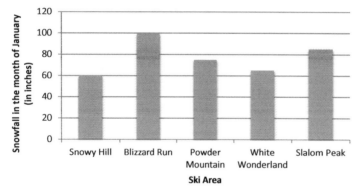

Snowfall in the month of January

What was the median snowfall in the month of January at these five ski areas?

(A) 60
(B) 65
(C) 75
(D) 80

First, we have to list out the snowfall at each area: 60, 100, 75, 65, and 85. Remember to use the edge of a piece of paper as a straightedge if there are not lines provided. Also, you may have to estimate a little, but remember that this is a multiple-choice test. Now we have to list those numbers in order from least to greatest: 60, 65, 75, 85, 100. From this we can see that the middle number is 75, so answer choice C is correct.

Mode

The mode of a data set is the number that shows up most often. Not every set of data has a mode.

- Mode is the number that shows up most often in a data set
- Not every set of data has a mode

Here is an example of how mode could be tested on the ISEE:

6. Mrs. Taylor made a stem and leaf plot of the grades that her class received on the last test.

6	2	5	6					
7	5	6						
8	3	3	3	5	6	6	7	9
9	0	0	2	4	5	6	6	8	9

What is the mode of the test scores in her class?

(A) 6
(B) 83
(C) 90
(D) 96

To answer this question, we have to remember to combine the first digit (on the left of the bar) with the numbers on the right to form a complete data point. (Remember that the number on the left is the tens digit and the number on the right is the units digit). That means that our data points are really: 62, 65, 66, 75, 76, 83, 83, 83, 85, 86, 86, 87, 89, 90, 90, 92, 94, 95, 96, 96, 98, and 99. From this, we can see that 83 shows up more often than any other number, so this is our mode. Answer choice B is correct.

Range

Range tells us the difference between the highest and the lowest points on the graph. Sometimes the questions will use the word "range" and sometimes they will just ask for the difference between the highest and lowest points on the graph.

- To find range, subtract the lowest number from the highest number

Here is an example of a question that tests range, even though it doesn't use the word "range" at all:

7. Mr. McGarry's class recorded the average rainfall for every month in the school year. Their results are shown in the graph below.

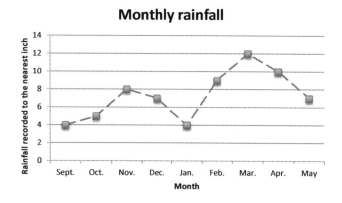

What was the difference between the highest and lowest amounts of rainfall recorded in a month?

(A) 4 inches
(B) 6 inches
(C) 8 inches
(D) 10 inches

To answer this question, we first have to figure out what the highest and lowest amounts of rain recorded were. From the graph, we can see that the lowest amount recorded was 4 inches. The highest recorded rainfall in a month was 12 inches. To find the difference, we simply subtract 4 from 12 and get a difference of 8. Answer choice C is correct.

The following question gives us the range and requires that we use the range to determine the answer:

8. The Tigers won an average of 11 games per season over a period of 10 seasons. If the team's greatest number of wins in a season was 17 and the range over the period was 13, what was the lowest number of wins in a season for the Tigers during the period?

(A) 2
(B) 4
(C) 6
(D) 10

This question gives us the highest value and the range, and asks us to figure out the lowest value. The highest value is 17 wins, and the range is 13. To find the lowest value, we subtract 13 from 17 to get 4. Answer choice B is correct.

The following question also requires using the range to determine the answer:

9. Terry answered a total of 80 questions correctly on a series of 5 quizzes. If 19 was the largest number he answered correctly on a quiz and the range of his scores was 8, which could NOT have been one of his scores?

   (A) 8
   (B) 11
   (C) 14
   (D) 17

This question gives us the highest value and the range, which we can use to figure out the lowest value. Subtracting the range of 8 from the highest value of 19 gives us the lowest value of 11. Answer choice A is less than the minimum score, so this could not have been one of his scores. Answer choice A is correct.

Basic probability

Probability tells us the likelihood of a certain event occurring.

$$\text{Probability} = \frac{\text{desired outcome}}{\text{total number of outcomes}}$$

For example, let's say that we have a bowl with three red candies and four blue candies. Let's say we want to know that probability of choosing a red candy.

$$\text{Probability of choosing red candy} = \frac{\text{desired outcome}}{\text{total number of outcomes}} = \frac{3}{7}$$

Our desired candy is red and there are 3 red candies in the bowl, so that is the top number in our probability. There are a total of 7 candies in the bowl, so that is our bottom number. The key is that you have to add together all the outcomes (including the desired outcome) to get the total number of outcomes.

Here is what basic probability problems look like on the ISEE:

1. There are 6 red cards, 5 green cards, and 8 blue cards in a pile. If a card is drawn at random, what is the probability that the card will be red?

    (A) $\dfrac{6}{13}$

    (B) $\dfrac{6}{19}$

    (C) $\dfrac{5}{13}$

    (D) $\dfrac{8}{19}$

If we add up the total number of cards, we get that there are a total of 19 cards. Of those cards, 6 are the desired outcome (or red). That means that the probability of drawing a red card is $\dfrac{6}{19}$, so answer choice B is correct.

Here is what a basic probability question could look like in the quantitative comparison section:

2. There are 4 red marbles, 4 green marbles, and 8 black marbles in a bag. A marble is to be chosen at random.

Column A	**Column B**
The probability that the marble drawn will be black	The probability that the marble drawn will not be black

(A) The quantity in Column A is greater
(B) The quantity in Column B is greater
(C) The two quantities are equal
(D) The relationship cannot be determined from the information given

Again, we start by adding up the total number of outcomes, which in this case is 16 marbles. Since there are 8 black marbles, or half of the total, the probability of drawing a black marble is equal to the probability of drawing something other than a black marble. This means that answer choice C is correct.

On the ISEE, the test writers love to use a spinner to illustrate probability. Here is what a basic type of this question looks like on the ISEE:

3.   A spinner is divided into 7 equal pieces. When it is spun, what is the probability that it will land on an even number?

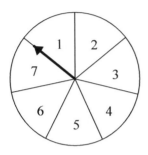

(A) $\dfrac{3}{7}$

(B) $\dfrac{3}{4}$

(C) $\dfrac{4}{7}$

(D) $\dfrac{4}{3}$

In this problem, there are 7 total outcomes (the spinner landing on each of the numbers 1-7), with 3 of those being the desired outcome (the spinner landing on 2, 4, or 6.) So the probability of the spinner landing on an even number is $\dfrac{3}{7}$, and answer choice A is correct.

Probability questions with multiple events

Another type of question that shows up on the ISEE is probability questions where first one thing has to happen, and then an unrelated second event must occur (there are also probability questions where the two events ARE related, but these will not show up on the Middle Level ISEE).

Sometimes, the easiest way to solve these problems is to list out the possible outcomes in a systematic way.

Here is an example where it is easiest just to list out the possible outcomes:

1. In a game, players must draw one numbered marble from each of two separate bags. In one bag, the marbles are numbered 1-3. In the other bag, the marbles are numbered 1-4. The numbers on the two marbles drawn are then added together.

Column A	**Column B**
The probability that the numbers on the marbles will add up to 3	The probability that the numbers will add up to 4

(A) The quantity in Column A is greater
(B) The quantity in Column B is greater
(C) The two quantities are equal
(D) The relationship cannot be determined from information given

Let's go ahead and list out the outcomes. We want to be sure to do it in a systematic way, so first we will list all the outcomes if we drew a 1 to begin with. Then we will list the outcomes if we drew a 2 first, and then we will list the outcomes if we drew a 3 first.

It would look something like this:

$$1+1=2$$
$$1+2=3$$
$$1+3=4$$
$$1+4=5$$
$$2+1=3$$
$$2+2=4$$
$$2+3=5$$
$$2+4=6$$
$$3+1=4$$
$$3+2=5$$
$$3+3=6$$
$$3+4=7$$

From this chart, we can see that the outcome of getting a sum of 3 shows up twice in our list of possible outcomes. We can also see that the outcome of getting a sum of 4 shows up 3 times. That tells us that the probability that the numbers will add up to 4 is greater than the probability that the numbers will add up to 3. This means that answer choice B is correct.

Sometimes you can just use a simple formula to solve for the probability of multiple events occurring. This formula is:

probability of event 1 occurring × probability of event 2 occurring
= probability of both events occurring

Here is an example of a question that uses this equation:

2. Sharon is using a random number generator. She has set her computer to randomly pick a number between 1 and 9. If she uses the random number generator twice to pick a number, what is the probability that both numbers will be odd?

(A) $\dfrac{1}{9}$

(B) $\dfrac{25}{81}$

(C) $\dfrac{4}{9}$

(D) $\dfrac{5}{9}$

We have two independent events occurring here. First the computer must choose an odd number. Since there are nine numbers, and five of them are odd, the probability of the first event occurring is $\dfrac{5}{9}$. Since the second event is the same as the first, the probability of the second event occurring is also $\dfrac{5}{9}$. Now, to get the probability of BOTH events occurring, we must multiply the two together.

$$\frac{5}{9} \times \frac{5}{9} = \frac{25}{81}$$

Answer choice B is correct.

Here is another problem that uses the same concept of multiplying together probabilities, only in this case there are three events occurring:

3. Kara has one red, one blue, one green, one yellow, and one brown shirt in her suitcase. She has one pair of red pants, one pair of blue pants, and one pair of tan pants in her suitcase as well. She also has one pair of red shoes and one pair of white shoes. If she randomly selects a shirt, a pair of pants, and a pair of shoes from her suitcase, what is the probability that they will all be red?

(A) $\dfrac{1}{30}$

(B) $\dfrac{3}{30}$

(C) $\dfrac{1}{6}$

(D) $\dfrac{1}{3}$

In order to answer this question, we have to first figure out the probability of each individual event occurring. Since she has 5 shirts in her suitcase, the probability of choosing the red shirt is $\dfrac{1}{5}$. Since she has three pairs of pants in her suitcase, the probability of choosing the red pants is $\dfrac{1}{3}$. Since she has only two pairs of shoes, the probability of choosing red shoes is $\dfrac{1}{2}$. To find the probability of all three events occurring, we simply multiply them together:

$$\frac{1}{5} \times \frac{1}{3} \times \frac{1}{2} = \frac{1}{30}$$

Answer choice A is correct.

If we make a table of outcomes and then highlight the outcomes that work, it is called outcome table.

- **Outcome table** lists ALL the possible outcomes in a systematic way and then highlights only the desired outcomes

Here is an example of a question that asks you to use an outcome table:

4. A bag has a red marble, a purple marble, and a yellow marble. A spinner has five equally sized sections that are numbered 1 through 5. Shane wants to use an outcome table to figure out the probability of choosing a purple marble and then spinning a number that is a multiple of 2. Which of the following tables is shaded to help Shane find the answer?

(A)

Red 1	Red 2	Red 3	Red 4	Red 5
Purple 1	Purple 2	Purple 3	Purple 4	Purple 5
Yellow 1	Yellow 2	Yellow 3	Yellow 4	Yellow 5

(B)

Red 1	Red 2	Red 3	Red 4	Red 5
Purple 1	Purple 2	Purple 3	Purple 4	Purple 5
Yellow 1	Yellow 2	Yellow 3	Yellow 4	Yellow 5

(C)

Red 1	Red 2	Red 3	Red 4	Red 5
Purple 1	Purple 2	Purple 3	Purple 4	Purple 5
Yellow 1	Yellow 2	Yellow 3	Yellow 4	Yellow 5

(D)

Red 1	Red 2	Red 3	Red 4	Red 5
Purple 1	Purple 2	Purple 3	Purple 4	Purple 5
Yellow 1	Yellow 2	Yellow 3	Yellow 4	Yellow 5

The tricky part of this question is just figuring out what the table means! In the first box, we see written "Red 1". That means that a red marble was chosen and then the spinner landed on a 1. If we further examine, we can see that the first line of the table lists out all the possible outcomes if a red marble is drawn first. The outcomes are listed in order so that none are missed. The second row of the table lists out the outcomes if a purple marble is drawn first and the third line of the table lists out the possible outcomes if a yellow marble is drawn first. We know that we are looking for a table that has only purple shaded, so we can rule out choice A. We are also looking only for shaded boxes that have a multiple of 2 for the number portion. Of the numbers 1 through 5, only 2 and 4 are multiples. So we are looking for the answer choice that has only Purple 2 and Purple 4 shaded. This means that answer choice C is correct.

Complementary events

Complementary events are events that occur if and only if the other event does not. Events are also said to be complementary if the probabilities of each event add up to one.

Here are some examples of complementary events:

- If you have a spinner labeled 1 through 6, landing on a number greater than or equal to 4 is complementary to landing on a number less than 4 because they can't happen at the same time and their probabilities add to 1.
- If you roll a die, landing on an even number is complementary to landing on an odd number because they can't both happen at once and the probabilities of these two events add to 1.
- If you have a bag of pink, brown, and violet marbles, choosing a pink marble and then choosing either a brown or a violet marble are complementary events because their probabilities add to 1 (assume that the pink marble is replaced after it is drawn.)

Here are some events that are NOT complementary:

- If you have a spinner labeled 1 through 6, spinning a factor of 6 and then spinning a factor of 2 are not complementary. The probabilities of these 2 events do add to 1, but there is overlap (1 and 2 are factors of both 6 and 2), so they can't be complementary.
- If you roll a die, landing on a 4 is not a complementary event to landing on a 2. The probabilities of these two events don't add to 1.
- If you have a bag of pink, brown, and violet marbles, choosing a pink marble and then a brown marble are not complementary events because the probabilities of these two events do not add to 1.

The following two questions demonstrate how complementary events could be tested on the ISEE:

1. Cheryl has a spinner with equally sized sections labeled 1-3. She is going to spin twice. Which of the following describes complementary events?

    (A) The spinner first stops on 1 and then on 2.
    (B) The spinner first stops on 2 and then on 2.
    (C) The spinner first stops on 3 and then on 2 or 3.
    (D) The spinner first stops on 2 and then on 1 or 3.

Answer choices A and B describe events with probabilities that don't add to 1. Choice C describes events with probabilities that do add to 1, but they are not complementary because of overlap. Choice D also describes events with probabilities that add to 1, and there is no overlap. Choice D is correct.

2. Jake has 4 blue socks and 6 gray socks in a laundry bag. Which of the following describes complementary events? Assume that Jake replaces a sock after choosing it.

(A) Jake chooses a blue sock, and then another blue sock
(B) Jake chooses a gray sock, and then another gray sock
(C) Jake chooses a blue sock, and then a gray sock
(D) Jake chooses a gray sock

Answer choices A, B, and D describe events with probabilities that don't add to 1. Choice C describes events with probabilities that do add to 1, so it is the correct answer.

Be sure to complete the data and probability practice set to reinforce what you have learned.

Data and probability practice set

1. There are 5 green shirts, 7 blue shirts, and 4 white shirts in a drawer. If a shirt is selected at random, what is the probability that it will be green?

   (A) $\dfrac{5}{11}$

   (B) $\dfrac{5}{16}$

   (C) $\dfrac{5}{7}$

   (D) $\dfrac{7}{16}$

2. Maria records the low overnight temperature over a period of 8 nights and creates the bar graph below with her measurements.

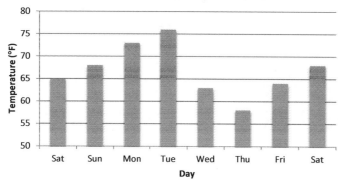

Daily Low Temperature (°F)

   What was the difference in degrees between the highest and lowest overnight low temperatures during the period?

   (A) 58
   (B) 76
   (C) 13
   (D) 18

3. A die is rolled that is numbered 1 through 6.

Column A	Column B
The probability of that the die will land with a factor of 5 on the side facing up	The probability that the die will land with a factor of 4 on the side facing up

(A) The quantity in Column A is greater
(B) The quantity in Column B is greater
(C) The two quantities are equal
(D) The relationship cannot be determined from the information given

4. Each of the seventh grade students kept track of how much mail their households received over the course of the week. The students then created the following histogram with the data.

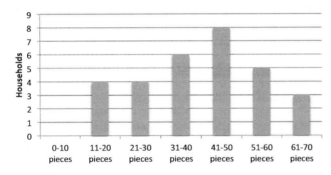

Pieces of mail received in 1 week

Which of the following could NOT be the median for the number of pieces of mail received for the week?

(A) 40
(B) 42
(C) 44.5
(D) 49.5

5. Cameron spins Spinner 1 and Spinner 2 (both of which have equally-sized sections). He then adds the results together.

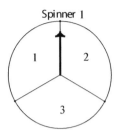

Spinner 1

Spinner 2

Column A	Column B
The probability that the sum will be greater than 4	The probability that the sum will be less than or equal to 4

(A) The quantity in Column A is greater.
(B) The quantity in Column B is greater
(C) The two quantities are equal.
(D) The relationship cannot be determined from the information given.

6. The Tigers created the following stem and leaf plot of the number of points they scored in each football game over the last two seasons.

0	3	6	7	7					
1	0	3	3	4	7	9			
2	0	1	1	4	7	8	8		
3	1	1	1	1	4	4	5	5	8

What is the mode of their data?

(A) 1
(B) 7
(C) 12.5
(D) 31

7. A spinner is divided into six equal parts.

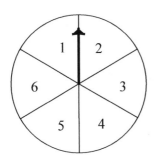

Column A	Column B
The probability that the spinner will land on an even number	The probability that the spinner will land on a number less than 4

(A) The quantity in Column A is greater.
(B) The quantity in Column B is greater
(C) The two quantities are equal.
(D) The relationship cannot be determined from the information given.

8. Joy kept track of the number of sunny days in each of the first 8 months of the year. She created the following line graph with her data.

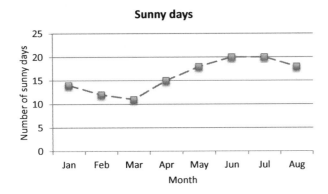

What is the average number of sunny days per month?

(A) 16
(B) 18
(C) 20
(D) 9

9. In a bag there are 5 red marbles, 3 green marbles, and 4 blue marbles. One marble is drawn and then replaced. Then a second marble is drawn. What is the probability that both of these marbles are red?

(A) $\dfrac{25}{144}$

(B) $\dfrac{5}{12}$

(C) $\dfrac{55}{144}$

(D) $\dfrac{10}{12}$

10. A seafood market kept track of the daily number of lobsters sold based on the price of the lobster that day and produced the scatter plot below.

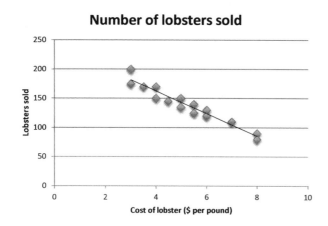

Number of lobsters sold

Today's price is $7.50 per pound. About how many lobsters are expected to be sold at the market today?

(A) 70

(B) 95

(C) 125

(D) 150

11. A library display has four novels, five non-fiction books, and six poetry books. The display contains the novel that is checked out the most often, the non-fiction book that is checked out most often, and poetry book that is checked out most often. If a student is to randomly choose a novel, a non-fiction book, and a poetry book, what is the probability that all three books that they choose will be the book that is checked out most often in that genre?

(A) $\dfrac{1}{120}$

(B) $\dfrac{1}{15}$

(C) $\dfrac{3}{120}$

(D) $\dfrac{3}{15}$

12. The 300 students at Washington Middle School were asked to name their favorite kind of cookie. The circle graph below shows the results.

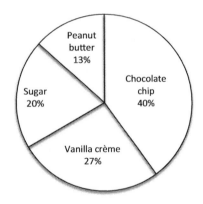

How many students said that their favorite kind of cookie is chocolate chip?

(A) 40
(B) 100
(C) 120
(D) 300

13. A bag contains four marbles. One is red, one is green, and two are blue. A marble is randomly chosen, then replaced in the bag, and then another marble is randomly chosen. Which of the following scenarios best describes complementary events?

(A) The first marble is red and the second marble is green.
(B) Both of the marbles drawn are blue.
(C) The first marble is blue and the second marble is green or blue.
(D) The first marble is green and the second marble is blue or red.

14. A class used to have 10 girls with an average height of 60 inches. A girl has since joined the class, and the average height is now 59 inches. What is the height of the girl who recently joined the class?

(A) 27 inches
(B) 49 inches
(C) 59 inches
(D) 65 inches

15. Karen has one red ribbon, one blue ribbon, and one green ribbon. She also has a box of six chips that are labeled 1 through 6. She is randomly going to select one ribbon and one chip. She wants to find the probability that she will select a blue ribbon and a number that is a factor of 4. Which of the following outcome tables is shaded in a way that will help her figure out this probability?

(A)

Red 1	Red 2	Red 3	Red 4	Red 5	Red 6
Blue 1	Blue 2	Blue 3	Blue 4	Blue 5	Blue 6
Green 1	Green 2	Green 3	Green 4	Green 5	Green 6

(B)

Red 1	Red 2	Red 3	Red 4	Red 5	Red 6
Blue 1	Blue 2	Blue 3	Blue 4	Blue 5	Blue 6
Green 1	Green 2	Green 3	Green 4	Green 5	Green 6

(C)

Red 1	Red 2	Red 3	Red 4	Red 5	Red 6
Blue 1	Blue 2	Blue 3	Blue 4	Blue 5	Blue 6
Green 1	Green 2	Green 3	Green 4	Green 5	Green 6

(D)

Red 1	Red 2	Red 3	Red 4	Red 5	Red 6
Blue 1	Blue 2	Blue 3	Blue 4	Blue 5	Blue 6
Green 1	Green 2	Green 3	Green 4	Green 5	Green 6

Answers to Probability Practice Set

1. B
2. D
3. B
4. A
5. C
6. D
7. C
8. A
9. A
10. B
11. A
12. C
13. D
14. B
15. C

Tips For the Essay

When you take the ISEE, you will be asked to complete an essay at the very end of the test. You will be given 30 minutes and two pages to write your response. You will also be given a piece of paper to take notes on.

- Essay is at the end of the test
- 30 minutes to complete
- Two pages to write on, plus one piece of paper for notes

Your writing sample will NOT be scored. Rather, a copy of it will be sent to the schools that you apply to. This essay is a great way for the admissions committee to get to know you better.

- Let your personality shine through so that admissions officers can get to know you better

You will be given a question to write from. The questions are topics that you can relate to your own life.

Here are some examples that are like the questions that you will see on the ISEE:

1. If you could change one thing about your community, what would it be? Describe what you would change and how it would improve your community.
2. Who is your favorite teacher? Describe how this person has influenced your thoughts and actions.
3. We live in a world that is rapidly changing. Describe one change that you have seen recently and whether or not you think it is an improvement.

(There are more sample questions in ERB's official guide, *What to Expect on the ISEE*)

To approach the essay, follow this three-step plan:

Step 1: Plan

- Take just a couple of minutes and plan, it will be time well spent
- Be sure to know what your main idea is and how each paragraph will be different
- Use the piece of paper provided

Step 2: Write

- Break your writing into paragraphs – don't do a two-page blob
- Write legibly – it does not have to be perfect and schools know that you are writing with a time limit, but if the admissions officers can't read what you wrote, they can't judge it
- Remember that each paragraph should have its own idea

Step 3: Edit/proofread

- Save a couple of minutes at the end to look over your work
- You won't be able to do a major editing job where you move around sentences and rewrite portions
- Look for where you may have left out a word or misspelled something
- Make your marks simple and clear – if you need to take something out, just put a single line through it and use a carat (^) to insert words that you forgot

The essay is not graded, but the schools that you apply to do receive a copy.

What are schools looking for?

Organization

There should be structure to your essay. You need to have an introduction, good details to back up your main point, and a conclusion. Each paragraph should have its own idea.

Word choice

Use descriptive language. Don't describe anything as "nice" or "good". Describe specifically why something is nice or good. Good writing shows us and DOESN'T tell us.

Creativity and development of ideas

It is not enough just to be able to fit your writing into the form that you were taught in school. These prompts are designed to show how you think. This is your chance to shine!

The writing sample is a place for you to showcase your writing skills. It is just one more piece of information that the admissions committee will use in making their decisions.

The best way to get better at writing an essay is to practice. Try writing about one or more of the questions above. Use the prompts from *What to Expect on the ISEE*. Have a trusted adult help you analyze your writing sample and figure out how you can improve.

- Practice writing an essay before the actual test
- Have a teacher or parent help you analyze your practice essays

Practice Test

Following is a practice test for you to try. It is a full-length practice test with the same number of questions and timing as the actual test.

When you complete this practice test:

- Time yourself for each section
- Try to do the whole test in one sitting, if you can
- Check your answers and figure out WHY you missed the questions that you miss
- Keep in mind that the percentile charts are a very, very rough guideline – they are included just so you can see how the scoring works

Section 1—Verbal Reasoning

40 questions
20 minutes

The Verbal Reasoning section has two parts. When you finish Part One, be sure to keep working on Part Two. For each answer that you choose, make sure to fill in the corresponding circle on the answer sheet.

Part One – Synonyms

The questions in Part One each have a word in all capital letters with four answer choices after it. Choose the answer choice with the word that comes closest in meaning to the word in all capital letters.

SAMPLE QUESTION:

1. SPEEDY:

   (A) loud
   (B) messy
   (●) quick
   (D) small

Part Two – Sentence Completions

The questions in Part Two each have a sentence with one blank. The blank takes the place of a word that is missing. The sentence has four answer choices after it. Choose the answer choice that would best complete the meaning of the sentence.

SAMPLE QUESTION:

1. Since the weather is getting warmer every day, it is particularly important to -------- more water.

   (A) create
   (●) drink
   (C) leave
   (D) waste

STOP: Do not move on to the section until told to.

Part One – Synonyms

Directions: Choose the word that is closest in meaning to the word that is in all capital letters.

1. FAVORABLE:

   (A) devout
   (B) overdue
   (C) positive
   (D) willowy

2. TREACHEROUS:

   (A) deceitful
   (B) earnest
   (C) obedient
   (D) simple

3. MEEK:

   (A) controversial
   (B) familiar
   (C) literal
   (D) shy

4. PIOUS:

   (A) beneficial
   (B) domestic
   (C) occasional
   (D) religious

5. RASH:

   (A) dismal
   (B) reckless
   (C) secure
   (D) timid

6. DIVINE:

   (A) abrupt
   (B) exaggerated
   (C) heavenly
   (D) valiant

7. INGENIOUS:

   (A) brilliant
   (B) disagreeable
   (C) nervous
   (D) relieved

8. RENOWN:

   (A) absence
   (B) damage
   (C) fame
   (D) jubilance

9. HARDY:

   (A) available
   (B) defensive
   (C) miserly
   (D) strong

10. CAPER:

   (A) disgrace
   (B) prank
   (C) reminder
   (D) tablet

Go on to the next page

11. HOODWINK:

(A) deceive
(B) employ
(C) observe
(D) smear

12. SUSPEND:

(A) diminish
(B) label
(C) stop
(D) translate

13. SPARSE:

(A) embroidered
(B) meager
(C) ridiculous
(D) tawny

14. PEDESTRIAN:

(A) boring
(B) flawless
(C) objective
(D) remorseful

15. FANATIC:

(A) adviser
(B) emigrant
(C) phantom
(D) zealot

16. SCURRY:

(A) dash
(B) graze
(C) inquire
(D) stalk

17. BOISTEROUS:

(A) fearless
(B) graceful
(C) loud
(D) ordinary

18. RIGHTEOUS:

(A) important
(B) moral
(C) possessive
(D) trespassing

19. SULLEN:

(A) efficient
(B) gloomy
(C) liable
(D) tarnished

Go on to the next page

Part Two - Sentence Completions

Directions: Choose the word to best complete the sentence.

20. Fertilizer runoff from farms has led to algae bloom in waterways, which means that the abundant growth of algae has -------- the growth of other plants and reduced food available to aquatic life that does not consume algae.

    (A) curbed
    (B) immersed
    (C) misguided
    (D) tolerated

21. Jackson Pollock revolutionized the art world when he started producing abstract paintings instead of the -------- pictures that more conventional artists had been creating.

    (A) borrowed
    (B) larger
    (C) majestic
    (D) realistic

22. When Richard Drew visited an automobile painting shop in 1925 and witnessed the difficulty the painters were having painting two differently colored sections without an adhesive strip, he came up with the -------- of masking tape.

    (A) calamity
    (B) examination
    (C) innovation
    (D) sequence

23. Styrofoam is often used in surfboards and boats because it is a lightweight material with a high level of ---------.

    (A) agreement
    (B) buoyancy
    (C) harmony
    (D) mythology

Go on to the next page

24. When animals are released into the wild after being in captivity for an extended period of time, it can be difficult for them to adapt because they are --------- to having food provided for them.

   (A) accustomed
   (B) employed
   (C) perplexed
   (D) removed

25. Because the Galapagos Islands are highly secluded, species survive there that have long ago ------- in other locations.

   (A) assisted
   (B) declined
   (C) maximized
   (D) thrived

26. Martha Graham considered dancing to be a(n) --------- part of her life that could not be avoided.

   (A) aggressive
   (B) dignified
   (C) inevitable
   (D) unusual

27. Clearly the conditions for growing corn on the plains were --------- given the tremendous harvest that was produced.

   (A) advantageous
   (B) delicate
   (C) static
   (D) tapering

28. During World II the supply of natural rubber from Southeast Asia was cut off and American scientists had to quickly develop a -------- replacement.

   (A) backward
   (B) fragrant
   (C) lagging
   (D) synthetic

Go on to the next page

29. It can be difficult to treat diseases that are -------- because symptoms often go away and then reappear later.

    (A) chronic
    (B) humbling
    (C) lazy
    (D) questionable

30. Opponents of the bridge project had to be -------- before construction could begin on the massive span crossing the Ohio River.

    (A) explained
    (B) fortified
    (C) pacified
    (D) replaced

31. Although it is possible to --------- a quick fix during a race, it is better for a sailing team to plan ahead for potential problems they might encounter during a long race.

    (A) appreciate
    (B) improvise
    (C) pronounce
    (D) shelter

32. Although many people consider air conditioning to be essential, it is often ------- if a house is built to capture surrounding winds and be sheltered from the sun by tall trees.

    (A) complimented
    (B) fraudulent
    (C) protective
    (D) superfluous

33. It is illegal to -------- secrets that are vital to maintain for national security.

    (A) convert
    (B) divulge
    (C) retain
    (D) trump

Go on to the next page

34. When pure olive oil has been ------- by other oils it must be discarded or relabeled so that consumers do not pay more for a product that has been mixed with other ingredients.

    (A) adulterated
    (B) eclipsed
    (C) hosted
    (D) thawed

35. Although many people believe that voter turnout was reduced by the weather, the effect of the rain on the number of voters was actually ---------.

    (A) flattering
    (B) massive
    (C) negligible
    (D) requested

36. Powerful thunder and lightning storms often crop up quickly on days when the weather is --------.

    (A) arid
    (B) cold
    (C) placid
    (D) torrid

37. In Victorian England there was a strong ------- against upper class women working outside the home so many women did not pursue careers.

    (A) approval
    (B) furrow
    (C) performance
    (D) taboo

38. When too much sediment builds up in a river bed then the river must be ------- in order to keep water flowing in the same path.

    (A) classified
    (B) dredged
    (C) lubricated
    (D) quenched

Go on to the next page

39. Bonnie and Clyde were famous for their ------- bank robberies, often entering a bank in broad daylight without wearing disguises.

(A) brazen
(B) honest
(C) mystical
(D) vivid

40. It is rude to wear a large hat in a movie theater because it might ------ the view of the people sitting in the back of the theater.

(A) astonish
(B) hound
(C) obscure
(D) smear

STOP. If you have time left, you may check your answers in ONLY this section.

Section 2—Quantitative Reasoning

37 questions

35 minutes

Each math question has four answer choices after it. Choose the answer choice that best answers the question.

Make sure that you fill in the correct answer on your answer sheet. You may write in the test booklet.

SAMPLE QUESTION:

1. What is the perimeter of a rectangle that has a length of 3 cm and width of 5 cm?

   $(P = 2l + 2w)$

   (A) 6 cm
   (B) 10 cm
   (C) 8 cm
   (●) 16 cm

The correct answer is 16 cm and circle D is filled in.

STOP. Do not move on to the section until told to.

Part One – Word Problems

1. Differently colored buckets were filled with water and then placed in a sunny spot. The temperature was measured when the buckets were filled and again one hour later. Recorded below is how many degrees the temperature rose by in each bucket.

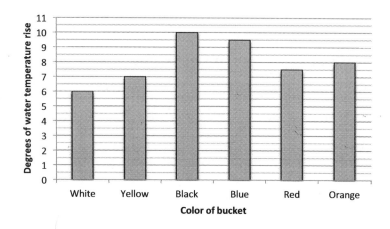

According to the above graph, what is the mean number of degrees that the temperature was raised?

(A) 6.5 degrees
(B) 7.0 degrees
(C) 7.5 degrees
(D) 8.0 degrees

2. A set of 6 numbers had a mean of 8. One number was removed and the mean of the remaining numbers was 7. What number was removed?

(A) 7
(B) 13
(C) 35
(D) 48

Go on to the next page

3. Grady has 8 coins, which are all either a penny or a nickel. If he traded in all 8 of his coins for 8 dimes, the value of his coins would increase by 56 cents. How many nickels does Grady have?

(A) 4
(B) 5
(C) 6
(D) 7

4. Use the picture below to answer the question.

What fraction of the picture above is shaded?

(A) $\dfrac{1}{6}$

(B) $\dfrac{1}{3}$

(C) $\dfrac{1}{2}$

(D) $\dfrac{2}{3}$

5. The area of the largest rectangle shown below is 90 cm².

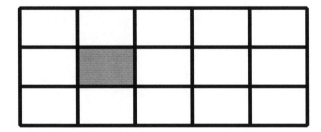

What is the area of the shaded region?

(A) 2 cm²
(B) 3 cm²
(C) 6 cm²
(D) 15 cm²

Go on to the next page

6. Which of the following numbers is closest to the square root of 130?

    (A) 5
    (B) 6
    (C) 10
    (D) 11

7. The two triangles shown below are similar.

Triangle 1

Triangle 2

A = 40 cm²

A = 10 cm²

What is the ratio of a side length in Triangle 1 to the side length of the corresponding side in Triangle 2?

    (A) 2 to 1
    (B) 4 to 1
    (C) 8 to 1
    (D) 16 to 1

8. Liam was playing a game with a made up currency system. He traded his 20 snamps in for 10 wurls. He then took 5 of those wurls and traded them in for 10 lins. How many wurls is equal to 2 snamps?

    (A) 1
    (B) 2
    (C) 5
    (D) 10

Go on to the next page

9. Brian and Meredith start at the same place and time walking along a straight path. If Brian walks twice as fast as Meredith and after 20 minutes they are 600 feet apart, which equation would give Meredith's speed (M) in feet per minute?

(A) $2M - M = 600$
(B) $40M - 600 = 20M$
(C) $40M = 600 - 20M$
(D) $20(M + 2M) = 600$

10. If $5w + 3 = 12$, then what is $15w + 9$ equal to?

(A) 3
(B) 4
(C) 36
(D) 60

11. City X decided to run an advertising campaign to increase the number of riders using the subway system. The graph below shows the relationship between the number of days that the campaign had been running and the number of riders on the various subway lines.

Number of riders

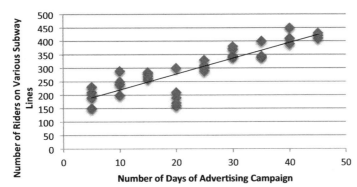

Using the line of best fit, about how many riders were there on each subway line after the advertising campaign had been running for 25 days?

(A) 300
(B) 600
(C) 900
(D) 1200

Go on to the next page

12. A population of 64 bats increased by 150%. What was the total number of bats after the increase?

(A) 72

(B) 96

(C) 128

(D) 160

13. A baseball team played 20 games during the summer. The attendance for the games is shown in the histogram.

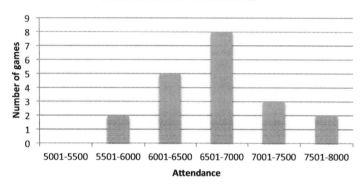

Attendance Statistics

Which measure of central tendency could never equal the attendance at one of the 20 individual games?

(A) median

(B) mode

(C) range

(D) mean

14. Perry is using a random number generator. He sets the computer to choose a whole number from 1 to 10 for each trial. What is the probability that both numbers chosen will be less than 5?

(A) $\dfrac{4}{25}$

(B) $\dfrac{2}{5}$

(C) $\dfrac{7}{10}$

(D) $\dfrac{4}{5}$

Go on to the next page

15. The net below is going to be folded into a cube.

If side D is going to be on the bottom of the cube, which side will be on the top?

(A) side A

(B) side B

(C) side C

(D) side F

16. A hardware store gives customers rewards points according to the pattern below.

Number of Items Purchased	Rewards Points
1	2
2	4
3	8

Tina received 32 rewards points. How many purchases did she make?

(A) 5

(B) 8

(C) 12

(D) 16

Go on to the next page

17. Jill stacked smaller cubes in order to build the larger cube below.

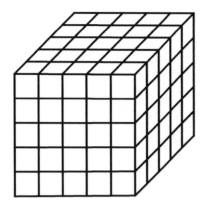

How many smaller cubes did she use?

(A) 50

(B) 75

(C) 100

(D) 125

18. A school buys books that are $13 each. An additional 10% service fee is added plus a shipping charge. The table below gives the total cost, including the shipping charge, of several orders.

Number of Books Ordered	Total Cost of Order
3	$45.90
5	$74.50
6	$88.80

What is the shipping fee per order?

(A) $2.50

(B) $3.00

(C) $3.50

(D) $4.00

Go on to the next page

19. An elementary school has set up a phone tree. At noon, the first person calls 4 people. At 1:00 PM those 4 people each call 4 more people. At 2:00 PM, those 16 people each call another 4 people. If this pattern continues, which expression would represent the total number of people who would be called by 4:30 PM?

(A) $1 + 4^5$
(B) $1 + 4^6$
(C) $1 + 4 + 4^2 + 4^3 + 4^4 + 4^5$
(D) $4 + 4^2 + 4^3 + 4^4 + 4^5$

20. Which graph shows a function whose y-values decrease at the greatest rate as the x-values increase?

(A)

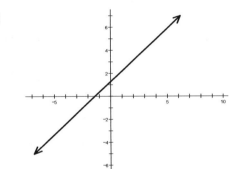

(B)

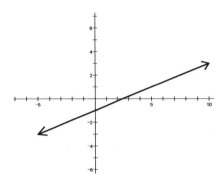

(C)

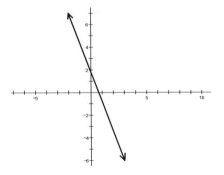

(D)

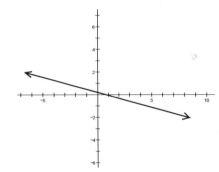

Go on to the next page

Part Two – Quantitative Comparisons

Directions: Use the information in the question to compare the quantities in Columns A and B. After comparing the two quantities, choose the correct answer choice:

- (A) Quantity in Column A is greatest.
- (B) Quantity in Column B is greatest.
- (C) The quantities in Column A and Column B are equal.
- (D) Cannot be determined from information given.

$$m = 3n + 7$$

	Column A	**Column B**
21.	The value of m when $n = 3$	The value of n when $m = 16$

Caleb has \$1.32 in quarters, dimes, nickels, and pennies. (Note: 1 quarter = \$0.25, 1 dime = \$0.10, 1 nickel = \$0.05, and 1 penny = \$0.01)

	Column A	**Column B**
22.	10	The smallest number of coins that Caleb could have

	Column A	**Column B**
23.	M	$\dfrac{1}{M}$

$$\frac{x}{6} + 5 = 11$$
$$2y - 10 = 62$$

	Column A	**Column B**
24.	x	y

Go on to the next page

Column A	**Column B**
25.	$\sqrt{4+36}$	$\sqrt{4}+\sqrt{36}$

Column A	**Column B**
26.	$(-2)^6$	-2^6

Triangle 1

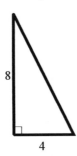

8

4

Triangle 2

2

1

Column A	**Column B**
27.	The area of a triangle that is similar to Triangle 1 with a scale factor of $\dfrac{3}{4}$	The area of the triangle that is similar to Triangle 2 with a scale factor of 3

A shirt originally cost $15.

Column A	**Column B**
28.	The price of the shirt after a 20% discount	The price of the shirt after two separate 10% discounts

Column A	**Column B**
29.	The slope of a line between (2, 4) and (4, 5)	The slope of a line that is perpendicular to the line $y = \dfrac{1}{2}x + 7$

Go on to the next page

Clara and James start at the same location and ride along the same straight bike path. Clara rides for twenty minutes at an average speed of 15 miles per hour and James rides for fifteen minutes at an average speed of 20 miles per hour.

	Column A	**Column B**
30.	Distance that Clara has travelled	Distance that James has travelled

Before an election, a survey was done in two separate towns to see which of two candidates voters were planning to vote for. This data was then used to predict who would win the election.

	Town 1	Town 2
Percent of town surveyed	50%	25%
Number of votes for Candidate A	200	175
Number of votes for Candidate B	150	225

	Column A	**Column B**
31.	The number of predicted votes for Candidate A in Town 1	The number of predicted votes for Candidate A in Town 2

Go on to the next page

The larger circle shown below is cut into 4 equal pieces by two diameters. The smaller circle shown has the same center as the larger circle. The area of the larger circle is 1.

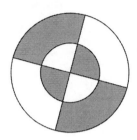

	Column A	Column B
32.	$\dfrac{2}{3}$	Area of the shaded region.

The spinner below is divided into six equally sized pieces.

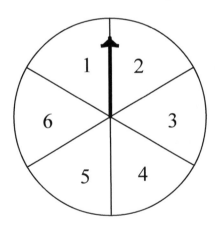

	Column A	Column B
	Column A	**Column B**
33.	For each spin, the probability that the hand will land on an even number	For each spin, the probability that the hand will land on a number greater than 3

Go on to the next page

G and *H* are points on the line shown below. *L* (not shown) is on the same line somewhere between *G* and *H*.

	Column A	**Column B**
34.	The distance between *G* and *H*	The distance between *L* and *H*

---

y is a whole number less than zero.

	Column A	**Column B**
35.	y^2	y^3

	Column A	**Column B**
36.	The number of multiples of 8 between 4 and 58	The number of multiples of 8 between 2 and 63

	Column A	**Column B**
37.	$0.31 \times 2.1 \times 31.5$	$0.21 \times 3.15 \times 31$

STOP. If you have time left, you may check your answers in ONLY this section.

Section 3—Reading Comprehension

36 questions

35 minutes

The Reading Comprehension section has six short passages. Each passage has six questions after it. Choose the answer choice that comes closest to what is stated or implied in the passage. You can write in the test booklet.

STOP. Do not move on to the section until told to.

Questions #1-6

1   Stretching approximately 2,200 miles over 14 states, the Appalachian Trail is a
2   popular hiking route that many hiking enthusiasts dream of one day completing. Some
3   hikers, called "section hikers," choose to cover the trail in smaller sections over the
4   course of multiple trips, or sometimes even several years. Others, who have the luxury
5   of time and seek a more difficult challenge, attempt to hike the entire length within one
6   hiking season. These adventurers are called "thru-hikers." Whether a section hiker or a
7   thru-hiker, anyone who successfully completes the trail in its entirety is designated a
8   "2,000 Miler" by the Appalachian Trail Conservancy. To date, there are more than
9   10,000 people who have been bestowed with that title.

10   Beginning in March or April, most thru-hikers set off from Georgia and travel
11   north along the trail toward Maine. Of the more than 1,000 people who begin the jour-
12   ney each year, only a few hundred actually complete it, usually within five to seven
13   months. Along the way, the main path is marked by white paint and any side trails that
14   extend to shelters are marked with blue paint. Hikers can stop at any of the more than
15   200 shelters to rest, go to the privy (bathroom) if there is one, and possibly meet up with
16   other hikers who are at the same location.

17   Many hikers would likely say that one of the best parts of the experience is the
18   camaraderie among the hikers. As with many specific interests, there is a particular
19   culture that surrounds the activity of thru-hiking. Many hikers give themselves a
20   special trail nickname or have one assigned to them by other hikers. Another custom is
21   for hikers to leave items, such as food, candy, or some other type of gift behind for a
22   fellow hiker to find. These gifts, called "Trail Magic," can make for a pleasant surprise
23   after a long day of intense hiking.

24   Because the majority of the trail passes through wilderness, many dangers lurk
25   along the path and threaten to interfere with hikers' mission of reaching their final post.
26   Each year only a small percentage of people who have intentions of thru-hiking accom-
27   plish the feat. Right from the beginning of the northbound journey, steep hills in
28   Georgia pose a difficult, often painful, challenge that defeats some hikers who are less-
29   seasoned mountain climbers. Similarly, overwhelming fatigue after months on the
30   road, and minor injuries, such as sprained and broken bones, are also common reasons
31   hikers depart from the trail early. And although animal attacks and animal-borne
32   illnesses are rare, they do occur on occasion.

33   For an adventurous thru-hiker who thrives on adrenaline, though, all of these
34   dangers are merely just part of the excitement of joining the exclusive club of 2,000
35   Milers.

Go on to the next page

1. Which best expresses the main idea of the passage?

    (A) The Appalachian Trail is approximately 2,000 miles long.
    (B) It is a great accomplishment to hike the entire Appalachian Trail.
    (C) There is a risk of injury with any hiking experience.
    (D) If hikers make it past Georgia, they are likely to complete the hike to Maine.

2. The passage implies that hikers along the Appalachian Trail

    (A) generally support one another.
    (B) are fiercely competitive.
    (C) prefer to be section-hikers.
    (D) usually finish the journey.

3. The author describes Trail Magic as

    (A) nicknames given to thru-hikers.
    (B) dangerous animal-borne diseases.
    (C) treats that hikers leave for one another.
    (D) thru-hikers.

4. Which question is answered by the passage?

    (A) What does black paint mean along the trail?
    (B) How many states does the Appalachian Trail pass through?
    (C) Who is the oldest person to have completed hiking the Appalachian Trail?
    (D) When was the Appalachian Trail built?

5. In line 24, the word "lurk" most nearly means

    (A) stumble.
    (B) finish.
    (C) create.
    (D) hide.

6. The main purpose of the fourth paragraph (lines 24-32) is to

    (A) explain why hiking the Appalachian Trail is a rare accomplishment.
    (B) detail the steps hikers must take to prepare for the Appalachian Trail.
    (C) offer a brief history of the Appalachian Trail.
    (D) create a sense of suspense for the reader.

Go on to the next page

Questions #7-12

1   How much difference can one person make in the world? Consider the life of Wangari
2   Maathi—the first African woman to win the Nobel Peace Prize. From fighting for change,
3   to helping others in need, to using words to inspire others, she is one person who left a
4   tremendous impact on the world that will have long-lasting effects beyond her lifetime.

5   Wangari Maathai was born in 1940 in Kenya. Because her family believed in the
6   importance of education, she attended school as a child and then later transferred to a
7   Catholic school, where she learned English. At a time when girls often did not have
8   the same opportunities as boys, it could be difficult for a girl to obtain a higher education.
9   However, Maathai was an exemplary student and was awarded a scholarship to study
10   at Mount St. Scholastica College in Kansas, where she received a degree in biology in
11   1964. This would be the first of many earned and honorary degrees she would receive
12   during her life. In 1966, she received a master's degree from the University of Pittsburgh
13   and then earned a doctorate in veterinary medicine from the University of Nairobi five
14   years later. This degree in particular was an extraordinary accomplishment. With it, she
15   became the first woman in East or Central Africa to ever receive a doctoral degree.

16   As a leader for the National Council of Women of Kenya, Maathai often fought for
17   women's rights. In addition to her desire to support women's interests, she was also
18   interested in protecting the environment. With these motivations in mind, Maathai
19   ultimately sought to develop a tree-planting program that could help the community
20   while improving the environment.

21   In 1977, she founded the Green Belt Movement. At that time in Kenya, the expanding
22   population created a demand for more homes and other buildings. And this increase in
23   development led to an increase in deforestation. With the Green Belt Movement,
24   Maathai encouraged women to go to work planting trees. The mission of the movement
25   was three-fold—it would plant trees to help the environment, create a source of firewood
26   for fuel, and also provide employment for women.

27   After the movement spread across Kenya, Maathai met with people from other African
28   countries to expand the program further. With the support of these additional countries,
29   the Green Belt Movement has planted more than 30 million trees in Africa.

30   Throughout her life, Maathai continued to fight for democracy, women's rights, and
31   environmental protection. Although she passed away in 2011, her work will continue
32   to influence environmental and equality programs in Africa and beyond. And her life
33   will continue to inspire people around the world.

Go on to the next page

7. Which statement best expresses the main idea of the passage?

   (A) Wangari Maathai struggled to find educational opportunities.
   (B) Without Wangari Maathai, women in Kenya would not be receiving doctoral degrees today.
   (C) Wangari Maathai fought to improve the lives of others.
   (D) Wangari Maathai helped developers responsibly build houses.

8. The passage implies that the Green Belt movement

   (A) was responsible for deforestation.
   (B) had trouble transitioning to countries outside of Kenya.
   (C) was only interested in increasing the number of trees in Kenya.
   (D) led to a greater number of trees in Africa.

9 It can be inferred from the passage that

   (A) no Kenyan women received doctorates in 1965.
   (B) Wangari Maathai came from a large family.
   (C) Wangari Maathai has not been recognized outside of Africa.
   (D) the number of African women employed has risen.

10. Which word best describes the author's tone concerning Wangari Maathai?

   (A) hesitant
   (B) admiring
   (C) doubtful
   (D) awkward

11. As used in the passage, the term "deforestation" most nearly means

   (A) to plant more trees.
   (B) to expand to other countries.
   (C) to cut down trees.
   (D) providing jobs for women.

12. Information from the passage supports which statement?

   (A) Women are more affected by deforestation than men.
   (B) In 1977 there was a need for more firewood in Kenya.
   (C) There were not other people fighting for women's rights in Kenya during Wangari Maathai's lifetime.
   (D) The Nobel Peace Prize is frequently awarded to Africans.

Go on to the next page

Questions #13-18

1   Many students and parents agree that our school district should install solar panels to
2   power some, if not all, of our school buildings. Not only would solar panels be beneficial to
3   our school community for several reasons, but they would also help protect the
4   environment in general.

5   First, unlike fossil fuels and other sources of nonrenewable energy, solar energy is a
6   renewable resource. At some time in the possibly near future, nonrenewable energy
7   sources will be completely depleted. Why should our schools create even more pollution
8   and contribute to this destruction of Earth when instead, we can do something beneficial
9   for the environment? By using solar energy, we will be drawing from an endless supply
10   of resources that can be renewed. Experts say that it would only take a small fraction
11   of the world's surface to be covered in solar panels to supply enough power for the entire
12   world. People who use solar energy prevent the use of over 70 million barrels of oil each
13   year.

14   Solar panels can also help the environment by being a source of educational lessons
15   for children and adults alike. The panels on display are likely to become a talking point
16   for environmental issues. Parents can teach their children about renewable energy
17   sources. They also can show them other ways to minimize their impact on the environment
18   at home and at school. Perhaps the schools' panels will even inspire other people to
19   install panels for their businesses and homes. Like a rock skipping across a pond, our
20   solar panels could create a ripple effect that ultimately benefits the greater community
21   and the world.

22   Likewise, many solar panel programs support this theory. They even offer special
23   initiatives for school districts willing to use their installed panels to educate students
24   and others in their community. We may even be able to apply for a grant from one of
25   these programs and have the panels installed at no cost to our taxpayers.

26   Even if the district has to pay the cost of installation, another major benefit of using
27   solar panels is the money that can be saved on energy costs. One district in California
28   saved almost 300,000 dollars after one year of using a solar system. Based on their best
29   projections, they are hoping that solar energy will save them millions of dollars over 25
30   years. Perhaps our district will benefit from such returns if we install solar panels, too.

31   Overall, with millions of dollars and the fate of the environment at stake, installing
32   solar panels in our school district is one possibility that should not be ignored.

Go on to the next page

13. What is the primary purpose of this passage?

    (A) to encourage a particular course of action
    (B) to inform the reader about the pros and cons of solar energy
    (C) to disprove a popular theory
    (D) to discourage the reader from polluting

14. What does the author mean by "ripple effect"?

    (A) An action by one person often influences one other person to do the same action.
    (B) Pollution will lead to more pollution.
    (C) The effect of a single action can often be much greater than just the immediate response.
    (D) A little water can lead to flooding.

15. Which word best describes the tone of the passage as a whole?

    (A) cynical
    (B) passionate
    (C) humorous
    (D) resigned

16. The passage implies that the economic effects of solar panels would be

    (A) greater than the educational effects.
    (B) disregarded by students.
    (C) negative for the school as a whole.
    (D) overall positive for the school.

17. According to the passage, solar energy

    (A) could potentially provide all of mankind's energy needs.
    (B) is limited by current technology.
    (C) is broadly supported by the community.
    (D) pollutes the environment more than fossil fuels.

18. Which best describes the organization of this passage?

    (A) An argument is presented and then proven wrong.
    (B) Several competing theories are presented.
    (C) Events are presented in chronological order.
    (D) An assertion is made and then evidence is provided to support that assertion.

Go on to the next page

1   In its over 80-year history, The Seeing Eye in Morristown, New Jersey has placed over
2   15,000 guide dogs with more than 8,000 visually-impaired people. Due to its long
3   history and reputation for success, along with its influence on the development of similar
4   organizations, The Seeing Eye has familiarized many people with the concept of service
5   dogs for the blind. Yet, few people are aware of how the group began. Thousands of dogs
6   may have passed through training and completed years of service, but as with the start of
7   most things, it all started with one. That one dog's name was Buddy. She was the first
8   seeing eye dog.
9   Buddy's human partner was a man named Morris Frank. Although many people often
10   refer to a dog's handler as a "master," the relationship between person and seeing eye
11   dog is more a dual partnership than a superior-subordinate match, and Buddy and
12   Morris' relationship exemplified this right from the start.
13   Morris was able to obtain a Seeing Eye dog due to the work of Dorothy Eustis and
14   Jack Humphrey. In 1927, Morris encountered an article in The Saturday Evening
15   Post, written by Dorothy Eustis, in which she described a school that trained German
16   Shepherd dogs to lead the blind. Dorothy and the dog-training school were located in
17   Switzerland, but that did little to discourage Morris Frank. Interested in obtaining a guide
18   dog of his own, Morris wrote a letter to Dorothy to inquire about the innovative program
19   discussed in her article. Her encouraging reply led Morris to take a trip to Switzerland.
20   There, he met with Dorothy and Jack Humphrey, the head trainer of the guide dog school.
21   In many ways, this historic meeting was the start of The Seeing Eye's development.
22   Morris was matched with a German Shepherd named Buddy, and together, they completed
23   five long weeks of intensive training. Then Morris and Buddy returned to America.
24   Charged with the task of demonstrating the worthiness of a guide dog, Morris and Buddy
25   walked along a busy New York City street, to the amazement of a group of on-looking
26   reporters. Undoubtedly, both dog and man were proud of what they accomplished in
27   that moment.
28   Shortly afterward, The Seeing Eye was officially formed, with Dorothy Eustis and Jack
29   Humphrey serving as president and vice president, respectively. Initially operating for
30   two years in Morris' home state of Tennessee, the agency later relocated to its current
31   location in New Jersey. With the help of Buddy, Morris gained a new independence,
32   self-confidence, and sense of purpose. Although Buddy died after 10 years of service,
33   every seeing eye dog Morris received in successive years was also bestowed with the
34   name Buddy in honor of the original heroine.

Go on to the next page

19. Which statement best expresses the primary point of the passage?

    (A) Morris Frank always wanted to be matched with a seeing eye dog.
    (B) It is important to maintain the master-dog relationship.
    (C) The hard work and perseverance of one person can benefit many.
    (D) The Seeing Eye organization started in Switzerland.

20. According to the passage, Dorothy Eustis

    (A) was vice president of the Seeing Eye.
    (B) lived in Switzerland.
    (C) trained the original Buddy herself.
    (D) was passionate about bringing seeing eye dogs to America.

21. Why were the reporters amazed to see Buddy and Morris Frank walking in New York City?

    (A) Dogs are generally not welcome on city streets.
    (B) Morris Frank did not live in New York City.
    (C) Buddy had not yet been trained.
    (D) Morris Frank was visually-impaired and the reporters had never seen a demonstration with a seeing eye dog before.

22. What does it mean when the passages states that the relationship between Buddy and Morris Frank was "more dual partnership than a superior-subordinate match"?

    (A) Buddy and Morris were equals in the relationship.
    (B) Morris was clearly the master of Buddy.
    (C) Morris and Buddy made the decision together to come to America.
    (D) Buddy was also visually impaired.

23. According to the passage, how did Morris Frank first find out about seeing eye dogs?

    (A) Dorothy Eustis sent him a letter.
    (B) He read an article in a newspaper.
    (C) On a trip to Switzerland, he was introduced to Dorothy Eustis.
    (D) He was contacted by The Seeing Eye in Tennessee.

24. Which word best describes the tone of the passage?

    (A) humorous
    (B) calculating
    (C) critical
    (D) informative

Go on to the next page

1   Seven-year-old Maggie lounged on the porch stoop, trapped in a perpetual state of
2   lethargy brought on by the unbearable heat choking the air around her. A persistent
3   wave of higher than normal temperatures had pounded the region for the past month
4   and only served to worsen the already bad conditions brought on by the severe drought.
5   Whenever Maggie heard her father talking with other farmers in town, this was all they
6   ever discussed—how 1934 was the worst drought year they had ever experienced; how
7   it was sure to be remembered as one of the worst droughts in history.

8   Although Maggie did not know if they were right since her less than decade of life
9   limited her frame of reference, she did know that the conditions were the worst she had
10   ever witnessed. This past season, their crops had withered and slumped over, like fallen
11   soldiers on a battlefield. The dry, hardened ground disintegrated into dust, and then the
12   dust was blown into large, swirling black clouds when harsh winds whipped through the
13   plains.

14   Maggie recalled one day at school when her class became trapped by a sudden storm.
15   As the barreling dust passed over the building, it covered the windows with dirt and debris.
16   In an instant, the bright light of midday turned as dark as night, and the class and teacher
17   were bound to the confines of the room's four walls. In the midst of nature's fury, they
18   huddled together and comforted each other as they waited several hours for the storm
19   to settle down and grant them their freedom.

20   That night at home, Maggie's father referred to the storm as a "black blizzard," and
21   Maggie observed that she would much rather experience a traditional blizzard than this
22   new dusty, dirty variety. At least a white blizzard created an occasion for fun. With any
23   significant accumulation, Maggie and her siblings would take leave from their household
24   duties early and spend the afternoon playing in the snow. In Maggie's view, there was
25   nothing quite as beautiful as a sparkling canvas of fresh snow covering the acreage of
26   their farm. She always paused to admire the untouched landscape before disturbing its
27   newness with her footprints.

28   Now today, in the blistering heat, Maggie looked out onto the cracked layer of dust
29   coating the earth and imagined it covered with a thick layer of snow. She envisioned
30   shimmering hexagonal flakes floating down from the heavens and landing one by one,
31   upon the layer of snow already before her. Slowly she stretched out her hand and
32   pictured the drops softly falling into the curve of her uplifted palm. It was not long
33   before the refreshing thoughts helped to soothe her scorching brain and eased her body
34   into a deep and peaceful sleep.

Go on to the next page

25. The passage implies that Maggie lives

    (A) in a small town.
    (B) on a farm.
    (C) in the mountains.
    (D) in a northern climate.

26. According to the passage, a "black blizzard" is

    (A) dirty snow.
    (B) a huge snow storm.
    (C) extremely common in the area that Maggie lives in.
    (D) a giant dust storm.

27. Which word best describes Maggie as she is portrayed in the passage?

    (A) imaginative
    (B) lonely
    (C) unruly
    (D) hungry

28. The passage provides evidence to support which statement about the farmers in the area where Maggie lives?

    (A) Many of them are planning to move away.
    (B) They have had to adapt new farming techniques to deal with drought.
    (C) They can't remember a worse year for their crops.
    (D) Heat stroke has become a major problem for them.

29. The primary purpose of this passage is to

    (A) provide background information about a bad drought.
    (B) describe the effect of a drought on the life of one child.
    (C) explain how drought can be prevented.
    (D) inform the reader about bad droughts throughout history.

30. The word "lethargy" in line 2 most nearly means

    (A) lack of energy.
    (B) emotion.
    (C) wonder.
    (D) peace.

Go on to the next page

1   Did you ever enter an elevator by yourself and stand with your back facing the
2   doors? If you are like most people, you probably haven't, and perhaps the thought of
3   facing that way has never even crossed your mind. Perhaps you have never even
4   considered why people in an elevator stand one way versus another. This is because
5   certain practices are social norms—unspoken rules of how people are expected to
6   behave in social situations. This includes facing the door when riding in an elevator,
7   joining an already-formed line by standing at the back of it, and practicing certain
8   manners when dining at a restaurant.
9   Yet, if these customs are not formal rules, why do people follow them so often?
10 Psychologists believe it is because of conformity. Although the term may have a negative
11 connotation for some people, particularly those who desire to be different, conformity is
12 simply a part of our nature as humans. Most people have the desire to be liked, and
13 accepted by, others—at least to some degree.
14   Even people who deny any need to conform may have difficulty resisting conformity
15 when faced with social pressures, and this is especially true when one person stands in
16 opposition to the majority. A majority influence can be very powerful. It can cause people
17 to give an incorrect answer they know to be wrong, to change their views, and even to
18 see things that do not exist.
19   Imagine yourself walking up to a group of people looking up at something in a tree.
20 They all claim to see a snake way up high on one of the branches. You join the group and
21 strain to see the slithering creature that supposedly lies there in plain sight, and yet,
22 you see nothing but a tree. What do you do? Do you report that you honestly cannot see
23 anything, or do you claim that you can see what everyone else is seeing?
24   Surprisingly, when faced with this situation, many people would admit to seeing a snake,
25 just like the rest of the group, even though there is no snake there. This trickery is effective
26 because on some subconscious level, people believe that if the majority says something
27 is true, then it must be so, despite the physical evidence to the contrary. When placed
28 in opposition to the group view, people begin to doubt themselves. Or perhaps they feel
29 confident in their view but do not want to be seen as strange or defiant by other members
30 of the group.
31   In many cases, conformity is harmless, or sometimes even beneficial; but in other
32 situations, it may be dangerous, or even harmful to others. One must rely on an
33 independent mind to appropriately discern the difference, though unfortunately,
34 deciding whether to conform is not always a conscious choice.

Go on to the next page

31. Which statement about conformity would the author be most likely to agree with?

    (A) Conformity should be avoided at all costs.
    (B) The results of conformity are always harmless.
    (C) People are not always aware that they are even making a choice to conform.
    (D) For the good of society, more people should conform.

32. In line 5, the term "social norms" refers to

    (A) rules that people in a society seem to follow.
    (B) interactions between people.
    (C) large gatherings of people.
    (D) data collected by social scientists.

33. The main purpose of the fourth paragraph (lines 19-23) is to

    (A) introduce a new topic.
    (B) keep the reader's attention with a humorous aside.
    (C) present evidence against a particular theory.
    (D) provide an example to illustrate the main point of the passage.

34. In lines 32-33, relying "on an independent mind" can be interpreted to mean

    (A) ignoring the influence of other people.
    (B) not listening to other people at all.
    (C) not joining social groups.
    (D) never agreeing with the majority opinion.

35. The organization of the passage as a whole can best be described as

    (A) a presentation of conflicting viewpoints.
    (B) a theory is presented and then illustrations are provided.
    (C) several unrelated stories.
    (D) a collection of facts.

36. The passage suggests that a person who faces the door in an elevator most likely does so

    (A) in order to get off the elevator first.
    (B) to limit interaction with other people.
    (C) because other people are facing the door.
    (D) for absolutely no reason.

STOP. If you have time left, you may check your answers in ONLY this section.

Section 4—Mathematics Achievement

47 questions
40 minutes

Each math question has four answer choices after it. Choose the answer choice that best answers the question.

Make sure that you fill in the correct answer on your answer sheet. You may write in the test booklet.

SAMPLE QUESTION:

1. Which number can be divided by 4 with nothing left over?

   (A) 6
   (●) 12
   (C) 15
   (D) 22

Since 12 can be divided by 4 with no remainder, circle B is filled in.

STOP. Do not move on to the section until told to.

1. Which is equal to the sum 8,765 + 5,678?

    (A) 13,443

    (B) 14,443

    (C) 14,453

    (D) 14,463

2. Which expression equals 7?

    (A) $2 \times (7 - 5) + 3$

    (B) $(2 \times 7) - 5 + 3$

    (C) $2 \times 7 - (5 + 3)$

    (D) $2 \times (7 - 5 + 3)$

3. The circle shown is divided into equal parts.

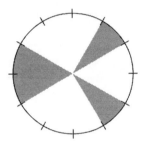

What part of the circle is shaded?

    (A) $\dfrac{1}{8}$

    (B) $\dfrac{1}{5}$

    (C) $\dfrac{1}{4}$

    (D) $\dfrac{1}{3}$

4. Which number has only itself and 1 as factors?

    (A) 2

    (B) 4

    (C) 6

    (D) 33

Go on to the next page

5. If 4 coins is equal to 3 stamps, and one stamp is equal to 12, what is the value of one coin?

   (A) 6
   (B) 8
   (C) 9
   (D) 12

6. The average monthly rainfall for one year was 8.2 inches in City X. The highest monthly rainfall recorded was 12.6 inches and the range was 6.2 inches. What was the lowest monthly rainfall recorded?

   (A) 0.68 inches
   (B) 4.4 inches
   (C) 6.2 inches
   (D) 6.4 inches

7. What is the greatest common factor of 8, 12, and 20?

   (A) 2
   (B) 4
   (C) 96
   (D) 1,920

Go on to the next page

8. While away at camp, the students measured the high temperature outside every day and displayed the results on the graph.

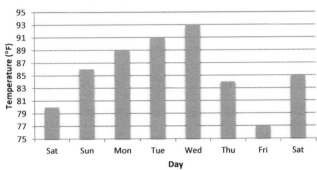

Daily High Temperature (°F)

What was the difference between the high temperature of the warmest day and the high temperature of the coolest day?

(A) 8
(B) 9
(C) 16
(D) 26

9. If $X = 3 \times (Y + Z)$, then what is X when Y is 16 and Z is 9?

(A) 75
(B) 100
(C) 288
(D) 432

10. A clothing shop had a storewide clearance that was 10% of all items in the store. They also had a sale on t-shirts that was an additional 20% off of the clearance price. If a t-shirt originally cost $20, what as the final price after all discounts?

(A) $12.00
(B) $14.00
(C) $14.40
(D) $16.00

Go on to the next page

11. Which is the best estimate of $\dfrac{59 \times 61}{600}$?

   (A) 6
   (B) 10
   (C) 60
   (D) 70

12. John and Grace kept track of their savings for 5 weeks and made the table below.

John's and Grace's Savings		
Week #	John's total	Grace's total
1	$3.70	$2.10
2	$4.50	$3.50
3	$5.30	$4.90
4	$6.10	$6.30
5	$6.90	$7.70

   Starting in week 2, how much did Grace save each week?

   (A) $0.40
   (B) $0.80
   (C) $1.40
   (D) $1.80

13. In the equation $\dfrac{b+4}{b} = \dfrac{1}{3}$, what is the value of b?

   (A) 6
   (B) 2
   (C) −2
   (D) −6

14. The expression $\dfrac{40(64+36)}{2}$ is equivalent to which of the following?

   (A) 1,000
   (B) 2,000
   (C) 3,092
   (D) 4,000

Go on to the next page

15. The cost for a taxi ride is $2.50 for the first mile and $1.50 per mile or fraction thereof after the first mile. Which equation could be used to find the total cost, C, of a taxi ride that is M miles if M is a whole number?

(A) $C = 2.50M + 1.50$
(B) $C = 2.50 + 1.50M$
(C) $C = 2.50 + 1.50(M - 1)$
(D) $C = 2.50(M - 1) + 1.50$

16. Yesterday, Sally had a collection of 150 pencils. Today, she has twice as many pencils. By what percent did her collection increase?

(A) 50%
(B) 100%
(C) 150%
(D) 200%

17. In the figure below, a circle is inscribed within a square.

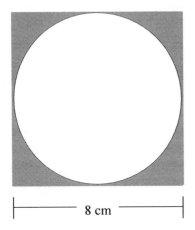

8 cm

What is the area that is shaded? (area of a circle $= \pi r^2$)

(A) $32 - 8\pi$ cm^2
(B) $32 - 16\pi$ cm^2
(C) $64 - 8\pi$ cm^2
(D) $64 - 16\pi$ cm^2

Go on to the next page

18. Which network represents the routes from point *A* to *B*, *A* to *C*, *A* to *D*, *B* to *C*, and *C* to *D* without including any other routes?

(A)
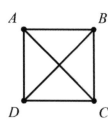

(B)
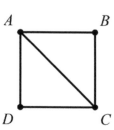

(C)
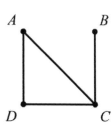

(D)
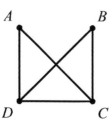

19. In a pet store, there are only cats and dogs. If there are 5 more dogs than cats in the store and there are 10 cats, what fraction of the pets are dogs?

(A) $\dfrac{1}{3}$

(B) $\dfrac{1}{2}$

(C) $\dfrac{3}{5}$

(D) $\dfrac{4}{5}$

20. Larry is driving away from the park. His distance from the park is given by the equation $y = \dfrac{1}{2}x + 5$, where *y* is his distance from the park in miles, and *x* is the number of minutes that he has been driving. What does 5 mean in this equation?

(A) Larry was 5 miles from the park when he started driving.
(B) Larry is driving at a speed of 5 miles per hour.
(C) Larry drives $\dfrac{1}{2}$ mile every five minutes.
(D) Larry drives 5 miles every minute.

Go on to the next page

21. On a map, 3 centimeters is equal to 400 kilometers. If two cities are actually 1,000 kilo-meters apart, how far apart are they on the map?

(A) 6 cm
(B) 7.5 cm
(C) 9 cm
(D) 133 cm

22. Use the scatterplot below to answer the question.

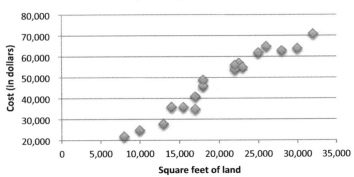

How much would you expect 20,000 sq. ft. of land to cost, based on the scatter plot above?

(A) $30,000
(B) $40,000
(C) $50,000
(D) $60,000

Go on to the next page

23. Use the trapezoid below to answer the question.

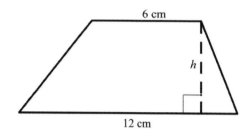

6 cm

h

12 cm

If the area of the trapezoid is 45 cm², what is the height, h?

Note: *Area of a trapezoid* $= \dfrac{1}{2}(b_1 + b_2)h$

(A) 4
(B) 5
(C) 11
(D) 12

24. Two spinners are divided into six equal sections labeled #1-6. Which scenario describes complementary events?

(A) The probability of landing on a 2 and then a 4.
(B) The probability of landing on a 3 and then landing on an even number.
(C) The probability of landing on a number less than 3 and then landing on a number greater than 3.
(D) The probability of landing on an even number and then landing on an odd number.

25. What is the value of $2\dfrac{2}{3} \div 1\dfrac{3}{5}$?

(A) $\dfrac{3}{5}$

(B) $1\dfrac{1}{5}$

(C) $1\dfrac{2}{3}$

(D) $2\dfrac{1}{2}$

Go on to the next page

26. Kim surveyed her friends to find out how many times they went swimming over the summer. She put her results into the stem-and-leaf plot below.

```
0 | 3 3 5 6 7
1 | 0 0 2 3 3 3 5 8
2 | 2 4 4 9
3 | 0 3 9
5 | 4
```

How many people did Kim survey?

(A) 5
(B) 8
(C) 21
(D) 54

27. Triangle *BCD* is similar to triangle *EFG*.

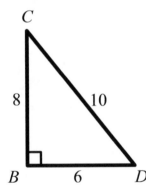 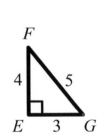

What is the ratio of the length of one side of triangle *BCD* to the corresponding side of triangle *EFG*?

(A) 3 to 1
(B) 2 to 1
(C) 1 to 3
(D) 1 to 2

Go on to the next page

28. If $\dfrac{B}{15} = \dfrac{12}{18}$, then what is the value of B?

(A) 10
(B) 12
(C) 18
(D) 24

29. What is the slope of a line that passes through the points $(-2, 3)$ and $(4, 6)$?

(A) $-\dfrac{3}{4}$

(B) $-\dfrac{1}{2}$

(C) $\dfrac{1}{2}$

(D) $\dfrac{3}{4}$

30. Gustav has four shirts, but only one of them is red. He has three pairs of shorts, but only one of them is red. He has five pairs of socks and only one of them is red. If he randomly selects a shirt, a pair of shorts, and a pair of socks, what is the probability that they will all be red?

(A) $\dfrac{1}{3}$

(B) $\dfrac{1}{4}$

(C) $\dfrac{1}{12}$

(D) $\dfrac{1}{60}$

Go on to the next page

31. Charlotte surveyed the students in her class about how they got to school that morning. Her results are shown in the circle graph below.

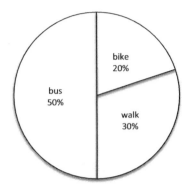

Which could have been the data that was collected?

(A) 10 bus riders, 4 bike riders, and 4 walkers
(B) 10 bus riders, 4 bike riders, and 6 walkers
(C) 10 bus riders, 6 bike riders, and 6 walkers
(D) 10 bus riders, 6 bike riders, and 8 walkers

32. Which expression is equivalent to $\dfrac{w}{y}\left(\dfrac{y}{x}-\dfrac{w}{x}\right)$?

(A) $\dfrac{wy-2w}{xy}$

(B) $\dfrac{wy-w^2}{y}$

(C) $\dfrac{w}{x}\left(1-\dfrac{w}{y}\right)$

(D) $\dfrac{w}{x}\left(1-\dfrac{1}{y}\right)$

Go on to the next page

33. There are 5 yellow, 4 green, and 6 blue marbles in a bag. If a marble is randomly selected, what is the probability that it will be a yellow marble?

(A) $\dfrac{1}{15}$

(B) $\dfrac{1}{5}$

(C) $\dfrac{1}{3}$

(D) $\dfrac{7}{15}$

34. In order for boats at a rowing club to go out on the water, the air temperature must be 15 °C. If it is currently −3 °C, by how many degrees does the temperature need to increase before boats can go out on the water?

(A) 5 °C

(B) 8 °C

(C) 15 °C

(D) 18 °C

35. If $m - 9 = n + 3$, what is the value of $n - m$?

(A) −12

(B) −9

(C) −3

(D) 3

36. The first four elements of a dot pattern are in the figure below

What is the fifth element of the dot pattern?

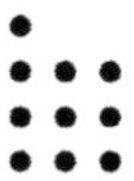

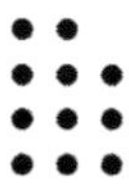

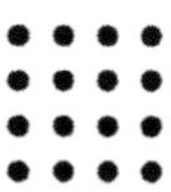

Go on to the next page

37. Of the 60% of the class that have a brother, $\frac{1}{3}$ also have a sister. What fraction of the class have both a brother and a sister?

(A) $\frac{1}{5}$

(B) $\frac{1}{3}$

(C) $\frac{2}{5}$

(D) $\frac{3}{5}$

38. The graph below shows the distance that four cars are from town hall over a ten-minute period.

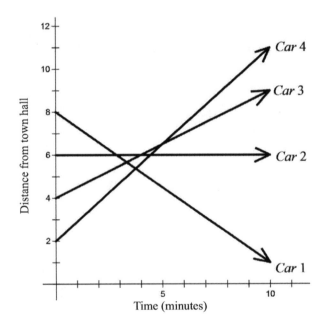

Which car is driving away from town hall at the greatest speed?

(A) Car 1
(B) Car 2
(C) Car 3
(D) Car 4

Go on to the next page

39. If $\frac{2}{5}$ of a glass can be filled in one minute, how many minutes would it take to fill the entire glass?

(A) 1.75 minutes

(B) 2.5 minutes

(C) 3.0 minutes

(D) 3.3 minutes

40. Emilio is playing a board game that uses a spinner and an 8-sided die to determine a move. The spinner has 2 equal sections labeled "up" and "down". The die has 8 equal sides labeled 1 through 8. Emilio put together an outcome table to determine the probability of moving up a number of spaces that is a factor of 8. Which table is shaded in a way to help Emilio figure out the answer?

(A)

Up 1	Up 2	Up 3	Up 4	Up 5	Up 6	Up 7	Up 8
Down 1	Down 2	Down 3	Down 4	Down 5	Down 6	Down 7	Down 8

(B)

Up 1	Up 2	Up 3	Up 4	Up 5	Up 6	Up 7	Up 8
Down 1	Down 2	Down 3	Down 4	Down 5	Down 6	Down 7	Down 8

(C)

Up 1	Up 2	Up 3	Up 4	Up 5	Up 6	Up 7	Up 8
Down 1	Down 2	Down 3	Down 4	Down 5	Down 6	Down 7	Down 8

(D)

Up 1	Up 2	Up 3	Up 4	Up 5	Up 6	Up 7	Up 8
Down 1	Down 2	Down 3	Down 4	Down 5	Down 6	Down 7	Down 8

Go on to the next page

41. Use the figure below to answer the question.

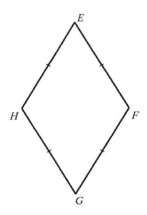

What is the most accurate name for quadrilateral *EFGH*?

(A) square
(B) rectangle
(C) rhombus
(D) trapezoid

42. Which equation is equivalent to $\dfrac{b}{2} = c - 3$?

(A) $2c - b = 6$
(B) $c - b = 3$
(C) $2(c - b) = -3$
(D) $\dfrac{1}{2}b - c = 3$

43. What is the value of the expression 0.42 + 0.3 + 2.6 + 3.45?

(A) 5.98
(B) 6.04
(C) 6.45
(D) 6.77

44. If the volume of a cube is 125 cm³, what is its surface area?

(A) 125 cm²
(B) 150 cm²
(C) 175 cm²
(D) 225 cm²

Go on to the next page

45. Which expression is equivalent to $\dfrac{8\left(\sqrt{64}+16x\right)}{\sqrt{4}}$?

(A) $\dfrac{8\sqrt{1024}}{\sqrt{4}}$

(B) $\dfrac{\sqrt{512}+128}{\sqrt{4}}$

(C) $4(4+8x)$

(D) $4(8+16x)$

46. Triangle HJK and NOP are similar.

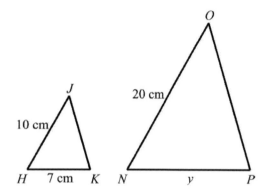

What is the value of y?

(A) 12

(B) 13

(C) 14

(D) 18

Go on to the next page

47. What is the equation for the line perpendicular to $\overline{AB}$ at (6, 2)?

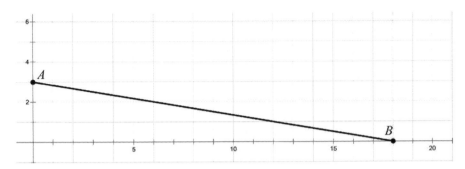

(A) $y = -\dfrac{1}{6}x + 3$

(B) $y = -\dfrac{1}{6}x - 3$

(C) $y = 6x + 34$

(D) $y = 6x - 34$

STOP. If you have time left, you may check your answers in ONLY this section.

Essay

You will be given 30 minutes to plan and write an essay. The topic is printed on the next page. *Make sure that you write about this topic. Do NOT choose another topic.*

This essay gives you the chance to show your thinking and how well you can express your ideas. Do not worry about filling all of the space provided. The quality is more important than how much you write. You should probably write more than a brief paragraph, though.

A copy of this essay will be sent to the schools that you apply to. Make sure that you only write in the appropriate area on the answer sheet. Please print so that the admissions officers can understand what you wrote.

On the next page is the topic sheet. There is room on this sheet to make notes and collect your thoughts. The final essay should be written on the two lined sheets provided in the answer sheet, however. Make sure that you copy your topic at the top of the first lined page. Write only in blue or black ink.

REMINDER: Please remember to write the topic on the top of the first lined page in your answer sheet.

What do you think is your strongest subject in school? Describe why you like the subject as well as why you think that you do well in that class.

- Write only about this topic
- Only the lined sheets will be sent to schools
- Use only blue or black ink

Notes

_____

_____

_____

_____

_____

_____

_____

_____

_____

_____

Answer Sheets

Student Name_____   Grade Applying For_____

Use pencil to fill in your answers below

Verbal Reasoning

1. (A)	(B)	(C)	(D)	21. (A)	(B)	(C)	(D)
2. (A)	(B)	(C)	(D)	22. (A)	(B)	(C)	(D)
3. (A)	(B)	(C)	(D)	23. (A)	(B)	(C)	(D)
4. (A)	(B)	(C)	(D)	24. (A)	(B)	(C)	(D)
5. (A)	(B)	(C)	(D)	25. (A)	(B)	(C)	(D)
6. (A)	(B)	(C)	(D)	26. (A)	(B)	(C)	(D)
7. (A)	(B)	(C)	(D)	27. (A)	(B)	(C)	(D)
8. (A)	(B)	(C)	(D)	28. (A)	(B)	(C)	(D)
9. (A)	(B)	(C)	(D)	29. (A)	(B)	(C)	(D)
10. (A)	(B)	(C)	(D)	30. (A)	(B)	(C)	(D)
11. (A)	(B)	(C)	(D)	31. (A)	(B)	(C)	(D)
12. (A)	(B)	(C)	(D)	32. (A)	(B)	(C)	(D)
13. (A)	(B)	(C)	(D)	33. (A)	(B)	(C)	(D)
14. (A)	(B)	(C)	(D)	34. (A)	(B)	(C)	(D)
15. (A)	(B)	(C)	(D)	35. (A)	(B)	(C)	(D)
16. (A)	(B)	(C)	(D)	36. (A)	(B)	(C)	(D)
17. (A)	(B)	(C)	(D)	37. (A)	(B)	(C)	(D)
18. (A)	(B)	(C)	(D)	38. (A)	(B)	(C)	(D)
19. (A)	(B)	(C)	(D)	39. (A)	(B)	(C)	(D)
20. (A)	(B)	(C)	(D)	40. (A)	(B)	(C)	(D)

Quantitative Reasoning

1. (A)	(B)	(C)	(D)		21. (A)	(B)	(C)	(D)
2. (A)	(B)	(C)	(D)		22. (A)	(B)	(C)	(D)
3. (A)	(B)	(C)	(D)		23. (A)	(B)	(C)	(D)
4. (A)	(B)	(C)	(D)		24. (A)	(B)	(C)	(D)
5. (A)	(B)	(C)	(D)		25. (A)	(B)	(C)	(D)
6. (A)	(B)	(C)	(D)		26. (A)	(B)	(C)	(D)
7. (A)	(B)	(C)	(D)		27. (A)	(B)	(C)	(D)
8. (A)	(B)	(C)	(D)		28. (A)	(B)	(C)	(D)
9. (A)	(B)	(C)	(D)		29. (A)	(B)	(C)	(D)
10. (A)	(B)	(C)	(D)		30. (A)	(B)	(C)	(D)
11. (A)	(B)	(C)	(D)		31. (A)	(B)	(C)	(D)
12. (A)	(B)	(C)	(D)		32. (A)	(B)	(C)	(D)
13. (A)	(B)	(C)	(D)		33. (A)	(B)	(C)	(D)
14. (A)	(B)	(C)	(D)		34. (A)	(B)	(C)	(D)
15. (A)	(B)	(C)	(D)		35. (A)	(B)	(C)	(D)
16. (A)	(B)	(C)	(D)		36. (A)	(B)	(C)	(D)
17. (A)	(B)	(C)	(D)		37. (A)	(B)	(C)	(D)
18. (A)	(B)	(C)	(D)					
19. (A)	(B)	(C)	(D)					
20. (A)	(B)	(C)	(D)					

Reading Comprehension

1. (A)	(B)	(C)	(D)		21. (A)	(B)	(C)	(D)
2. (A)	(B)	(C)	(D)		22. (A)	(B)	(C)	(D)
3. (A)	(B)	(C)	(D)		23. (A)	(B)	(C)	(D)
4. (A)	(B)	(C)	(D)		24. (A)	(B)	(C)	(D)
5. (A)	(B)	(C)	(D)		25. (A)	(B)	(C)	(D)
6. (A)	(B)	(C)	(D)		26. (A)	(B)	(C)	(D)
7. (A)	(B)	(C)	(D)		27. (A)	(B)	(C)	(D)
8. (A)	(B)	(C)	(D)		28. (A)	(B)	(C)	(D)
9. (A)	(B)	(C)	(D)		29. (A)	(B)	(C)	(D)
10. (A)	(B)	(C)	(D)		30. (A)	(B)	(C)	(D)
11. (A)	(B)	(C)	(D)		31. (A)	(B)	(C)	(D)
12. (A)	(B)	(C)	(D)		32. (A)	(B)	(C)	(D)
13. (A)	(B)	(C)	(D)		33. (A)	(B)	(C)	(D)
14. (A)	(B)	(C)	(D)		34. (A)	(B)	(C)	(D)
15. (A)	(B)	(C)	(D)		35. (A)	(B)	(C)	(D)
16. (A)	(B)	(C)	(D)		36. (A)	(B)	(C)	(D)
17. (A)	(B)	(C)	(D)					
18. (A)	(B)	(C)	(D)					
19. (A)	(B)	(C)	(D)					
20. (A)	(B)	(C)	(D)					

Mathematics Achievement

1. (A) (B) (C) (D)
2. (A) (B) (C) (D)
3. (A) (B) (C) (D)
4. (A) (B) (C) (D)
5. (A) (B) (C) (D)
6. (A) (B) (C) (D)
7. (A) (B) (C) (D)
8. (A) (B) (C) (D)
9. (A) (B) (C) (D)
10. (A) (B) (C) (D)
11. (A) (B) (C) (D)
12. (A) (B) (C) (D)
13. (A) (B) (C) (D)
14. (A) (B) (C) (D)
15. (A) (B) (C) (D)
16. (A) (B) (C) (D)
17. (A) (B) (C) (D)
18. (A) (B) (C) (D)
19. (A) (B) (C) (D)
20. (A) (B) (C) (D)
21. (A) (B) (C) (D)
22. (A) (B) (C) (D)
23. (A) (B) (C) (D)
24. (A) (B) (C) (D)
25. (A) (B) (C) (D)

26. (A) (B) (C) (D)
27. (A) (B) (C) (D)
28. (A) (B) (C) (D)
29. (A) (B) (C) (D)
30. (A) (B) (C) (D)
31. (A) (B) (C) (D)
32. (A) (B) (C) (D)
33. (A) (B) (C) (D)
34. (A) (B) (C) (D)
35. (A) (B) (C) (D)
36. (A) (B) (C) (D)
37. (A) (B) (C) (D)
38. (A) (B) (C) (D)
39. (A) (B) (C) (D)
40. (A) (B) (C) (D)
41. (A) (B) (C) (D)
42. (A) (B) (C) (D)
43. (A) (B) (C) (D)
44. (A) (B) (C) (D)
45. (A) (B) (C) (D)
46. (A) (B) (C) (D)
47. (A) (B) (C) (D

Write your essay topic below
_____

_____

_____

Write your essay below and on the next page
_____

_____

_____

_____

_____

_____

_____

_____

_____

_____

_____

_____

_____

Answers to Practice Test

Answers to Verbal Reasoning

Correct Answer	Your Answer	Put a check mark here if you answered the question correctly
1. C		
2. A		
3. D		
4. D		
5. B		
6. C		
7. A		
8. C		
9. D		
10. B		
11. A		
12. C		
13. B		
14. A		
15. D		
16. A		
17. C		
18. B		
19. B		

20. A		
21. D		
22. C		
23. B		
24. A		
25. B		
26. C		
27. A		
28. D		
29. A		
30. C		
31. B		
32. D		
33. B		
34. A		
35. C		
36. D		
37. D		
38. B		
39. A		
40. C		
Total Questions Answered Correctly _____		

Interpreting your Verbal Reasoning Score

On the ISEE, your raw score is the number of questions that you answered correctly on each section. Nothing is subtracted for the questions that you answered incorrectly.

Your raw score is then converted into a scaled score. This scaled score is then converted into a percentile score. Remember that it is the percentile score that schools are looking at. Your percentile score compares you just to other students in your grade.

Below is a chart that gives a very rough conversion between your raw score on the practice Verbal Reasoning section and a percentile score.

Please keep in mind that the purpose of this chart is just to let you see how the scoring works, not to give you an accurate percentile score. You will need to complete the practice test in *What to Expect on the ISEE* in order to get a more accurate percentile score.

Middle Level Verbal Reasoning

Applicants to Grade 7			
Percentile Score	25th	50th	75th
Approximate raw score needed	19-20	25-26	29-30

Applicants to Grade 8			
Percentile Score	25th	50th	75th
Approximate raw score needed	24-25	28-29	32-33

Answers to Quantitative Reasoning

Correct Answer	Your Answer	Put a checkmark here if you answered the question correctly
1. D		
2. B		
3. A		
4. B		
5. C		
6. D		
7. A		
8. A		
9. B		
10. C		
11. A		
12. D		
13. C		
14. A		
15. A		
16. A		
17. D		
18. B		
19. D		
20. C		
21. A		
22. A		
23. D		

24. C		
25. B		
26. A		
27. C		
28. B		
29. A		
30. C		
31. B		
32. A		
33. C		
34. A		
35. A		
36. C		
37. C		
Total Questions Answered Correctly _____		

Interpreting your Quantitative Reasoning Score

On the ISEE, your raw score is the number of questions that you answered correctly on each section. Nothing is subtracted for the questions that you answered incorrectly.

Your raw score is then converted into a scaled score. This scaled score is then converted into a percentile score. Remember that it is the percentile score that schools are looking at. Your percentile score compares you just to other students in your grade.

Below is a chart that gives a very rough conversion between your raw score on the practice Quantitative Reasoning section and a percentile score.

Please keep in mind that the purpose of this chart is just to let you see how the scoring works, not to give you an accurate percentile score. You will need to complete the practice test in *What to Expect on the ISEE* in order to get a more accurate percentile score.

Middle Level Quantitative Reasoning

Applicants to Grade 7			
Percentile Score	25th	50th	75th
Approximate raw score needed	16-17	20-21	24-25

Applicants to Grade 8			
Percentile Score	25th	50th	75th
Approximate raw score needed	20-21	23-24	26-27

Answers to Reading Comprehension section

Correct Answers	Your Answer	Put a checkmark here if you answered the question correctly
1. B		
2. A		
3. C		
4. B		
5. D		
6. A		
7. C		
8. D		
9. A		
10. B		
11. C		
12. B		
13. A		
14. C		
15. B		
16. D		
17. A		
18. D		
19. C		
20. B		
21. D		
22. A		
23. B		
24. D		
25. B		
26. D		

27. A		
28. C		
29. B		
30. A		
31. C		
32. A		
33. D		
34. A		
35. B		
36. C		
Total Questions Answered Correctly _____		

Interpreting your Reading Comprehension Score

On the ISEE, your raw score is the number of questions that you answered correctly on each section. Nothing is subtracted for the questions that you answered incorrectly.

Your raw score is then converted into a scaled score. This scaled score is then converted into a percentile score. Remember that it is the percentile score that schools are looking at. Your percentile score compares you just to other students in your grade.

Below is a chart that gives a very rough conversion between your raw score on the practice Reading Comprehension section and a percentile score.

Please keep in mind that the purpose of this chart is just to let you see how the scoring works, not to give you an accurate percentile score. You will need to complete the practice test in *What to Expect on the ISEE* in order to get a more accurate percentile score.

Middle Level Reading Comprehension

Applicants to Grade 7			
Percentile Score	25th	50th	75th
Approximate raw score needed	11-12	17-18	22-23

Applicants to Grade 8			
Percentile Score	25th	50th	75th
Approximate raw score needed	16-17	21-22	25-26

Mathematics Achievement Answers

Correct Answers	Your Answer	Put a checkmark here if you answered the question correctly
1. B		
2. A		
3. D		
4. A		
5. C		
6. D		
7. B		
8. C		
9. A		
10. C		
11. A		
12. C		
13. D		
14. B		
15. C		
16. B		
17. D		
18. B		
19. C		
20. A		
21. B		
22. C		
23. B		

24. D		
25. C		
26. C		
27. B		
28. A		
29. C		
30. D		
31. B		
32. C		
33. C		
34. D		
35. A		
36. B		
37. A		
38. D		
39. B		
40. D		
41. C		
42. A		
43. D		
44. B		
45. D		
46. C		
47. D		
Total Questions Answered Correctly _____		

Interpreting your Mathematics Achievement Score

On the ISEE, your raw score is the number of questions that you answered correctly on each section. Nothing is subtracted for the questions that you answered incorrectly.

Your raw score is then converted into a scaled score. This scaled score is then converted into a percentile score. Remember that it is the percentile score that schools are looking at. Your percentile score compares you just to other students in your grade.

Below is a chart that gives a very rough conversion between your raw score on the practice Mathematics Achievement section and a percentile score.

Please keep in mind that the purpose of this chart is just to let you see how the scoring works, not to give you an accurate percentile score. You will need to complete the practice test in *What to Expect on the ISEE* in order to get a more accurate percentile score.

Middle Level Mathematics Achievement

Applicants to Grade 7			
Percentile Score	25th	50th	75th
Approximate raw score needed	32-33	37-38	42-43

Applicants to Grade 8			
Percentile Score	25th	50th	75th
Approximate raw score needed	35-36	39-40	43-44

Books by Test Prep Works

	Content instruction	Test-taking strategies	Practice problems	Full-length practice tests
ISEE				
Lower Level (for students applying for admission to grades 5-6)				
Success on the Lower Level ISEE	✓	✓	✓	✓ (1)
30 Days to Acing the Lower Level ISEE		✓	✓	
The Best Unofficial Practice Tests for the Lower Level ISEE				✓ (2)
Middle Level (for students applying for admission to grades 7-8)				
Success on the Middle Level ISEE	✓	✓	✓	✓ (1)
The Best Unofficial Practice Tests for the Middle Level ISEE				✓ (2)
Upper Level (for students applying for admission to grades 9-12)				
Success on the Upper Level ISEE	✓	✓	✓	✓ (1)
The Best Unofficial Practice Tests for the Upper Level ISEE				✓ (2)
SSAT				
Middle Level (for students applying for admission to grades 6-8)				
Success on the Middle Level SSAT	✓	✓	✓	
The Best Unofficial Practice Tests for the Middle Level SSAT (coming soon)				✓ (2)
Upper Level (for students applying for admission to grades 9-12)				
Success on the Upper Level SSAT	✓	✓	✓	✓ (1)
30 Days to Acing the Upper Level SSAT		✓	✓	
The Best Unofficial Practice Tests for the Upper Level SSAT				✓ (2)

TEST PREP WORKS, LLC.

Looking for more practice?

Check out our other book for the Middle Level ISEE:

The Best Unofficial Practice Tests for the Middle Level ISEE

✓ 2 full-length practice tests (different from the practice test in *Success on the Middle Level ISEE*)

Was ***Success on the Middle Level ISEE: A Complete Course*** helpful to you?

Please consider leaving a review with the merchant where you purchased the book.

We welcome your suggestions at *feedback@testprepworks.com*.

TEST PREP WORKS, LLC.

Made in the USA
Middletown, DE
14 November 2016